Strategies for School Equity

Strategies for School Equity

Creating Productive Schools

in a Just Society

Edited by Marilyn J. Gittell

Yale University Press

New Haven & London

To Brett, Molly, and Rose

Set in Garamond and Stone Sans types by the Composing Room of Michigan, Inc. Printed in the United States of America.

Library of Congress Cataloging-in-Publication Data
Strategies for school equity : creating productive schools in a just society / edited by Marilyn J. Gittell.
    p.   cm.
Includes bibliographical references and index.
ISBN 0-300-06992-8 (cloth : alk. paper)
    1. Educational equalization—United States.   2. Education, Urban—United States.   3. Education—United States—Finance.   4. School management and organization—United States.   I. Gittell, Marilyn.
LC213.2.S76   1998
379.2'6'0973—dc21   97–44949
                                                             CIP

A catalogue record for this book is available form the British Library.

The paper in this book meets the guidelines for permanence and durability of the Committee on Production Guidelines for Book Longevity of the Council on Library Resources.

10 9 8 7 6 5 4 3 2 1

Contents

050853

Foreword

History, above all other disciplines, has an insistent way of reminding us where we have been as a nation and, if we are wise about understanding the various streams of history, where we might be going. The history of the universal public education system is a little more than 150 years old, and it is full of turning points and paradoxes. No other nation on earth has been more committed to providing free and effective primary and secondary school education for all its children, but the United States has also produced a legacy of unequal and inadequate schooling, especially for its most disadvantaged students.

Recently, we celebrated the fiftieth anniversary of *Brown v. Board of Education,* in which the United States Supreme Court found that segregated education was unconstitutional because it was "inherently unequal." In 1996, we marked—but did not celebrate—the hundredth anniversary of another landmark Supreme Court decision, *Plessy v. Ferguson,* in which the Court accepted segregated educational institutions for blacks as long as they were equal to those for whites. One view of this hundred-year history recognizes that the *Brown* decision successfully overturned *Plessy.* Certainly, *Brown* reversed the legal legitimacy of segregated education. But another view of this same history would suggest that, judicial findings to the contrary, African American children, and increasingly children of color, continue to enter an educational system that is as segregated by race and ethnicity as it was at the turn of the century or even in 1960. In fact, scholars such as Gary Orfield claim that since *Brown,* schooling in America's inner cities and vast rural poverty belts has become even more segregated. And though this de facto segregation has no legal standing, it is deeply entrenched, and it results in a fundamentally unequal education system because of the ways in which government raises funds to pay for public schooling. When nearly 90 percent of the support for education comes primarily from the local tax base and state appropriations, there are built-in and often "savage inequities," as Jonathan Kozol proclaimed in his 1991 critique of school finance schemes.

The most recent wave of education reform, begun in 1983 with the publication of the federal report *A Nation at Risk,* shifted the public discourse away from a concern with equity and equal opportunity for all students. Instead, it embraced the conclusion that American schooling was largely mediocre for even its best students. Critics claimed that the drive for equality during the previous two decades had left schools inadequate to prepare students for an increasingly competitive global labor market. Excellence needed to replace equity in order to get schools, teachers, and especially students back on track.

To anyone who thinks that excellence and equity represent a trade-off, I would counter that it need not be a zero-sum game. Educators who give greater attention to the needs of "at-risk" students are not sacrificing excellence for mediocrity. Rather, they are attempting to provide the best possible education for those with the greatest need. The only way in which trade-offs may affect the excellence-equity calculus is if the resource base for schools and schooling is not growing with the needs of students but rather shrinking. Moreover, a renewed call for "quality and excellence" has the political advantage of not demanding expanded funding but redirecting existing support from the most needy to the most able. Behind all the rhetoric lies the disturbing fact that many in our society believe that we are spending too much to educate "the wrong students"—new and illegal immigrants, inner-city blacks trapped in generations of poverty, unwed teenage mothers and their often-violent, irresponsible boyfriends. I would counter that there are no "wrong" students, only ineffective schools.

In 1992, the Ford Foundation asked a distinguished City University of New York professor of political science, Dr. Marilyn Gittell, to convene a group of scholars, policy analysts, education reformers and practitioners, and legal rights advocates to examine the current state of litigation as well as legislation focused on equity issues in financing public education and restructuring it to give more individuals a stake in school decision-making. Papers were commissioned and a conference was held to discuss the papers (which became the chapters of this book) in New York City in the spring of 1994. It was the first time in more than a decade that the "fiscal equity" lens was applied to determine whether the new wave of education reform, otherwise known as the excellence movement, had taken account of the needs of those whom the system has largely failed in the past.

I recall hearing the aphorism "a rising tide lifts all boats" as part of the rationale for redirecting funds and energies toward improving education for the best and brightest. I never wholly endorsed it. If some boats are already listing, a rising tide will not carry them but rather swamp them more quickly. The chapters in this book offer models of bailing out the schools, students, and school districts in gravest danger. More money and more equitable finance schemes are necessary. In twenty-nine states there is pending litigation addressing finance inequities. Although more money is necessary, it is not sufficient, as the various authors report. Sound educational reform includes devolving decision-making and accountability to the school site and the local community. But none of these equity-driven fiscal and governance changes will last unless teachers, parents, politicians, and administrators are fully committed to the philosophy that all students can learn—and that increasing the societal investment in public education is more than a statement of hope; it is a hallmark of a democratic society.

Alison Bernstein

Preface

I have been writing about urban school reform for thirty years. My earliest research was a study of decision-making in the New York City school system that was the subject of my first book, *Participants and Participation: A Study of School Policy in New York City.* As a political scientist I was shocked to find the closed political structure of a large city school system. This failure of democratic governance, I concluded, resulted in a system that was not responsive to the needs of new populations in the city. Several years later I studied six urban school systems (those of Baltimore, Chicago, Detroit, New York, Philadelphia, and St. Louis). My observations confirmed the fact that power was concentrated in the central bureaucracies in large city school systems. The public was excluded from the decision-making but also from any discourse about education options or choices. In *Six Urban School Districts* I described the limited number of stakeholders in education and how closed political systems failed to make needed changes in urban education. My research on school reform for the next decade was concentrated on the need to decentralize large city systems, engage the public in decision-making at the school and the district levels, and enhance community control of schools. Although system-wide reforms seemed impossible to achieve, some changes in selected cities did open school systems to more stakeholders.

This book is a continuation of my personal campaign to achieve urban school reform and to address the inequities in urban school systems. The book includes a compilation of papers presented at a seminar held at The City University of New York in 1996. The seminar was conceived as an update on the issue of (in)equality and urban school reform. It was organized to include scholars, lawyers, and school activists who were addressing these issues from three different perspectives: those of financial equality, school governance, and educational policy. Their collective work concludes that comprehensive reform and community activity are essential to achieving reform.

Alison Bernstein, then director of the Ford Foundation, and Janice Petrovich, its deputy director of education, knowledge, and religion, provided the encouragement and insight to see the value of the discourse, as well as the funding support necessary to bring together the seminar participants. Both added much to the discussion of the importance of joining the various approaches to school reform. That enterprise and this book owe much to their support.

I want to thank all the participants in that seminar for providing different but important insights into what is essential in urban school reform. My students, John McCabe and Kirk Vandersall, staffed the seminar, provided insights on the subject, and contributed to the content and structure of the book. Most of all I want to thank Laura McKenna, who contributed significantly to the task of conceptualizing the structure and content of the book and performed the task of editing and organizing the papers. Her editing skills and constant attention to detail made the book possible. She was a valuable collaborator, and I am sure she will go on to write more about the subject herself. I also want to thank Kay Powell, the administrator of the Howard Samuels Center, who kept us all on target for the seminar and the completion of the volume.

At Yale University Press I want to particularly thank Gladys Topkis, Richard Miller, Margaret Otzel, and Jane Zanichkowsky.

Marilyn Gittell

Introduction: The Ends and the Means in Education Policy

Marilyn Gittell and Laura McKenna

The demand for educational reform has been growing as the need for an educated workforce has increased, as the number of low-skill jobs has diminished, as inequities have expanded, and as inefficiencies and scandals have been exposed. In every recent election, candidates have put forth their vision of how to reform a system that is obviously inefficient and unfair in distributing its resources. Almost everyone, regardless of ideology, feels that the current system requires reform whether the solution takes the form of finance reform, charter schools, governance reform, or vouchers. Creating an excellent and equitable public education system has become a priority, but the means for achieving this goal have remained elusive.

Throughout the country various plans to reform the existing system have been presented. There have been school education district governance reforms in Chicago, voucher proposals in Pennsylvania, recentralization in New York City, comprehensive reform in Kentucky, decentralization reform in Texas, and court challenges in most states. Some of these plans have resulted in effective legislation, whereas others have languished in legislative committees or have been derailed by powerful interest groups. This book looks at the politics behind education reform and presents a strategy for reform based on the successes and failures of various states and cities.

This book is a collection of articles from a broad spectrum of reformers who have had direct involvement in shaping policy in states that include New Jersey, Texas, Alabama, Illinois, Washington, and Kentucky. They have participated in these reforms as members of advocacy groups, lawyers, members of the business community, academics, and education professionals. Because of their diverse, hands-on backgrounds in education reform, their conclusions are fresh and different from the usual academic studies.

Each chapter presents the author's experiences and observations on the politics behind one particular state reform. We have organized the book according to certain themes that we feel are important in drawing together a viable strategy for achieving workable education reform policies. Yet, each chapter provides a much richer source of information than this collection's overarching theme. The case study approach of each chapter yields a myriad of facts and conclusions on a wide variety of states that we hope will be useful to scholars and practitioners alike.

POLITICS AND EDUCATION

Education policy is conceived, modified, and enacted in the political arena—a fact often forgotten by scholars in the field of education. As a result, education reform must consider the interests of many key stakeholders including governors, state legislators, mayors, the courts, business groups, unions, professional associations, and interest groups. Their involvement certainly complicates the policy process, but it is essential. Ivory-tower reform efforts that neglect the political dimension of democratic policy-making face certain failure.

Even state supreme court decisions are not immune to politics. Court challenges to educational inequities and inadequacies have become increasingly popular but have had varying degrees of success. Experiences in New Jersey and Texas have shown that, nationwide, favorable court decisions do not guarantee a smooth implementation process. The political environment of each state must be considered.

Because education is primarily a function of the states in the United States, the development of education policy must also take into account individual state cultures and political institutions. Attention to the politics within state legislatures and the rise of new conservative state regimes is required within any strategy for reform. On a more positive note, however, the authors demonstrate how our decentralized educational system has resulted in the states' truly functioning as laboratories of democracy.

Another element that must be considered in the politics of American education reform is the role of grassroots community and advocacy groups. In many states, they have profoundly affected the success of a policy through lobbying efforts and publicity campaigns. In addition, these groups strengthen participation by providing an essential link between the public, the bureaucracy, and elected officials.

The chapters in this book describe the political realities of education reform and present the successes and failures of recent reform efforts. Together, they present a strategy for reform. This strategy calls for recognition of the key stakeholders in education (as well as their interests), the constraints on action imposed by the political culture and political institutions, the limitations of court decisions, and the impact of including business groups and community organizations in coalitions.

Part I looks at the pros and the cons of the legal road to reform. In Part II, the importance of understanding state politics, including the role of the governor and the state legislature, is discussed. In Part III, the authors discuss the various stakeholders in education policy who must be involved in any legislation. And in Part IV, the role of community and advocacy groups in forging successful education legislation is addressed.

VALUES AND EDUCATION

The chapter authors have a common understanding of the significance of politics in the education reform process, but they have differing views of what reform should look like. Some seem to favor the establishment of charter schools, whereas others feel that equalizing the financing system is most fundamental. Yet, the premise common to all reform proposals discussed in this book is the need to bring both excellence and equality to American education. Although these two goals have torn American education in different directions at times, they must both be pursued.

A historic struggle between the concepts of excellence and equality has pervaded the politics of American education since its inception. The problem is not a simple one; how can a country afford to provide a truly excellent education to all sectors of a population? Tocqueville's early-nineteenth-century prediction that the United States would struggle with the conflict between its values of liberty and equality has been reflected most dramatically in debates over the priorities of American education.

These two competing beliefs about American education have had a real impact on our school systems. The belief that education should promote equality has resulted in universal access, equitable standards, and a just distribution of resources. The countervailing value of educational excellence gave priority to the preparation of an educated elite, concentrated on professionally defined goals and standards of performance, and attempted to develop exclusionary tracking of students and rewards based on competitive performance.

Although advocates for excellence and equality declare their support for both goals, the concepts, translated into public policy, are competitive. The reason has much to do with financial constraints and the politics of resource allocation. Educational excellence can be satisfied by the investment of limited new resources and assurance that the most-endowed receive the rewards of the system. Equity goals are far more costly, because they require that larger numbers of students receive the same benefits. The conflict occurs when resources are insufficient to fulfill the demands of competing reformers.

In actuality, the only way public education will ever become excellent is through pursuing a plan of equity. The educational system must be improved for all children. Those who have espoused excellence without equity have only improved the system for a select few—hardly an acceptable result in a democratic society. To eliminate this historical struggle, priority must be placed on equity with the necessary financial support from the public to assure an excellent education for all students.

Although the states have held center stage in recent years in the promotion of equity—and this book certainly stresses their importance—the federal government should be playing a larger role. Perhaps equity and excellence can be brought together through a more active federal role in the promotion of equity in education, with state reform efforts concentrating on the need for excellence. In *Choosing Equality* I outlined a theory of progressive federalism based on this division of power.[1] Progressive federalism embraces local governance of local schools while significantly broadening the participation of stakeholders. It embraces public ownership in education that requires "a democratic process guiding the governance process, which goes beyond the election of school boards or public officials." It calls for expanded public discourse. Because states control the largest portion of education funding and institutional resources, progressive federalism views them as the center of political activity and the focal point for reform; they are potential "[agencies] for redistributing school resources and control and for mediating the direction of national and local action."[2] Progressive federalism thus "affirms that government action is the central instrument for achieving egalitarian goals" and holds that it is the duty of the national government to provide leadership to work toward those goals.[3] Our federal system allows us to retain local control and responsiveness through the states and localities while utilizing federal leadership to sustain the values of equity and fairness.

Values and politics must be brought together. In order to maintain our democracy, we must retain our commitment to a quality education for all children. To do this, however, we must work within the political restraints and obstacles that face us in a democratic society. Democracy is paradoxically both the goal and the stumbling block. This book aims to bring us closer to an understanding of the ends and the means of education reform.

NOTES

1. See Ann Bastian, Norm Fruchter, Marilyn Gittell, Colin Greer, and Kenneth Haskins, *Choosing Equality: The Case for Democratic Schooling* (Philadelphia: Temple, 1986), especially chap. 6, "Governance and Funding: Toward Progressive Federalism," 134–58
2. Ibid., 145.
3. Ibid.

Part One Constitutional
Issues and Legal Reform

Financial inequities in education have been challenged in state supreme courts since 1971, commencing with California's *Serrano v.
Priest.* Many state constitutions contain provisions for the public
education of children requiring that all children be provided with an
equal and adequate education. Constitutional requirements typically
state that education must be provided in a "free," "uniform," "efficient," "thorough," "ample," or "basic" way (see John Augenblick's
chapter). Although most cases brought in the 1970s sought to address
only financial inequality under states' equal protection clauses, more
recent cases have used the same constitutional requirements to challenge other inequities (i.e., facilities, equipment, teaching) as a part of
the adequacy concept. The adequacy arguments also allow reformers
to include governance and restructuring as areas for court review and
reform. Pursuing litigation as a means to reform may prove advan-
tageous in forcing a recalcitrant legislature to action and in providing
an impetus for necessary tax increases or reformulations. If the court
disregards political realities, however, legislative action and implementation are likely not to occur.

As Kirk Vandersall argues in Chapter 1, modern attempts to achieve equity in school finance followed the landmark U.S. Supreme Court decision in *Brown v. Board of Education* (1954). Equity advocates first sought action to redress gross financial inequities from the U.S. Congress and succeeded in getting passage of the Elementary and Secondary Education Act, which produced the federal title programs. Because only a small fraction of financial support is provided by the federal government, this action was scarcely able to overcome inequities stemming from local property taxation, which remained the largest source of education funding. Equity advocates then sought to overturn state education finance systems in the federal courts under the federal equal protection clause but were roundly defeated in *San Antonio v. Rodríguez* (1973), wherein the Supreme Court ruled that education was not a fundamental right under the Constitution. Advocates then turned to state constitutional challenges.

State court challenges of state school finance systems usually seek either resource parity or educational "adequacy." The first round of state litigation following *Rodríguez* focused on the high correlation between school district property wealth and per-pupil expenditures, arguing that state school aid formulas should be fiscally neutral and that equal tax efforts should produce equal revenues. In many cases, low-property-wealth school districts were taxing themselves at nearly twice the rate of high-wealth districts but yielding far smaller per-pupil revenues. Some litigation sought to expand the range of inputs considered, thus broadening the definition of resource disparity (see Peter Roos's chapter). More recent cases have sought to establish minimum levels of constitutionally acceptable educational outcomes (see, e.g., the discussion of *Rose* and *Harper* in the chapters by Kirk Vandersall and Helen Hershkoff) and were quite successful in overturning state systems in the late 1980s and early 1990s. The most recent cases are returning to arguments made in *Brown* and are seeking to join issues of de facto segregation with educational equity and adequacy in order to result in solutions that involve both housing policy and education policy (*Sheff v. O'Neill* and *NAACP v. State of Minnesota*).

Hershkoff focuses on *Harper v. Hunt,* which challenges the adequacy and equity of the Alabama public school systems. An ACLU lawyer involved with the planning and the litigation of this case, her perspective provides insight into the legal path for achieving school reform. In her chapter, "School Finance Reform and the Alabama Experience," she explains how features of the case fostered constituency-building efforts.

In January 1991, the ACLU challenged the Alabama public school systems as inequitable, inadequate, and in violation of the Alabama constitution's guarantee of a "liberal education." The finance disparities included expenditures that ranged from $2,200 per student in the wealthy districts to $150 per student in the poor districts. At trial, plaintiffs established the unconstitutionality of Alabama's education system through a multi-prong approach that emphasized the interrelation between educational inputs—the resources that form the enabling conditions for learning—and educational outputs—the cognitive and noncognitive goals of an educational system.

This case was significant because it not only challenged the financial equity of the state educational system, as early state litigation had done, but expanded the examination of inequities to ask whether total funding was sufficient to meet the programmatic mission. Education had to be not only equitable but adequate. In seeking to improve the adequacy of all schools, the ACLU consciously brought together a diverse coalition of support for action. Hershkoff argues further that state-driven reform must become part of a federal strategy that preserves local discretion but assures national standards of excellence.

In Chapter 3, Peter Roos describes the role of state court cases in rectifying inequities as defined in broader terms than mere financial disparities. His chapter, "Intradistrict Resource Disparities: A Problem Crying Out for a Solution," examines *Rodríguez v. Los Angeles Unified School District,* which dealt not only with intradistrict financial inequities but also with teacher and facility inequities that affected black and Latino communities in Los Angeles. Poor communities suffer greatly from inexperienced and underqualified teachers and overcrowded classrooms, the result of receiving less money per pupil than wealthier communities.

In 1986 representatives of Latino and African American students sued the Los Angeles Unified School District, claiming that teacher, facility, and dollar disparities between minority and white schools denied the minority children equal protection under the California constitution. The plaintiffs proposed remedies for the faculty and facility inequities including accelerated recruitment of new teachers and improved physical conditions of schools (which would also serve to attract better-qualified teachers). Owing in part to California's own financial crisis, the remedy was less ambitious; it focused primarily on equalizing intradistrict spending on education. Although the outcome was a positive start toward improving educational conditions in poor communities, it has not fully resolved the inequities.

Roos also examines the merits of legal recourse in reducing educational inequities. The decision to press one's case in court, he notes, depends on the particular state's constitution and whether the state exhibits a strong correlation between the ethnicity of the disadvantaged population and the disparities of resources. State constitutional provisions that assure equal protection under the law have been used in the past, and if plaintiffs establish that such disparities exist, proof of discrimination can be established. Roos points to other avenues for litigation opportunities but concludes with the hope that court intervention will not always be necessary. Improving conditions within minority school districts has advantages for the entire community and should be pursued without the pressure of litigation.

The shortcoming of litigation is often lack of adequate implementation. As Alexander Hamilton stated in Federalist Paper 78, the court lacks the power of both the sword and the purse; it is dependent on the legislature and the executive branch to carry out its decisions. If court decisions ignore the political environment, inadequate legislative responses may be forthcoming.

In Chapter 4, Tom Corcoran and Nathan Scovronick describe reform efforts in New Jersey and point to the mistakes the court made in formulating the decision that resulted in two failed legislative attempts at achieving equity. The political problems that were in part created by the court's decision made it difficult for any redistributive law such as Quality Education Act I (QEA I) to be passed and implemented. They believe that the court must provide the tools for the legislature and the governor to forge consensus but that *Abbott v. Burke* failed to do so.

This case did not attack the inequities of the local property tax, which reinforces the political fragmentation of New Jersey, a state with a large suburban population. In addition, comprehensive reform could have broadened a New Jersey reform coalition to include suburban and rural interests by incorporating the issues of governance and adequacy into that of financial equity. If the court had focused on program parity instead of on spending parity, perhaps the wealthier districts would have been less alienated and reacted less strongly to the changes in the tax structure recommended by the governor as a response to the court decision.

Part I provides an overview of state court action and a look at the strategies and outcomes of court cases in Alabama, New Jersey, and California. Descriptions of other court cases in such states as Kentucky and Texas are also available in this text. All of the evidence suggests that although litigation may appear to be the best course of action to correct inequities in school finance and even to promote broader school reform efforts, positive court decisions do not guarantee effective implementation, especially when the political environment is unreceptive to the changes proposed. These chapters point to the need for the development of new strategies to promote equitable school systems that take into account the importance of state politics.

Chapter 1 Post-*Brown* School Finance Reform

Kirk Vandersall

State courts have been the central battleground in the struggle to achieve educational equity. Convinced that reducing dramatic inequities in educational resources and achievement was vitally important to creating real equality of opportunity, reformers first sought relief in Congress. The states, however, have primary authority over elementary and secondary education, and the struggle quickly focused on them. Advocates first challenged state finance systems under the federal Constitution's equal protection clause but were roundly defeated. They next turned to state constitutional challenges and began a series of successful suits under state equal protection clauses. After the ascendance of the excellence movement and a brief hiatus, the equity movement entered a new era of successful challenges using state constitutional education clauses and in the process has become more closely linked to the broader education reform movement. This chapter traces the history of these efforts to reform school finance systems from the mid-1950s to the present, discusses the legal strategies used in the major legal challenges, and places the equity movement in the context of other education reform efforts during the same time period.

Brown v. Board of Education (1954) marks the beginning point of modern attempts to achieve educational equity through its impact on school desegregation and its resurrection of the equal protection clause from the separate-but-equal doctrine of *Plessy v. Ferguson* and the concurrent and consequent elevation of the value of equality. *Brown* highlighted and gave official sanction to protests against the tremendous inequities in American education lodged by civil rights activists. Gerald Rosenberg convincingly argues, however, that despite the culmination in *Brown* of years of litigation, little progress was made in reducing school segregation until the federal government addressed the issue in the 1964 Civil Rights Act, made it a matter of federal education policy in the Elementary and Secondary Education Act, and included it in the 1968 Housing Act (Rosenberg, 1991). This unified federal approach proved able to overcome some of the most egregious forms of school segregation, but it did more to highlight than to redress gross inequities in the distribution of educational resources. Federal K–12 education resources, even when carefully targeted, were scarcely able to overcome gross and increasing disparities between property-rich, growing suburbs and poor rural, urban, and suburban districts. While southern schools gradually desegregated and, together with some northern cities, began busing, rapid suburbanization continued to produce increasingly class-stratified housing patterns. Continuing reliance on property taxes assured that this created differential access to educational resources. Education advocates seeking greater equality of opportunity sought redress of the resulting educational inequities in the federal courts under the U.S. Constitution.

FEDERAL COURT ACTION

The first federal lawsuits brought to light major political and evidential gaps in strategies to achieve equity. In *McInnis v. Shapiro* (1968), an important early case filed against the state of Illinois, a federal district court rejected the plaintiff's claims that wide variation in expenditures that failed to accord with educational needs were unconstitutional under the equal protection clause of the Constitution. The court found that equality of per-pupil expenditures was an inappropriate standard and that in the absence of a judicially manageable standard, the issue was nonjusticiable. Further, the court was unable to independently produce an equitable funding plan. *Burruss v. Wilkerson* (1969) followed a similar argument in Virginia. These early cases raised a number of serious deficiencies in the case against the existing system of school finance. Very little information was available regarding the effects of various finance systems or the cost-effectiveness of various educational practices (La Morte, 1989, p. 5). There was no obvious emerging consensus about the definitions of educational equity, equality, or opportunity (Berne and Stiefel, 1984). There was a substantial lack of consensus over the final ends of schooling. And the historic leadership of state legislatures and governors in education policy meant that courts lacked the experience and undisputed authority necessary to drive the change.

University researchers, foundation officials, public advocates, and community organizers responded to the difficulties by collaboratively embarking on a program of research and action. The Ford Foundation was a key sponsor of several concurrent efforts: development of the legal strategy at the U.C. Berkeley law school, community organizing in California and Texas, and university and think-tank research in education finance. This effort resulted in work by Coons, Clune, and Sugarman, who proposed a legal strategy that called for fiscal neutrality in the relationship between education spending and local district property wealth under the federal equal protection clause. The strategy was first used in *Serrano v. Priest* (Van Slyke et al., 1995).

The school finance reform movement won its first major victory and significantly increased its momentum with the California Supreme Court's 1971 *Serrano v. Priest* decision (*Serrano I*). *Serrano I* was the first time a court of last resort declared a state school finance system unconstitutional. The court altogether sidestepped the issue of educational need while applying strict scrutiny to a judicial standard of fiscal neutrality, the absence of which was declared a violation of both the California and U.S. constitutional guarantees of equal protection. Minnesota's *Van Dusartz v. Hatfield* (1971) pursued the same argument as *Serrano I:* that differences in school district tax bases that led to different revenue-raising ability at the same tax rates was an equal protection violation. Although the district court agreed that there was an equal protection violation, it declined to act until the legislature did so. The Minnesota Miracle, enacted that year by the Minnesota State Legislature, dramatically reduced inequities in educational funding, instituting a system of revenue sharing and substantially increasing state education aid distributed through a combined foundation-aid and power-equalizing-type program.[1] The lawsuit was withdrawn.

Community organizers and attorneys in Texas attempting to establish a right to fiscal neutrality under the federal equal protection clause eventually argued before and lost in the U.S. Supreme Court in *San Antonio School District v. Rodríguez* (1973). The decision contradicted the California Supreme Court's *Serrano I* decision, finding 5–4 that education is not a fundamental right and does not fall under the equal protection clause of the U.S. Constitution. The litigants had sought application of the federal equal protection clause to the state system of school finance. Because the Court denied education the status of a fundamental right and further questioned the standing of school districts under constitutional rights, it upheld the constitutionality of variation in spending and service provision between wealthy and poor school districts. The Court declared that "the key to discovering whether education is 'fundamental' is not to be found in comparisons of the relative societal significance of education as opposed to subsistence or housing. Nor is it to be found by weighing whether education is as important as the right to travel. Rather, the answer lies in assessing whether there is a right to education explicitly or implicitly guaranteed by the Constitution" (*Rodríguez,* cited in Van Slyke et al., 1995, p. 5). By deciding that the Constitution contained no such guarantee, this decision effectively closed off the federal courts to advocates of state educational resource equity.

STATE STRATEGIES

Although the conventional wisdom after *Rodríguez* anticipated a declining judicial role in school finance, state courts were able to find judicially manageable standards for judgment under state constitutions (La Morte, 1989). This move to the state courts, a deliberate strategy pursued by education equity advocates, was emphatically embraced by the California Supreme Court in *Serrano v. Priest* (1977) (*Serrano II*). *Serrano II* reaffirmed the judicial standard of fiscal neutrality applied in *Serrano I* and found a fundamental right to education under the California constitution. Most state court challenges in the 1970s followed the *Serrano* logic, alleging fault under the equal protection clause of the state constitution. The table at the end of Part I summarizes state legal decisions in courts of last resort, or in a few cases, lower court rulings that were unchallenged. Early victories for equity advocates were won in California (*Serrano I,* 1971, and *Serrano II,* 1977), Connecticut (1977), New Jersey (1973), Washington (1978), West Virginia (1979), and Wyoming (1980). State courts upheld finance systems in Arizona (1973), Colorado (1982), Georgia (1981),

Idaho (1975), Illinois (1973), New York (1982), Ohio (1979), Oregon (1976), Pennsylvania (1979), and Washington (1974, overturned 1978) (Fulton and Long, 1993; Van Slyke, 1995).

CONSTITUTIONAL THEORIES

Most scholars divide state court challenges to school finance systems into those alleging a violation of the state or federal equal protection clause and those alleging violations of the state constitutional education clauses (Barton, Coley, and Goertz, 1991; Van Slyke, 1995; Thro, 1989; Odden and Picus, 1992; Fulton and Long, 1993). On one hand, litigation that employs an equal protection argument usually seeks parity in per-pupil revenues to remedy state school finance systems that discriminate against identifiable groups of people in terms of funding or educational resources. Advocates aim to demonstrate that such discrimination violates the state constitutional guarantee of the right to fair and equal protection of the laws (Van Slyke, 1995). Most early cases used this type of argument to claim violations in the high correlation between school district wealth and the revenue generated at a given tax rate (Odden, 1992). In many cases school districts with low property wealth taxed themselves at double the rates of high-wealth districts but realized lower tax yields. On the other hand, litigation that uses state education clauses or adequacy arguments usually seeks additional state resources for low-performing districts to reach constitutionally mandated levels of educational quality (Van Slyke, 1995). In New Jersey, for example, the state court determined that the resources made available to the twenty-eight poorest districts in the state were insufficient to provide an adequate education and must be raised. Most recent cases use the adequacy strategy (Odden, 1992).

Categorizing cases by legal strategy is not easy, however, because a finding of fault under an equal protection clause depends heavily on the status of education in the particular state constitution. All states have variation across districts in per-pupil spending. State courts usually follow the federal equal protection standards of review in assessing the constitutionality of these variations, choosing between strict-scrutiny and rational-basis review standards. Under strict scrutiny, the defendants must demonstrate a compelling state interest in the differential treatment of the group(s) in question. Under the rational-basis test, the defendants must demonstrate that the differential treatment serves a legitimate state interest and is rationally established. State courts will only apply the strict-scrutiny standard if they find that education is a fundamental right under their state constitution. As Barton et al. note, generally, when courts applied a strict-scrutiny standard of review, the school finance system was struck down. When they applied a rational-basis standard, the school finance system was generally upheld (1991, p. 16).

EARLY STATE CHALLENGES

In addition to *Serrano II,* several early cases represent advances in the theory and strategy of challenges to state school finance systems. Variations in state constitutional provisions, however, make it difficult to generalize the judicial findings and constitutional readings across states. The Connecticut Supreme Court's *Horton v. Meskill* decision (1977) is notable because it found a fundamental right to education in Connecticut not based on an explicit constitutional provision but established through the state's assumption of an implicit constitutional obligation through providing a high degree of state support for education throughout its history. The New Jersey Supreme Court chose to strike down the state school finance system for violating New Jersey's constitutional provision for a thorough and efficient state system of education. In doing so, the court chose to overlook the state equal protection clause, even though plaintiffs had sued under both in *Robinson v. Cahill* (1973). The court found that the state's school finance system was not providing equal educational opportunity and required the legislature to produce a more equalized system of funding. In an early use of what has come to be known as the adequacy strategy, *Seattle School District No. 1. v. State* (1978) overturned the previous Washington Supreme Court finding, which upheld the state school finance system (*Northshore School District v. Kinnear,* 1974). The court ruled that because the funding system failed to make ample provision for constitutionally minimal levels of education, it was inadequate for the plaintiff district (Thro 1989). Rather than ruling on interdistrict variation or its relation to tax bases or resident income, *Kinnear* ruled on the minimally acceptable level of financial support.

Finally, New York's *Levittown v. Nyquist* (1982, 1987) and Maryland's *Somerset County Board of Education v. Hornbeck* (1983) attempted to expand the interpretation of state education clauses by introducing the concept of municipal overburden. The plaintiffs in these cases alleged that their state education finance systems failed to account for the overburdening of urban areas due to their increased costs of operating schools, greater level of student educational needs, high level of required public services (particularly for poor people), and increased level of student absenteeism (Barton, Coley, and Goertz, 1991; Van Slyke, 1995; *Levittown*, 1982).[2] A brief filed on behalf of the *Levittown* plaintiffs claims that, whereas the public education fiscal burden of the large urban districts is by far the greatest in the state, the levels of state education assistance they receive are almost the lowest (cited in Barton, Coley, and Goertz, 1991, p. 17). Although the courts agreed that schooling was more expensive in cities due to increased costs of physical plant and operations, they also argued that cities have greater fiscal capacity, that strict scrutiny was thus not warranted, and that the present system of finance was therefore constitutional.

THE EXCELLENCE MOVEMENT

The effort to attain equitable school finance systems faltered in the early 1980s despite achieving legal and legislative overhauls of most state school finance systems. From 1971 to 1985, actual and threatened legal action produced substantially revised or altogether new systems of school finance in more than thirty-five states (Barton, Coley, and Goertz, 1991, p. 17). Yet many state courts chose to uphold the existing systems of finance, and the legislatures in most of those states were unreceptive to committing new resources or reallocating existing funds. States in which the courts struck down the finance system had considerable difficulty implementing the decisions. And the Reagan administration in general and the educational excellence movement in particular focused attention away from equity issues and toward achievement and standards.

The rise of the excellence movement coincided with a period of reflection and pause in the equity movement that produced some disheartening assessments of the prior decade of legal work and activism. Carroll and Park, for example, found that despite many changes in and increased scrutiny of school finance, states most often achieved taxpayer equity rather than resource equity; states used increased state shares of education funding to assure a leveling of property tax rates throughout the state rather than to reduce the association between income and per-pupil revenue and to reduce the overall variation in revenues (Carroll and Park, 1983). Their comparison of school finance reforms in California, Florida, Kansas, Michigan, and New Mexico found that Florida and Kansas actually slipped backwards in the association of average household income and per-pupil revenues within school districts, a matter that, they point out, would be decidedly worse if variations in classroom expenditures rather than per-pupil revenues were examined. Using forty-nine states' data, Schwartz and Moskowitz found that despite (limited) moderating effects of increased state education revenues, there was only slight change in intrastate spending inequity between 1976 and 1985 (Schwartz and Moskowitz, 1988; Barton, Coley, and Goertz, 1991).

The release of *A Nation at Risk* quickly spurred the rise of the "educational excellence" movement and produced a flurry of state legislative and gubernatorial education policy activity. The response contrasts vividly with attempts by equity advocates to achieve state action. Where equity advocates faced resistance and reluctance, governors and legislators raced to do their part to overcome the rising tide of mediocrity by being the first to propose increased graduation requirements, teacher testing, merit pay, expanded standardized testing, and tightened state curricular standards. Nearly every state enacted a subset of these proposals in the early and mid-1980s.

These initial responses to *A Nation at Risk* were largely unsuccessful if their goal was substantial if not radical reform of state education systems. States had, though, shown that they were able and willing to take strong action in education. A maturing school reform movement began to produce several lines of thinking about education policy: systemic reform, the small schools movement, school choice, and a renewed finance equity movement. Systemic reformers, leading up to and following O'Day and Smith (1991), viewed the standards reforms of the early 1980s as superficial responses to systemwide problems. In their view, education systems, as complex sets of institutions, actors, interests, and purposes, need to be thoroughly redesigned from top to bottom. After deciding what students should know and be able to do, school systems would then be reengineered to deliver that product. Advocates of small schools also envision a dramatic reworking of the education system. They seek release from all curricular and regulatory requirements so that they have the freedom to rethink the education process. And choice proponents surfaced from several groups of people: those who grant no special status to public as opposed to private education institutions; those who seek to provide urban and poor students access to quality education; and those who are committed to market forces as the only viable means for reforming the education system.

THE EQUITY MOVEMENT RENEWED

New Victories

Amid this rethinking of education reform, equity advocates returned to court and won important victories in *Rose v. Council for Better Education* (1989), *Edgewood Independent School District v. Kirby* (1989), *Abbott v. Burke* (1990), and *Tennessee Small School Systems et al. v. McWherter et al.* (1989). Much had changed since the first round of cases. States, though faced with recession, federal cutbacks, and antitax fervor in the late 1970s and early 1980s, were experiencing significant though uneven growth in revenues from property taxes and other revenue sources (Wulf, 1992).[3] The strong gains in property wealth exacerbated school funding inequities, even as they filled state and local coffers, by creating deeper mismatches between school district property wealth and tax capacity, and the education needs of schoolchildren. Many state education systems adopted state standards of student achievement for the first time, a practice that opened new avenues for adequacy suits by providing state-sanctioned, justiciable benchmarks. And the growing state share of education revenues made the states increasingly capable of addressing fiscal disparities in education.

In each of these four cases plaintiffs sued under the respective state education clause and won a broad ruling. In the most noteworthy case, *Rose v. Council for Better Education,* the entire system of Kentucky common schools was declared to be constitutionally deficient (p. 2.) under the efficiency clause in the education section of the constitution (Kentucky Constitution, sec. 183). Finding the totality of the education code and prior attempts to reform it inadequate to the task of appropriately educating Kentucky youth, the court ordered the General Assembly to devise an altogether new system in which the tax effort was evenly spread, uniform resources necessary for providing an adequate education were provided, and proper management was assured (p. 57). The children of the poor and the children of the rich, the children who live in the poor districts and the children who live in the rich districts, must be given the same opportunity and access to an adequate education (p. 58a). The legislature and the governor responded in the Kentucky Education Reform Act, which is widely hailed as the foremost example of comprehensive statewide school reform in the country (see the chapters by Sexton, Hershkoff, and Gittell).

New Jersey's *Abbott v. Burke* and Texas's *Edgewood v. Kirby* both highlight the extraordinary political struggle of which the court decisions are a part. Legislative plans to meet the *Edgewood* mandates were rejected several times by the Texas courts and were a brief episode in a twenty-five-year political struggle dating to the filing of *Rodríguez.* As recently as December 1995, New Jersey area papers covered intense battles over a proposal developed by the New Jersey State Education Commissioner to reconfigure the state system of education aid, testifying to the enduring lack of closure to the struggle first begun when *Robinson* was filed in 1969. The New Jersey Supreme Court ultimately decided to overturn the system in 1973, but four more judicial decisions were required to force the legislature to enact a new school funding statute, Public Law 1975, ch. 212, which took effect in 1976–77 (Morheuser, 1993). Despite reservations about the plan, the supreme court justices allowed it to stand, only to watch the state education department fail to implement key sections of the law as the legislature voted in 1979 to reduce the equalizing factor of the court-approved funding formula. Equity advocates then filed *Abbott v. Burke* in 1981 but were delayed by a series of missed discovery deadlines and other state education department maneuvers until 1986, whereupon a nine-month trial was held. Then, more than two decades into the struggle, the New Jersey Supreme Court ruled in 1990 that the present arrangements were unconstitutional for the twenty-eight poorest school districts in New Jersey because they failed to provide students in those districts with an adequate education. The court ordered the state to raise expenditures in these districts to the level of the twenty-eight wealthiest districts of the state. In anticipation of the decision, Governor Jim Florio pushed the Quality Education Act, a $1.3 billion tax increase and school finance plan, through the New Jersey legislature. This, however, provoked a vigorous taxpayer revolt resulting in a substantial rollback of the bill (see the chapters by Goertz and Corcoran and Scovronick). As Hershkoff, Moore, and Gittell discuss at length elsewhere in this book, litigation is seldom able to achieve reform in the absence of committed involvement of a broad coalition of education stakeholders.

New Strategies

The hallmark of this new round of suits is the use of the state education clause to claim student rights to an adequate education. In *Rose,* for example, Chief Justice Stephens declared that the premise for the existence of common schools is that all children in Kentucky have a constitutional right to an adequate education (*Rose,* [1989], p. 60). The Alabama court in *Harper v. Hunt* (1993), an astonishingly sweeping decision, ruled that "the present system of public school in Alabama violates the . . . Alabama Constitution, because the system of public schools fails to provide equitable and adequate educational opportunities to all schoolchildren . . . and fails to provide appropriate instruction and special services [to children with disabilities]" (*Harper v. Hunt* 624 So. 2d 107, 110 [Ala 1993]). Adequacy claims in these instances mean "adequate for student achievement" and therefore focus questions on educational outcomes rather than resource inputs (Clune, 1993, p. 391).

An adequacy approach seeks to define minimum achievement standards for all students and to fashion an education system and a means of financing that system that achieve the minimum standards. This approach is very closely connected to the national goals approach of system redesign. Plaintiffs in an adequacy case typically include a group of students suing as representatives of a class of similarly situated students who allege that the serious underperformance of their schools violates the state constitutional guarantee of a free and adequate education. The precise definition of an adequate education may vary by state and be difficult to define, but state standards adopted in the mid-1980s provide some benchmarks. Some schools in Kentucky and Alabama were so abysmally equipped and run that a factual finding of inadequacy was not difficult to obtain. The most challenging aspect of the adequacy suits is convincing the court to rule that the factually established inadequacies are a violation of the state constitution (see the chapter by Hershkoff).

The explicit focus on student achievement in the adequacy cases highlights the growing ties between finance reforms and other segments of the education reforms movement. Questions regarding what students ought to know and be able to do and whether public school systems have sufficiently met those goals differ substantially from questions about taxing power or efficient distribution of resources. Not surprisingly, schools with fewer human and financial resources tend to be less able or likely to provide adequate educational opportunities. When combined with the emerging shift to high minimum standards for all students as embodied in statements from the National Governors Association and President Bill Clinton's flagship education program, Goals 2000, states whose constitutions leave room for adequacy claims are under increasing pressure to respond (National Governors Association, 1990).

Finally, two recent court challenges bring us full circle from *Brown* to the present. *Sheff v. O'Neill* in Connecticut and *NAACP v. State of Minnesota* in Minneapolis combine desegregation and educational adequacy claims in an attack on de facto segregation, "[weaving] a new theory of unequal educational opportunity due to a high concentration of poor children in an urban school district" (Brittain, 1993, p. 167). The cases, which seek metropolitan-area-wide solutions under state constitutions that deconcentrate race and poverty within schools, can be seen as a direct attempt to overcome the U.S. Supreme Court's *Milliken v. Bradley* (1974) decision. Whereas the *Sheff* plaintiffs seek a range of remedies through changes in school boundaries and admissions, plaintiffs in *NAACP* seek (among other things) new uses of strict land-use zoning to redistribute low-income housing, together with metropolitan education system changes. The Minneapolis case was filed in September 1995 and barring a settlement is expected to go to trial in 1998. Plaintiffs in *Sheff* won on appeal to the Connecticut Supreme Court and continue to negotiate with the state legislature over the scope of the state's response. Although the Minneapolis case has not yet been tried, and although the state's response to the *Sheff* ruling has been considerably narrower than hoped for by the plaintiffs, both cases point to an increasing recognition in the courts of the connections between housing and school segregation, school finance, and educational adequacy.

Equity reformers have made concrete progress in improving equality of educational opportunity, and through the adequacy strategy they have been able to achieve more comprehensive and substantive reform of state education systems. But oncoming changes in educational practice and system organization are leading to fundamentally different school finance systems that reopen questions about equity. School vouchers, public school choice, charter schools, site-based management and budgeting, and accountability systems linked to student performance goals all make significant challenges to the present finance system (Odden, 1992), and legislatures, jurists, governors, and bureaucracies are proceeding with these new initiatives. Whether and how these new systems will better serve urban and poor students will doubtless need to be explored through research and legal action. But as the remaining chapters in this book suggest, achieving equity in the new systems may depend at least as much on the ability of parents and urban advocates to establish a voice and a presence in the reform process as it does on the particular legal strategies and actions pursued.

NOTES

1. Foundation-aid programs typically guarantee that schools that tax at the minimum rate receive enough state aid to raise their per-pupil revenues to a set minimum foundation. Power-equalizing programs assure that each school district yields the same tax revenue per millage of property tax by supplementing local revenue with state funds or by a system of tax-base sharing.

2. Average daily attendance rather than average enrollment figures are traditionally used in state aid formulas. Higher levels of student absenteeism in urban areas therefore reduce their share of state aid.

3. Average state general sales tax revenues, for example, grew 9.9 percent from 1987 to 1988 and 7.4 percent from 1988 to 1989. In 1989, individual income tax and corporate net income tax revenues grew by 10.8 percent and 10.4 percent, respectively (U.S. Department of Commerce, Bureau of the Census, cited in Wulf, 1992).

REFERENCES

Paul E. Barton, Richard J. Coley, and Margaret E. Goertz. 1991. *The State of Inequality.* Princeton: Educational Testing Service Policy Information Center.

Robert Berne and Leanna Stiefel. 1984. *The Measurement of Equity in School Finance: Conceptual, Methodological and Empirical Dimensions.* Baltimore: Johns Hopkins University Press.

John C. Brittain. 1993. Educational and Racial Equity Toward the Twenty-first Century: A Case Experiment in Connecticut. In *Race in America: The Struggle for Equality,* edited by Herbert Hill and James E. Jones, Jr. Madison: University of Wisconsin Press.

Stephen J. Carroll and Rolla Edward Park. 1983. *The Search for Equity in School Finance.* Cambridge, Mass.: Ballinger–Rand Corporation.

William H. Clune. 1993. The Shift from Equity to Adequacy in School Finance. *The World and I* 8, no. 9 (September).

Mary Fulton and David Long. 1993. *School Finance Litigation: A Historical Summary.* Denver: Education Commission of the States.

Harper v. Hunt. 1993. no. CV-91-0117-R (Ala. Cir. Ct. Montgomery County).

Michael W. La Morte. 1989. Courts Continue to Address the Wealth Disparity Issue. *Educational Evaluation and Policy Analysis* 11, no. 1:3–15.

Marilyn Morheuser. Testimony Before the U.S. Senate Subcommittee on Education, Arts, and Humanities, August 3, 1993.

National Governors Association. 1990. *Educating America: State Strategies for Achieving the National Education Goals.* Washington, D.C.: National Governors Association.

Jennifer A. O'Day and Marshall S. Smith. 1991. Systemic School Reform. In *The Politics of Curriculum and Testing,* edited by Susan Fuhrman and B. Malen. Philadelphia: Falmer.

Allan R. Odden. 1992. School Finance and Education Reform: An Overview. In *Rethinking School Finance: An Agenda for the 1990s,* edited by Allan R. Odden. San Francisco: Jossey-Bass.

Allan R. Odden and Lawrence Picus. 1992. *School Finance: A Policy Perspective.* New York: McGraw-Hill.

Rose v. Council for Better Education. 1989. 790 S.W.2d 186 (Ky. 1989).

Gerald Rosenberg. 1991. *The Hollow Hope: Can Courts Bring About Social Change?* Chicago: University of Chicago Press.

Myron Schwartz and Jay Moskowitz. 1988. *Fiscal Equity in the United States.* Washington, D.C.: Decision Resources.

William E. Thro. 1994. Judicial Analysis During the Third Wave of School Finance Litigation: The Massachusetts Decision as a Model. *Boston College Law Review* 35:597–617.

———. 1989. To Render Them Safe: The Analysis of State Constitutional Provisions in Public School Finance Reform Litigation. *Virginia Law Review* 75:1669.

Dore Van Slyke, Alexandra Tan, and Martin Orland with Anna Danegger. 1995. *School Finance Litigation: A Review of Key Cases.* Washington, D.C.: Finance Project.

Henry S. Wulf. 1992. State Government Finances, 1990. In *The Book of the States.* 1992–93 ed. Vol. 29. Lexington: Council of State Governments.

Chapter 2 School Finance
Reform and the Alabama
Experience

Helen Hershkoff

In communities across the country, parents are increasingly going to court to enforce their children's state constitutional right to education.[1] Many of these lawsuits claim that public schools have insufficient resources to provide their students with even a minimally adequate education. Conditions in the children's schools are often bleak: dilapidated and unsafe buildings, dirty and poorly maintained facilities, and widespread deficiencies of essential resources such as textbooks and equipment. Moreover, such schools are said to have low expectations of their students' ability to succeed, and standardized test scores and other conventional measures of learning are frequently unacceptably low.[2]

In response to these lawsuits, courts in about one-third of the states have struck down school funding methods and in some states have even found entire public school systems to violate state constitutional mandates. Judicial declarations that a state public school system is inadequate and inequitable have precipitated legislative efforts to increase school funding, to restructure public schools, and to hold school systems accountable for the achievement of students.[3]

This chapter addresses efforts by civil rights advocates in one southern state to use a state constitutional right to education as a lever to precipitate systemic school reform. The discussion proceeds from the perspective of a lawyer involved in the planning and litigation of education cases for the American Civil Liberties Union.[4] The first part presents an abbreviated case study of *Harper v. Hunt* (the author served as one of plaintiffs' counsel), a lawsuit that successfully challenged the inadequacy and inequity of the public school system in Alabama. Because the case is pending, it is premature to offer conclusions about the lawsuit's effectiveness as a catalyst for educational improvement. But even if the comments of this chapter are provisional, it seems clear that the lawsuit can already claim at least one major victory: it has encouraged new constituencies to participate in the school reform process, thereby altering the political climate for educational change. The second part of this chapter describes three features of *Harper* that seem to have contributed to the lawsuit's constituency-building capacity: plaintiffs' use of a state constitutional adequacy theory; plaintiffs' reliance on the state court as the focus of judicial activity; and plaintiffs' collaboration, at both the liability and the remedial stages of the lawsuit, with legislative and executive officials. The chapter concludes with the suggestion that judicially precipitated reform may be most enduring when it is able to facilitate a more inclusive public discourse on the need for institutional change. But it also questions the sufficiency of deliberative dialogue as a solution to the problem of underresourced, underachieving schools.

HARPER V. HUNT

In January 1991, the American Civil Liberties Union and its Alabama affiliate filed a class action lawsuit in Montgomery County Circuit Court challenging the public school system of Alabama as inequitable, inadequate, and in violation of the Alabama constitution's guarantee of a "liberal education."[5] In the lawsuit, the ACLU represented a class of schoolchildren from school systems across the state who alleged that they were being denied an adequate and equitable education. A companion case, brought by separate counsel, involved parents and school districts constituting an advocacy group called the Alabama Coalition for Equity. In addition, students in need of special education moved to intervene in the consolidated lawsuits and were certified as a statewide subclass, and the Alabama Disabilities Advocacy Program also intervened as a plaintiff.[6]

When the *Harper* complaint was filed, Alabama ranked forty-ninth in the nation in its per capita expenditures for public education.[7] The state contributed only about $850 for each child's education, and school districts depended to a significant extent on local revenue for education spending. As in other parts of the United States, property wealth is not evenly distributed among Alabama school districts: at the time the lawsuit was filed, the wealthiest system in Alabama had $4,820 per student from state and local revenues for education spending, the poorest, only $2,371.[8]

As a result of Alabama's system of school financing, plaintiffs alleged, many public schools in low-wealth districts throughout the state did not have sufficient funding to provide students with the most basic components of a minimally adequate education. Their complaint recounted that in one system in which a plaintiff child resided, students had to carry bottles of water to class because the water at school was contaminated; in others, the plumbing did not work. Elsewhere, schools were so overcrowded that portable trailers served as classrooms for elementary schoolchildren, and some trailers often leaked when it rained. Some schools so lacked for resources that students and teachers had to take time from classroom instruction to conduct candy and bake sales to raise money for basic supplies such as paper towels and writing paper. The plaintiff children attended schools with no infirmary and no school nurse, no guidance counselors, and few course offerings—no art, no music, no advanced math.

The *Harper* complaint further contended that Alabama's underfunded and inadequate public school system related directly to the state's segregationist past.[9] In 1956, Alabama amended its constitution to disclaim any public responsibility for the education or training of the state's children. The history of this amendment—which included an explicit authorization for parents to choose to send their children to schools "provided for their own race"—reflected the state's goal of circumventing the desegregation mandate of *Brown v. Board of Education*.[10] Plaintiffs alleged that Alabama spent less money on education than virtually any other state in the union because of the continued existence of a well-funded and government-supported network of all-white private schools that evolved during the state's period of "massive resistance" to desegregation rulings of the federal judiciary.

In an early threshold victory, the *Harper* court declared that the 1956 amendment to the state constitution was void ab initio under the Fourteenth Amendment to the U.S. Constitution because it had the intent and continuing effect of depriving African American children of their state constitutional right to equal and adequate educational opportunities.[11] The court effectively restored a right to education to the Alabama constitution. The question as to whether the state's system of public school funding currently deprives schoolchildren of their enjoyment of this right was left to trial.

In preparing the case for trial, plaintiffs forged an early and important alliance with the Alabama Department of Education. Named as a defendant in the lawsuit, the department nevertheless declined to defend the existing educational system and instead obtained permission from the court to switch sides and join the *Harper* plaintiff class as plaintiffs. Moreover, although the governor vigorously opposed the lawsuit, he was forced to admit at his deposition that the state's public schools were inadequate for their educational mission.[12]

At trial, plaintiffs established the unconstitutionality of Alabama's educational system through a multi-prong approach that emphasized the interrelationship between educational inputs (the resources that form the enabling conditions for learning) and educational outputs (the cognitive and noncognitive goals that an educational system is expected to achieve).[13] Like many other states, Alabama has a variety of legislative and administrative standards governing important educational inputs, such as school buildings, curriculum, and teaching staff, as well as an output-based system of performance-based accreditation.[14] Plaintiffs presented extensive empirical evidence to demonstrate that schools in low-wealth systems were unable to meet the state's own resource and accreditation requirements—despite the fact that Alabama's standards in many respects did not themselves comport with evolving standards of educational adequacy. In addition, because local education authorities may have political incentives to construct regulatory standards that underenforce norms, plaintiffs urged the court to consider nationally recognized educational standards as part of its constitutional assessment of programmatic adequacy. These national standards provided the court with guidance on such matters as special education, dropout rates, and programs for socially and economically disadvantaged students.

Plaintiffs presented their evidence through the direct testimony of parents, schoolchildren, teachers, principals, and school staff. Plaintiffs also relied on a number of in-state and nationally recognized experts whose fields include school finance, educational psychology, and curriculum development. One of the plaintiffs' lead expert witnesses, Margaret E. Goertz of Rutgers University, analyzed the state's school finance formula to show how it prevents low-wealth school districts from having the funds needed to provide basic educational opportunities and creates broad interdistrict disparities. In particular, she showed that the top quintile of high-wealth school districts in Alabama had $750 more per pupil per year than the bottom quintile of low-wealth schools, or roughly $18,000 more per classroom and more than $4,000,000 in an average-sized school district. Goertz further showed that with the extra money that wealthy school districts have, poor districts could buy, for each classroom in a district, new textbooks for every student in six subjects; an increase in the teacher's salary to that offered in the higher-wealth systems; five laminated wall maps and one globe; four bulletin boards; and twelve microscopes.[15] Expert testimony showed further that the state school funding formula causes resource disparities not only among school districts but also at the school level. Steven E. Ross of Memphis State University, together with professors from the University of Alabama and Auburn University, conducted a comprehensive field study of conditions in forty-five low-wealth and high-wealth schools, focusing on staff levels, curriculum offerings, school facilities, and school equipment and supplies. On each of these measures, low-wealth schools were worse off than high-wealth schools and on many measures did not reach levels of educational adequacy.[16]

Finally, plaintiffs' experts demonstrated the ways in which resource deficiencies in low-wealth public schools adversely affect educational outcomes, broadly measured by such assessments as student achievement, dropout rates, labor market success, and economic development. For example, Alan Krueger, professor of economics and public affairs at the Department of Economics and Woodrow Wilson School at Princeton University, presented affidavit testimony on the relation between school quality and economic return to education. He urged that in assessing program adequacy the court look beyond standardized test scores and include student labor market success as an indicator. His conclusions in Alabama are consistent with findings elsewhere that school quality (as measured by pupil-teacher ratio and average teacher salary) is an important determinant of student income levels following entry into the labor market.[17]

Based on plaintiff's evidence and its interpretation of the governing law, the *Harper* court in March 1993 issued a landmark liability decision holding that the Alabama constitution requires public education to be both equitable and adequate and that the education currently being provided in Alabama fails to meet that standard. In its decision, the court defined educational adequacy in terms of nine capacities that all Alabama students must have the opportunity to achieve.[18] The nine capacities include the development of skills in oral and written communication, math, and science; economic, social, and political knowledge sufficient for civic participation; knowledge of the arts to appreciate cultural heritage; academic and vocational training to

pursue intelligent life's work and to compete in world markets; and sufficient guidance and support "so that every student is encouraged to live up to his or her full human potential."

The court assigned to the defendants responsibility for translating the liability order into an operational plan that will bring the Alabama educational system into constitutional compliance. In a development that is somewhat unusual in institutional reform litigation, the defendants agreed to work collaboratively with the plaintiffs to develop the remedial plan, in a process reflecting the broad political context of educational reform in Alabama. Throughout the summer of 1993, the parties worked under the auspices of a court-appointed facilitator to develop defendants' reform proposal, engaging the participation of experts, community representatives, and others in their discussions. The governor also convened a special task force on education reform that sponsored public meetings and solicited citizen input on how the state should restructure its public school system to meet constitutional requirements. At the same time, A+, a local group of civic and business leaders, sponsored a series of "town meetings" that directed community discussion on specific plans for education reform. In addition, the Coalition of Alabamians Reforming Education mobilized grassroots support for reform through a series of local educational summits.

This multifaceted approach implicated virtually every aspect of educational reform and involved intense public scrutiny. During this period, school change was the major story in the state's leading newspapers and talk shows. After the defendants submitted their remedial proposal to the court for approval, the court ordered a public hearing pursuant to the state's class action statute to review the fairness of the state's plan. Two days before the court hearing, a group of parents and taxpayers who were opposed to the reform effort moved to intervene in the action. The court denied their motion but provided them, as well as others, an opportunity to present views in open court and through written submissions. The dissident contingent later appealed the denial of their motion to intervene to the Supreme Court of Alabama.[19]

Before entering defendants' proposal as its remedy order, the court ordered a few modifications in response to the comments and views presented during the class-action fairness hearing. As finally entered, the remedy order is based on the assumptions that all Alabama students can achieve "at significantly higher levels" and that learning environments must enable students "to achieve educational success."[20] Among the topics covered by the court's remedy order are the need for:

- adequate and equitable school funding;
- clean, safe, and adequate school facilities;
- services to overcome social and economic barriers to learning;
- adequate and safe transportation;
- adequate textbooks and instructional materials;
- early childhood education;
- school-based decision-making;
- increased staff development;
- improved use of technology.[21]

Significantly, the remedy order does not specify how these areas are to be brought into constitutional compliance. Instead, it articulates broad principles as a framework for reform and assigns to the state Board of Education and the superintendent responsibility for developing more detailed plans to effectuate its terms. Although plaintiffs participated in the development of the remedy order, the order reserves their right to seek to modify the decree if it fails in practice to redress the school system's constitutional violations. In addition, the court retains power to monitor enforcement and to enter additional orders as necessary.

Fob James, subsequently elected governor, mounted a major legal challenge to the remedy order and to the idea of court-precipitated change. In January 1997, the Alabama Supreme Court upheld the authority of the Alabama courts in cases such as *Harper* to issue a remedy where a constitutional violation has been found. The court stressed, however, the importance of deferring in the first instance to remedial plans proposed by the other branches. Governor James moved the court to reconsider its decision. As of June 1997 that motion had not yet been decided by the court.[22]

LITIGATION AND SCHOOL REFORM

The Alabama school case illustrates how litigation aimed at educational adequacy can affect a community's broader thinking about public schools and the value of public education. At the same time, *Harper* raises a number of questions about the capacity of a rights-based, court-centered, state-focused strategy to achieve meaningful school reform. This part discusses the structural features of the *Harper* litigation that seem most important for affecting public discourse and facilitating a more inclusive politics of educational reform.

Rights-Based Approach

Like other school cases before it, the *Harper* litigation depends on a rights-based strategy that is doctrinally grounded in state and not federal law.[23] But *Harper's* approach differs in significant respects. Earlier school cases enforcing state constitutional rights to education emphasized equality as the main constitutional end and made fiscal equity the prime remedial goal. These cases looked exclusively at the allocation of education funds within a state, without asking whether total funding was sufficient to meet the schools' programmatic mission.[24] The Alabama school case, by contrast, sought to enforce a right to education that is both equitable and adequate. *Harper* thus broadened the litigation focus, asking what the mission of public schools ought to be, given the state constitutional mandate, and whether the state's schools have sufficient resources to enable all children to attain shared educational goals. *Harper* signals a broader strategic shift in education reform litigation, marking an evolution parallel to that of welfare rights theory, which moved from an emphasis on the formal equality of poor persons to the provision of "just wants."[25]

The Alabama experience also highlights the role that race continues to play in local educational politics and emphasizes the need to link the right to an adequate education with multicultural concerns. In *Harper* the inadequacy of the state's public schools had its roots in the state's segregationist past and its conscious effort to subvert the Supreme Court's mandate in *Brown*. The harmful effects of the state's "massive resistance" to the federal constitutional requirement of equal educational opportunity continue to this day in terms of inferior and inadequate facilities and resources. The remedy order makes respect for cultural diversity one of its basic assumptions and calls for participation by all groups in the process of constitutional implementation.[26]

The lawsuit, however, does not seek to desegregate the state's schools.[27] Indeed, the civil rights community embraced an adequacy approach to education reform only after changes in federal equal protection doctrine rendered interdistrict remedies virtually impossible to achieve and changes in demographic patterns made intradistrict remedies futile.[28] Recognizing integration as only a contingent tool, the new wave of education reform litigation seeks to implement *Brown* by placing educational adequacy at the decision's core.[29]

Some scholars have criticized litigation reform efforts that rely on a rights-based approach, contending that they tend to isolate the process of constitutional change from ordinary political life. Without entering this debate, it is important to note that such criticisms focus largely on institutional reform litigation in federal court aimed at the enforcement of equality-based rights.[30] Litigation in state court seeking to enforce rights of a more substantive nature may have different implications for citizen participation and for long-term political change. In particular, the right to an adequate education may have a generative capacity that is absent from litigation seeking to enforce rights of formal equality. In a world in which resources seem to be shrinking, the right to an adequate education arguably benefits not only plaintiffs but also the broader community by facilitating a higher quality of life in which all members share. In addition, implementation of adequacy-based remedies can entail broad changes in governance that may alter the political power structure in affected communities. And because the goal of educational adequacy is in part outcome-driven, enforcement of such a right allows taxpayers to associate their remedial dollars with better test scores, safer buildings, and more accountable forms of governance.

Finally, in defining an adequate education, the court plays an important pedagogic function by articulating the social values of public schooling and enlisting the entire community in their support.[31] These values resonate deeply in our democratic life. By giving judicial voice to a shared goal of school improvement, the court's declaration has the potential to draw diverse players together in a collaborative, rather than antagonistic, enterprise.

Some commentators may criticize an adequacy approach because it compels judges to decide questions of educational standards and quality, questions that may be portrayed as beyond the court's institutional competence. Indeed, such a concern—if widely held—could undermine the constituency-building capacity of adequacy claims by calling into question the legitimacy of judicial intervention in educational matters. A court assessing a claim of constitutional inadequacy is likely, however, to draw significant guidance from educational standards that the state itself has enacted as indicia of programmatic sufficiency.[32] Because these standards come with the stamp of democratic approval, they lend majoritarian appeal to the court's analysis. Moreover, as *Harper* illustrates, once the court has entered its constitutional declaration, it is likely at the remedial stage to assign to the legislative and executive branches the task of drawing up (at least in the first instance) detailed plans to satisfy the constitutional mandate. In *Harper*, for example, the court broadly defined the nature of the children's constitutional right to a "liberal" education, allowed the parties and others an extensive opportunity to elaborate on that right in programmatic and other operational terms, ordered the state Board of Education and other defendants to design an education system to effectuate that right, and retained jurisdiction to ensure enforcement. In this way, the court constrained its activities within conventionally accepted norms of institutional legitimacy.

Role of State Courts

Like many other education reform efforts, the *Harper* case relied on state courts as an institutional catalyst for structural change. In a few states, legislatures have initiated education reform efforts without judicial action or even the threat of judicial action. But states that are most advanced in systemic change have had the benefit of court decrees.[33] Although individual legislators may be sympathetic to the reform process, litigation is often necessary to overcome political inertia or to provide political cover against ballot-box pressure.

For many years, civil rights advocates purposefully avoided state courts on the view that the federal courts offered a more sympathetic and open forum for the enforcement of individual rights.[34] The Alabama experience suggests, however, that the education reform process may enjoy specific benefits from litigation in a state, rather than a federal, court. In particular, state courts share certain institutional features that may enable them to facilitate a more inclusive public discourse than is currently possible in federal courts, and the development of such a discourse may affect the long-term viability of progressive change.[35] Some of these institutional features relate to technical rules of procedure that shape the legitimate boundaries of constitutional decision-making. A full discussion of these procedures goes beyond the scope of this chapter. But an example may suffice.

"Standing" is a constitutional doctrine that determines which individuals can assert claims in court. Outside the First Amendment context, federal courts typically do not permit taxpayers qua taxpayers to challenge allegedly unconstitutional governmental practices. State courts, by contrast, tend to have more relaxed rules of standing, thus affording greater judicial access to citizen groups and enhanced receptivity to citizen claims.[36] The open, porous nature of state court adjudication may tend to encourage the formation of "intermediate" community groups that some commentators believe essential to the functioning of a robust democracy.[37] When such groups come to court to press their claims, they are expected to work out their differences within the principled framework of constitutional discourse, which differs significantly from the rough and tumble of legislative bargaining. The Alabama court's standing rules afforded citizen groups such as the Alabama Coalition for Equity a role in the judicial reform process that might have been foreclosed in federal court. By encouraging the participation of previously excluded groups in constitutional decision-making, the *Harper* court potentially encouraged a more inclusive political discourse on the need for long-term educational change.

One should not assume, however, that judicially sponsored dialogue inevitably can or should produce social consensus.[38] Whatever shared assumptions a community may have about public schooling, education remains a deeply personal and potentially divisive issue. The process of deliberative dialogue assumes that rational discourse is the best approach to public problems. Some situations, however, may require a healthy dose of idealism or other "non-commodity" values for change to be effective.[39]

Under certain circumstances, dialogue may enhance cooperation from affected interests.[40] But it may also exacerbate differences and harden positions.[41] In Alabama, for example, focus groups, court-facilitated discussion, a governor's task force, editorial pages, and a court-ordered fairness hearing enlarged the scope of public dialogue and gave greater voice to many underrepresented interests and values. It also, however, enabled those favoring the status quo to oppose reform in a systematic way.

One should not underestimate the effect that community opposition can have on state court decision-making. Unlike federal judges, who have the guarantee of life tenure during good behavior, state judges in many states are elected officials.[42] Despite the comparatively long tenure of many state judicial officers, a mobilized electorate can wield considerable influence against judges who are perceived as indifferent to majoritarian sentiment or ahead of community standards in the enforcement of constitutional rights.[43] In Alabama, for example, the *Harper* trial judge was unsuccessful in a bid for a seat on the Alabama appellate bench and ultimately yielded to public pressure to recuse himself from the monitoring stage of the school case.[44] Despite temporary setbacks in the litigation process, however, the court case has galvanized public discussion. In slow but steady steps, a reform agenda moves forward.

Role of States and Localities

Finally, the Alabama school case shows the preeminent role that states and localities are currently playing in education reform. This leadership role derives in part from the state constitutional duty to provide an adequate educational system and the historical reliance on local property wealth to fund the public schools. It also fits comfortably with the long tradition in America of regarding education as primarily a local obligation subject to local control and local preference.[45] For these reasons, state-based education reform carries an aura of political legitimacy because it seems to emerge from the will of the people.

At the same time, however, a state-based reform strategy comes with inherent limitations.[46] As we have seen, the task of translating a court's constitutional decree into detailed programmatic reform is typically assigned to the legislative and the executive branches. In particular states, serious technical limitations can impede the reform process because existing departments of education may lack the capacity or expertise to design meaningful remedial plans. Moreover, although we refer to the state as a single juridical unit, it in fact comprises a complex system of governance, with both vertical and horizontal elements, and coordination of the various aspects of reform presents structural difficulties that may be hard to overcome in a bureaucracy that is protective of existing prerogative. In addition, many departments of education or other educational authorities may be captive to ordinary electoral politics, making it difficult for less favored groups, even armed with a court's decree, to press educational reforms.

Continued judicial oversight of the enforcement efforts of state departments of education is only a partial solution to this problem. Governance through self-monitoring must become part of a locality's political structure.[47] In addition, state-driven reform must become part of a federal strategy that preserves opportunities for local discretion but assures funding sufficient to meet high quality goals for all students. At least since *Brown v. Board of Education,* the federal government has shown the capacity to play a galvanizing role in education reform. Decisional law under the U.S. Constitution provided a necessary impetus to the states in moving toward equal educational opportunity regardless of race and gender. Federal legislation such as the Elementary and Secondary Act of 1965 provided incentives to states to meet the educational and fiscal challenges of children with special needs. And federal commissions such as the President's National Commission on Excellence in Education in 1983 spurred the states throughout the 1980s to enact legislative minimum performance standards. Despite the strong local tradition that characterizes education in the United States, the problem of inadequate public schooling is a national problem in need of a national solution.[48]

Harper v. Hunt is an example of how advocates in one state used state constitutional rights to attempt to reform public schooling. The state constitutional guarantee of an equitable and adequate education became the basis for a potential restructuring of the governance, financing, and educational program of the Alabama public school system. Because the court's liability decision has not yet been implemented, it is too early to assess the effectiveness of the litigation as a catalyst for reform. In other structural reform settings, such as prisons and mental hospitals, litigation has produced significant improvement in institutional conditions,[49] and it can be expected that the *Harper* case will also positively affect the public schools of Alabama. But whatever the results, the Alabama school case has already mobilized new constituencies in education reform and affected the structure of institutional change.

NOTES

1. The constitution of every state explicitly addresses the provision of free public schools. State constitution education articles are collected in Allen W. Hubsch, "The Emerging Right to Education Under State Constitutional Law," *Temple L. Rev.* 65 (1992): 1325, 1343–48.

2. For a description of school conditions in selected communities, see Jonathan Kozol, *Savage Inequalities: Children in America's Schools* (New York: Crown, 1991).

3. See Michael Heise, "State Constitutions, School Finance Litigation, and the 'Third Wave': From Equity to Adequacy," *Temple L. Rev.* 68 (1995): 1151.

4. This chapter is adapted from a presentation at a seminar on school finance cosponsored by the Howard Samuels State Management and Policy Center and the Ford Foundation in May 1994. The author was associate legal director of the American Civil Liberties Union from 1987 through 1995 and represented plaintiffs or appeared as amicus curiae on behalf of plaintiffs in school reform cases in Alabama, California, Connecticut, Louisiana, Maryland, Massachusetts, and New York. Other members of the Alabama litigation team, past and present, include Robert Segall, Martha I. Morgan, Adam S. Cohen, Eileen Hershenov, Julie Fernandes, Christopher A. Hansen, and Robin Dahlberg. The author notes the extraordinary contribution of Olivia Turner, executive director of the Alabama Civil Liberties Union, to the struggle for education reform in Alabama, and thanks Chris Hansen, Julie Fernandes, and Martha Morgan for comments on an earlier draft of this chapter and Kara Schiffman for helpful research assistance. The ideas expressed in this chapter are those of the author and do not necessarily reflect the views of the American Civil Liberties Union or of the other members of the Alabama litigation team. The author is now an assistant professor of law at the New York University School of Law and is grateful to the Filomen D'Agostino and Max E. Greenberg Faculty Research Fund at the New York University School of Law, which provided generous financial support for this research.

5. Alabama Constitution, art. 14, sec. 256.

6. *Harper v. Hunt (Harper)*, No. CV-91–0117-R (Ala. Cir. Ct. Montgomery County), was consolidated with *Alabama Coalition for Equity, Inc. v. Hunt*, No. CV-90–833-R (Ala. Cir. Ct. Montgomery County). The procedural history of the Alabama lawsuit is set out in the decision on liability, *Alabama Coalition for Equity, Inc. v. Hunt*, Nos. CV-90–833-R, CV-91–0117-R (Ala. Cir. Ct. Montgomery County, filed Apr. 1, 1993), reprinted in

Opinion of the Justices No. 338, 624 So. 2d 107 app. (Ala. 1993). This chapter refers to the consolidated cases as *Harper.*

7. See, e.g., National Education Association, *Rankings of the States, 1988* (Washington, D.C.: NEA, 1988); State Department of Education, *Alabama Where Do We Stand? A Comparative View of Key Educational and Financial Statistics* (Alabama: 1989).

8. *Opinion of the Justices,* 624 So. 2d at 115, 120.

9. This discussion draws on an earlier account, Helen Hershkoff and Adam S. Cohen, "School Choice and the Lessons of Choctaw County," *Yale L. & Pol'y Rev.* 10 (1992): 1, 4–12.

10. 347 U.S. 483 (1954).

11. Order, *Alabama Coalition for Equity, Inc. v. Hunt,* Nos. CV-90–833-R, CV-91–0117-R (Ala. Cir. Ct. Montgomery County August 13, 1991).

12. *Opinion of the Justices,* 624 So. 2d at 137.

13. This discussion draws on an earlier account; see Martha I. Morgan, Adam S. Cohen, and Helen Hershkoff, "Establishing Education Program Inadequacy: The Alabama Example," *U. Mich. J.L. Ref.* 28 (1995): 559.

14. See, e.g., Alabama Education Improvement Act of 1991, 1991 Ala. Acts 602 (codified in scattered sections of 16 Ala. Code [Supp. 1994]), *repealed in part by* the Accountability Act, 1995 Ala. Acts 313.

15. *Opinion of the Justices,* 624 So. 2d at 117.

16. Ibid. at 121–23.

17. See David Card and Alan B. Krueger, "Does School Quality Matter? Returns to Education and the Characteristics of Public Schools in the United States," *J. Political Economy* 100 (1992): 1.

18. *Opinion of the Justices,* 624 So. 2d at 166.

19. See *Pinto v. Alabama Coalition for Equity, Inc.,* 662 So. 2d 894 (Ala. 1995). On appeal, the Supreme Court of Alabama reversed the trial court's denial of intervention with respect to the remedy—but not the liability—phase of the litigation.

20. See Remedy Order, *Alabama Coalition for Equity, Inc. v. Folsom,* Nos. CV-90–883-R, CV-91–0117-R (Ala. Cir. Ct. Montgomery County Oct. 22, 1993), reprinted in *Ex parte James,* 1997 WL 7736 at *65.

21. Ibid. at *64–*80.

22. In October 1995, the *Harper* trial court issued an order denying motions to dismiss or vacate the remedy order, certifying it as a final order, and setting the case for argument on whether newly enacted legislation achieved the mandate of the remedy order. In November 1995, defendants appealed the remedy order to the Supreme Court of Alabama. In January 1997, the court held that the remedy order was not final for the purposes of appeal and that implementtion of the order should be delayed for one year in order to give the legislative and executive branches an opportunity to act. See *Ex parte James,* Nos. 19500300, 1950031, 1950240, 19959241, 195048, 195049, and 1950917, 1997 WL 7736 (Ala. Jan. 10, 1997).

23. The *Harper* complaint also includes a federal due process claim, and the court found that the education system violates this right. See *Opinion of the Justices,* 624 So. 2d at 112, 161–62.

24. See William H. Clune, "The Shift from Equity to Adequacy in School Finance," *Educ. Pol'y* 8 (1994): 376.

25. See Frank I. Michelman, "The Supreme Court, 1968 Term—Foreword: On Protecting the Poor Through the Fourteenth Amendment," *Harv. L. Rev.* 83 (1969): 7.

26. The remedy order provides: "The diversity, including racial and ethnic, that parents, teachers, and students bring to Alabama's education system must be respected, and all education must be provided in an atmosphere free from prejudice of whatever variety."

27. Compare *Sheff v. O'Neill,* 238 Conn. 1, 678 A.2d 1267 (1996), wherein the Connecticut Supreme Court held that plaintiff schoolchildren were deprived of equal educational opportunity by racial and economic isolation in the public schools and required the legislature to take affirmative remedial measures. The author was one of plaintiffs' counsel until 1995.

28. See Chris Hansen, "Are the Courts Giving Up? Current Issues in School Desegregation," *Emory L. Rev.* 42 (1993): 863, 864.

29. See Derrick S. Bell, "*Brown v. Board of Education* and the Interest-Convergence Dilemma," *Harv. L. Rev.* 93 (1980): 518.

30. See, e.g., Peter Gabel and Paul Harris, "Building Power and Breaking Images: Critical Legal Theory and the Practice of Law," *N.Y.U. Rev. L. & Soc. Change* 11 (1982): 369.

31. Compare Christopher L. Eisgruber, "Is the Supreme Court an Educative Institution?" *N.Y.U. L. Rev.* 67 (1992): 961, 967–68.

32. See James S. Liebman, "Implementing *Brown* in the Nineties: Political Reconstruction, Liberal Recollection, and Litigatively Enforced Legislative Reform," *Va. L. Rev.* 76 (1990): 349.

33. See Gail F. Levine, "Meeting the Third Wave: Legislative Approaches to Recent Judicial School Finance Rulings," *Harv. J. Legis.* 28 (1991): 507, 537–38.

34. See Burt Neuborne, "The Myth of Parity," *Harv. L. Rev.* 90 (1977): 1105.

35. See Helen Hershkoff, "State Courts, Welfare Rights, and the Hart & Wechsler Paradigm," *N.Y.U. Rev. L. & Soc. Change* (forthcoming).

36. See William A. Fletcher, "The 'Case or Controversy' Requirement in State Court Adjudication of Federal Questions," *Calif. L. Rev.* 78 (1990): 263.

37. See Cass R. Sunstein, "Beyond the Republican Revival," *Yale L.J.* 97 (1988): 1539, 1589.

38. See Robert M. Gordon, "The Dangers of Deliberation," *Yale L.J.* 106 (1997): 1313 (reviewing *Democracy and Disagreement* by Amy Gutmann and Dennis Thompson [1996]).

39. Compare Richard B. Stewart, "Regulation in a Liberal State: The Role of Non-commodity Values, *Yale L. J.* 92 (1983): 1537.

40. See Susan P. Sturm, "A Normative Theory of Public Law Remedies," *Georgetown L.J.* 79 (1991): 1355, 1390–1410.

41. See Michael A. Fitts, "Look Before You Leap: Some Cautionary Notes on Civic Republicanism," *Yale L.J.* 97 (1988): 1651, 1657.

42. See Council of State Governments, *The Book of the States, 1996–97,* vol. 31, 127–46 (Lexington, Ky., 1996).

43. See Note, "Unfulfilled Promises: School Finance Remedies and State Courts," *Harv. L. Rev.* 104 (1991): 1072, 1084.

44. See Order of August 23, 1995, *Alabama Coalition for Equity v. James,* Nos. CV-90–883-R, CV-91–0117-R (Ala. Cir. Ct. Montgomery County, Apr. 1, 1993).

45. See Richard A. Briffault, "Our Localism: Part II—Localism and Legal Theory," *Colum. L. Rev.* 90 (1990): 346, 384.

46. See Susan H. Fuhrman, "Challenges in Systemic Education Reform, CPRE Policy Briefs (Consortium for Policy Research in Education, RB-14–9/94).

47. See Charles F. Sabel, "Learning by Monitoring: The Institutions of Economic Development," in *The Handbook of Economic Sociology,* 137–66, ed. Neil J. Smelser and Richard Swedberg (New York: Russell Sage Foundation, 1994).

48. Compare John C. Pittenger, "Equity in School Finance: The Federal Government's Role?" *Conn. L. Rev.* 24 (1992): 757.

49. This view is contested in Gerald N. Rosenberg, *The Hollow Hope: Can Courts Bring About Social Change?* (Chicago: University of Chicago Press, 1991).

Chapter 3 Intradistrict Resource Disparities: A Problem Crying Out for a Solution

Peter D. Roos

In 1954, *Brown v. Board of Education* initiated an era of hope that educational disadvantage suffered by students of color would be overcome by breaking down segregation in our schools. Significant inroads were made in dismantling black-white segregation in the South, and cases were won in the North and the West that led to integration orders on behalf of Latino pupils, as well as African Americans. Yet today, four decades after *Brown,* few blacks and even fewer Latinos see desegregation as the panacea it was considered in 1954. A number of factors have led to this judgment, including demographics and the limited reach of the legal integration movement. Recent statistics confirm what we visually observe—most minority pupils attend neighborhood schools in which their own race predominates. Court rulings that have required intent to compel integration or made it difficult to remedy interdistrict disparities have hindered efforts to address housing-based school segregation.

Other factors have also served to undermine the desegregation strategy. Much of the desegregation that was ordered placed heavier burdens on minority students than on white students, and courts often failed to follow through when it came to making white institutions change their behavior and attitudes toward minority students who were "integrated." These shortcomings gave desegregation a bad name in many minority communities. Further, minority communities did not see much academic improvement resulting from desegregation. Yet another factor has operated in Latino communities, where desegregation was often perceived as a black-white issue that would only complicate the educational opportunities open to Latinos. With few exceptions, desegregation cases were initiated by black communities; a review of most of the desegregation cases involving Latinos would show that they generally intervened to assure that desegregation plans were fairly implemented and did not undermine bilingual programs. In short, as legally and morally compelling as desegregation was at the outset, particularly to African Americans, its vitality has been greatly sapped. Today black and Latino children in segregated schools continue to have educational failure rates that assure the perpetuation of poverty and misery.

There are many reasons why integration is valuable for both minority and white children. One key argument has always been that the placement of minority children in predominately minority schools facilitated discrimination. Integration, it was argued, makes it more difficult for whites and middle-class power brokers to discriminate against minority children because their own children are in the same schools.

The failure to desegregate has indeed perpetuated a number of disparities within school districts, and even where there has been some level of desegregation, it has frequently been accompanied by in-school segregation that has enabled an unequal allocation of resources.

Amazingly, there has been little effort in the past few decades to attack intradistrict resource disparities even though they obviously contribute to the differences in educational outcomes between white and middle-class pupils on the one hand and poor and minority pupils on the other. Indeed, there has been only a vague recognition that the problem even exists. In this chapter I will outline the problem, discuss one major legal effort to attack a portion of it, and argue that other litigators and advocates will fail the cause of equal opportunity if they do not use available tools to get at the root cause of this continuing disparity.

COMMON AREAS OF RESOURCE DISPARITY

Teacher Inequality

The single most important input a school system can offer a pupil is a skilled and trained teacher. Although all students need the best teaching that can be offered, poor children are even more dependent on teachers than are middle-class pupils; rarely does a poor child have family or community resources to fall back on if the teacher fails. Yet, providing this all-important resource is becoming increasingly difficult for poor school districts as supply falls farther behind demand and better teachers become more expensive.

A number of researchers present evidence suggesting that segregated schools are significantly more likely to have novice teachers teaching minority students.[1] Although research suggests that there may be a leveling off of teacher effectiveness after five to eight years of teaching, a strong body of research as well as ample anecdotal evidence reveals that first- and second-year teachers are considerably less effective than those who have some experience.[2] This lack of proficiency translates into inability to plan lessons well, to deal with classroom diversity, and to maintain the classroom order needed for instruction. In addition, placing inexperienced, and thus generally ineffective, teachers in inner-city schools serves to create a vicious cycle. Teachers whose first experience is one of failure and frustration transfer out of poor schools or the profession at a much higher rate than similar teachers who are assigned to middle-class schools, thus creating openings that must be filled with more inexperienced teachers.[3]

Not only do inner-city children disproportionately receive inexperienced teachers, but they also receive more than their share of teachers who lack the requisite teaching credentials.[4] This is the result of many of the same factors that produce disparities in teacher experience in urban schools: high turnover, inability to attract properly credentialed teachers, and the unwillingness of school districts to tackle the traditional prerogatives of seniority.[5]

Inequality in the allocation of scarce teacher resources also exists within schools. Researchers have suggested recently that even in schools where there is a mix of pupils, white students are likely to get better-trained teachers than minority students.[6] Students in the more advanced tracks—mostly white students—are taught by the school's better-trained teachers, leaving the remainder for students in the lower tracks—mostly minority students.[7] By placing inexperienced teachers—or those perceived as the least able to teach—in classes disproportionately attended by minority students, schools directly undermine minority students with bad teaching and also convey a message of futility to both teachers and pupils in those "low classes."

In short, a key input resource—the teacher—is disparately allocated to minority pupils who are grouped together in segregated schools or segregated tracks within schools. Rather than give the most to those with the greatest need we give the least. Is it any wonder that the gaps these children bring to school widen as they progress through the system? In addition to the misallocation of teacher resources, many minority students, particularly Latino students, increasingly find themselves substantially shortchanged in what may be the second most important tangible resource a school can provide: an educationally viable facility.

Facility Disparities

From Miami to New York, to Houston, to the inner city of Los Angeles, Latino children frequently attend school in facilities that are overcrowded, oversized, and outdated.

In some instances overcrowding has resulted in effective exclusion from school.[8] In others it has forced students to travel several hours a day to attend school—thus breaking the already tenuous but crucial link between parents and schools.[9]

The disparities are graphically reflected in Los Angeles. At Latino elementary schools in 1992–93 there were 254 square feet per pupil, whereas the corresponding figure for white schools was 555; 34 percent of Latino elementary schools exceeded district size goals, but no white schools exceeded these goals. These differences held at all three levels of schooling.

Whereas the problems occasioned by overcrowding are self-evident, a growing body of research tells us that oversized facilities, without substantial corrective action, tend to undermine the sense of community and adult-student relationship necessary for school success. A study by the Public Education Association of New York concludes that

> Students learn better in small schools because accountability and feeling part of the community is cultivated to a greater degree in a smaller school than in a larger one. An environment where individual participation thrives, where there is greater day-to-day attraction to learning, where there is peer pressure to take part in activities whether they be verbal or physical exchanges, and where shared cultural and moral values are strongly reinforced, creates a more positive learning environment. In other words, a small school's inherent smallness is its strongest weapon against illiteracy and low achievement.[10]

The reasons why inadequate facilities are more commonly found in minority communities include the unprecedented and tremendous growth of communities with large numbers of immigrants, the failure of an aging, predominantly white voting population to support school building in inner cities, and outright discrimination. Whatever the causes, those with the greatest needs often attend schools that are wholly inadequate and are taught by teachers who do not meet the standards expected, indeed demanded, by more affluent parents.

Dollar Disparities

One consequence of this situation is that school districts often spend less per pupil of their basic resources for students in inner-city schools. Faculty expenditures comprise approximately 80 percent of school-based expenditures in most districts. Better trained, more experienced teachers cost more than inexperienced, undercredentialed teachers. Further, a school district that jams large numbers of pupils into certain schools creates economies of scale. The result is that districts often spend less of their own money on poor and minority pupils than on those who are more affluent.[11]

THE *RODRIGUEZ* CONSENT DECREE

In 1986, representatives of Latino and African American schoolchildren sued the Los Angeles Unified School District, challenging the allocation of resources within the district. The *Rodríguez* case alleged that teacher, facility, and dollar disparities between predominantly minority (Latino and African American) schools and white schools denied the minority children equal protection of the law under the California constitution.[12]

Evidence gathered over five years of discovery generally supported the allegations, indicating that new and undercredentialed teachers tended to be concentrated in overcrowded, oversized schools serving a disproportionate number of minority children.[13] Although there were exceptions, on the whole this led to lower district per-pupil expenditures in minority schools. As one would expect, the disparities were generally greatest at the elementary level, where schools more closely reflected the demographics of small, more coherent communities.

Negotiations to resolve these issues culminated, after several weeks of hearings in August 1992, in a consent decree approved by the court. A history of those negotiations and of the challenges to the decree is instructive.

Proposed Teacher Remedy. The position of the plaintiffs was that the district had an obligation to increase recruitment of properly trained teachers, to alter the conditions that made teachers seek transfers to other communities, and to restrict transfer opportunities. Although equalization could theoretically have been accomplished by wholesale transfers of teachers, this was seen as counterproductive. Teachers forced into schools where they did not want to be were unlikely to report for work. More important, such teachers were likely to be the least enthusiastic about teaching poor and immigrant children, thus perpetuating their disadvantage.

Discussion with experts led counsel for the plaintiffs to conclude that although extra economic rewards might be of some value in addressing the problem, altering the conditions of employment in these schools offered the best format for success.[14] We urged the adoption of reduced class sizes (with an emphasis on the beginning teacher), expansion and improvement of mentor teacher programs, use of the professional development center concept propounded by Linda Darling-Hammond and her colleagues at Teachers College,[15] greater release and educational sabbatical opportunities, improved safety, and economic enhancements.

Proposed Facility Remedy. The plaintiffs saw the facility issue as relating closely to the teacher issue. Teachers forced to instruct in anonymous, overcrowded, unpleasant situations were less likely to commit their best teaching years to working in such schools.

The proposals were straightforward: increased building, the development of schools within schools to break down larger facilities, and the removal of inequities that had arisen from the placement of multi-track year-round schools in Latino neighborhoods.

The Settlement. The negotiations took place during a time of deep financial stress in the California schools in general and in the Los Angeles Unified School District in particular. In the 1990s, as a result of a number of factors including Proposition 13 and the deepest recession since the 1930s, California plunged from fifth in per-pupil expenditures nationwide to thirty-fourth. The Los Angeles schools teetered on the brink of bankruptcy, cutting teachers' salaries in the process. These factors led to a decision that would not have been made in more affluent times. It was agreed that the primary vehicle for equalization would be per-pupil dollar equalization. The positive aspects of such a plan were real: millions of dollars would move from more affluent schools to poorer schools. The agreement also hastened the movement toward school-based budget control. Under the agreement, each school would get the same dollar amount of basic educational resources per pupil and would have to "buy" services out of their budget. The chief disadvantage of this approach was that there was no commitment to add supplemental and needed resources for inner-city schools. All additions would be funded from the equalization—a considerable sum, but substantially less than was needed to do the job properly.

The teacher disparity is primarily addressed through the fiscal equalization program. First, schools above budget must reduce their expenditures to the average for a given grade level. Schools with below-average levels will be brought up to the average. Because teacher salaries are the primary cost of running a school, there will be fewer jobs available in the more affluent schools for highly paid teachers. This should prevent some of the movement of teachers from the inner city to more affluent areas of the city. In addition, there are provisions that require the central administration to take experience and training level into consideration when assigning teachers who have no other claim to a particular school, such as teachers new to the district. Possibly the most important piece is the requirement that schools separate their teacher budget from other expenditures. When a school is unable to use up its teacher budget because it cannot attract expensive teachers, it must use the excess to assist less experienced or less well-trained teachers. This should result in increased mentoring in these schools, greater released-time in-service work, and possibly smaller class size.

The provision for remedying inadequate facilities also reflects significant compromise, although it is a step in the desired direction. Possibly the most significant limitation is the inability to obtain new funding for facilities. Virtually all funding for facilities is derived from the state, which was not a party to the lawsuit. Although it is not clear that the outcome would have been different if the state had been a party, it might be wise to name the state in future lawsuits of this kind. In recognition of the district's limitations in generating funding for schools, the agreement merely mandates a mechanism to ensure that the district captures all of the state money available—something it had not always done in the past.

A greater effort was made to address the problem of large schools, although the final agreement on this issue also reflects a compromise. The decree sets caps on school building that can only be exceeded if the district conducts a written feasibility assessment study demonstrating its inability to adhere to the cap. Perhaps even more important is the requirement that whenever schools exceed a certain size, they must work with parents and community members to determine how to create schools within schools or make similar arrangements. This process is to be facilitated by a central office staff with expertise in the area. Locally developed plans must be adopted unless the central staff specifically rejects them and gives a written explanation of its objections. Appeals can be taken to the school board.

As is common with agreements of this sort, there are numerous reporting requirements. There is also a phase-in of the fiscal provisions, which will become fully operational in the 1997–98 school year. Court jurisdiction, which can be extended for cause, continues until 2005.

In sum, it is clear that *Rodríguez* will significantly alter the way the Los Angeles schools function, and it should result in enhanced resources for predominantly poor minority schools. It is not the perfect remedy but one that should serve as a starting point for addressing the shameful inequality in the delivery of key resources to the neediest members of our school population.

The agreement was challenged by the local teachers' union, strongly supported by the American Federation of Teachers. Their primary concern was that teachers not be forced to accept reassignment against their will—something that the plaintiffs abjured from the beginning. Their further concern, that site-based budget control would increase the power of principals, interestingly led to intervention by the administrators' union and unions representing nonprofessional staff. The distrust between each of these groups, as well as the general distrust of parents and other consumers toward school staff, clearly needs to be considered as systems seek to develop fiscal responsibility at school sites. Finally, a middle-class parents' group sought to scuttle the agreement on the grounds that poor children who receive compensatory assistance should not also receive an equalized base education. After several weeks of hearings, the concerns of each of these groups were rejected and the agreement became law in the Los Angeles Unified School District.

THE LEGAL UNDERPINNINGS OF INTRADISTRICT
RESOURCE ALLOCATIONS CHALLENGES

A key question for litigators seeking to challenge intradistrict disparities is whether to proceed in a state or a federal forum. The question can be resolved by reviewing the law of the state in which the problem has arisen and by assessing the strength of the relationship between the ethnicity of the disadvantaged population and the disparities in educational resources.

Disparities in the treatment of groups of individuals are commonly challenged on the basis of constitutional requirements that all individuals be provided "equal protection of the laws." The Fourteenth Amendment to the United States Constitution contains the federal equal protection clause. Most state constitutions have similar provisions but they are not always construed identically. A state clause may be more (but not less) vigilant against disparities than the Fourteenth Amendment. Certain states have identified education as a "fundamental interest" requiring a high level of justification for any meaning-ful disparity—even where race is not a factor.[16] Conversely, the United States Supreme Court has ruled that education is not fundamental under the Four-teenth Amendment.[17] This means that disparities challenged pursuant to the Fourteenth Amendment are likely to be viewed more tolerantly *unless* the plaintiffs can establish that intentional racial animus is at the root of the unequal treatment.[18]

Thus, if one is in a state in which education is deemed fundamental, a challenge based on the state constitution should almost certainly be the pri-mary vehicle for an attack on intradistrict disparities. If a state constitution has not been so construed there are other possibilities. First, of course, might be an assessment that intent to discriminate on racial grounds can be established. That would allow judgment on the basis of either state or federal constitutions. If race is clearly a dividing line but intent is more questionable, it is possible to challenge disparities using the regulations issued pursuant to Title VI of the 1964 Civil Rights Act.[19] Suits under these regulations may be maintained if a federally funded entity offers a benefit on different terms to students of differ-ent ethnicities or races.[20] Intent to discriminate need not be shown, although a school district can certainly show that no meaningful disparity does exist or that there are other grounds for justification.[21]

In short, state constitutional provisions *may* avoid the necessity of showing that intentional racial discrimination or indeed any racial discrimination is a factor. Mere establishment of meaningful disparities should sustain a claim. A federal claim will need to be predicated on race, although establishment of intent may not be necessary. In some districts, especially in certain predomi-nantly minority urban districts, disparities may owe more to class than to race. In most situations, the use of state provisions will be the primary vehicle for an attack on discrimination.

Plaintiffs can marshal powerful factual arguments that the disparities in question cause educational harm. Few courts have had the opportunity to consider such arguments, but in several desegregation cases, courts have found that disparities in faculty experience and credentials constitute denial of equal educational opportunities.[22] In *Hobson v. Hansen* (*Hobson I*), the district court observed that "It remains beyond denial that other factors being equal, experi-ence is a real asset for a teacher . . . moreover, it can not be questioned that the initial few years of teaching make an enormous contribution to a teacher's competence."[23] Another court has observed, "Indeed, it is a truism that the more the child is disadvantaged by other factors, the greater the need of the child for skillful teaching. Certainly it is fatuous to make declarations regarding the educational handicaps imposed upon a child by being in a segregated school and not to take reasonable measures to assure that such child is given teachers at least equal in qualification to those not so disadvantaged."[24]

The existence of overcrowding in predominantly minority schools led one court to conclude that "the adverse educational effects of overcrowding are . . . obvious."[25] Although the legal effect of oversized facilities has yet to be tested, the fact that most states and districts set goals for school size, coupled with expert testimony concerning the dangers of exceeding such goals, should easily lead courts to find legal failure.

Finally, monetary differences have been the subject of two decades of legal wrangling. Although some courts have concluded that education is not fundamental and thus permitted disparities, many have struck down per-pupil differences as violations of either state equal protection clauses or provisions requiring thorough and efficient delivery of educational services.[26]

In short, common sense, expert opinion, and case authority argue forcefully for court intervention when significant disparities in teacher experience, facilities, or dollars exist within a school district; "a child of the poor assigned willy-nilly to the inferior state school takes on the complexion of a prisoner complete with a minimum sentence of 12 years."[27] The situation cries out for relief.

A FINAL PLEA: CAN WE SOLVE THESE PROBLEMS WITHOUT LITIGATION?

There is little dispute that the widespread assignment of new and undercredentialed teachers to poor children, coupled with the provision of schooling in inadequate facilities, is a recipe for disaster. If we can't do more for those who are most in need, we will all suffer for it.

The intervention of the unions in the Los Angeles case, although a cause for dismay, also contained seeds of hope. The teachers' union was, in the plaintiffs' view, paranoid about the reassignment of teachers, but the solutions it proposed for the problem of teacher inadequacy actually matched those initially proposed by the plaintiffs. Both saw the provision of greater support for beginning teachers and improved conditions in inner-city schools as the ideal solutions. School board associations should also be expected to recognize the wisdom of this approach. This suggests that before embarking on an acrimonious round of litigation, we should look for common ground. Commonsense solutions, even those that cost money, may well be accepted by state legislatures that are increasingly aware that if we fail to turn our public schools around, we all will sink together.

NOTES

1. See, e.g., Choy and Gifford, "Resource Allocation in a Segregated School System: The Case of Los Angeles," *Journal of Education Finance* no. 6 (1980): 44–45; Bruno, "Teacher Compensation and Incentive Programs for Large Urban School Districts," *Elementary School Journal* no. 86 (1986): 425.

2. See, e.g., Featherstone, "First Year Teachers: What Are They Learning?" *The Harvard Education Letter* vol. 5, no. 4, July–August 1989.

3. See, e.g., Gifford, Choy, and Guttenberg, "Race, Ethnicity and Equal Employment Opportunity: An Investigation of Access to Employment and Assignment of Professional Personnel in New York City's Public Schools," Board of Education of the City of New York, 1969–74 (1977).

4. In Los Angeles, discovery undertaken in pursuance of *Rodriguez v. LAUSD,* Superior Court of the State of California, County of Los Angeles, C611358 (henceforth *Rodriguez*), revealed inter alia that 14.7 percent of the teachers in predominantly black elementary schools, and 14.4 percent of the teachers in predominantly Latino elementary schools, teach with incomplete credentials; the corresponding figure for white schools was 6 percent. With respect to teachers with a year or less of experience, the figures at the elementary school level were black schools, 20 percent; Latino schools, 16 percent; and white schools, 12 percent. The pattern held through all three levels of schooling.

5. See Bruno, "Teacher Compensation." See also the study of the Los Angeles Unified School District, "Hard to Staff Schools Report" (Evaluation and Training Institute, 1984).

6. Oakes, "Multiplying Inequalities: The Effects of Race, Social Class and Training on Opportunities to Learn Mathematics and Science" (Rand Corporation, 1990).

7. Ibid.

8. In the West Contra Costa School District in California, students missed more than nine hundred days of school in 1994–95 due to overcrowding and problems of finding adequate and convenient placement for them. Most were minorities. *Fudge v. West Contra Costa Unified School District,* Superior Court of California, County of Contra Costa, C9403756.

9. See generally Torres-Guzman, "Recasting Frames: Latino Parent Involvement," in *In the Interest of Language: Contexts for Learning and Using Language,* ed. Faltis and McGroarty (in press). See also Henderson, A., ed., "The Evidence Grows: Parent Participation and Student Achievement" (Columbus, Md.: National Committee for Citizens in Education, 1981).

10. "Small Schools and Savings: Affordable New Construction, Renovation, and Remodeling" (New York: Public Education Association, 1992). A study of Chicago schools found that school size accounted for 15.4 percent of the variation in achievement of students—second only to socioeconomic status. Hess and Corsino, "Examining the Effect of Intra-

District Variation of School Size and Resources," paper presented at the American Educational Research Association, March 1989. A major report by the Carnegie Council on Adolescent Development strongly indicts large anonymous schools for the failings of inner-city middle-school students. "Turning Points: Preparing American Youth for the 21st Century" (New York: Carnegie Council on Adolescent Development, 1989).

11. A study of the Los Angeles Unified School District revealed that several predominantly white administrative areas spent $500 per student more than was spent in two predominantly Chicano administrative areas. Expenditures per student in the white schools were $300 larger than those in a predominantly black area. "Excellence for Whom?" (The Achievement Council, 1984), 11. Similar findings have been made with respect to the New York City schools. "Promoting Poverty: The Shift of Resources away from Low-Income New York City School Districts" (New York: The Community Service Society of New York, 1987). This is not to say that overall expenditures on poor pupils may not be higher. Federal and state compensatory education funds are often focused on such pupils. See, e.g., 20 U.S.C. sec. 3701 et seq. ("Title 1"). Such funds, however, are allocated in recognition of the fact that poor children often need more than advantaged children. They clearly anticipate that funds provided will normally be laid on top of an equal base. See, e.g., 20 U.S.C. sec. 2728.

12. California constitution, art. 1, sec. 7a.

13. The facilities issue in Los Angeles, and probably in other urban areas, affects immigrant children much more forcefully than African American children.

14. See, e.g., discussion in Darling-Hammond and Green, "Teacher Quality and Equality," in *Access to Knowledge: An Agenda for Our Nation's Schools* (The College Board, 1990).

15. Ibid., 254–56.

16. See, e.g., *Serrano v. Priest*, 487 P.2d 1241 (Cal. 1971); *Horton v. Meskill*, 376 A.2d 359 (Conn. 1977); *Rose v. Council for Better Education*, 790 S.W.2d 186 (Ky. 1989).

17. *Rodríguez v. San Antonio ISD*, 411 U.S. 1 (1973).

18. Intentional discrimination on the basis of race invites strict scrutiny under federal and state constitutions.

19. 20 U.S.C. sec. 2000(d).

20. 34 F.R.D. 100.3.

21. See *Alexander v. Choate*, 469 U.S. 287 (1985). See also *Grimes by and Through Grimes v. Sobel*, 832 F. Supp. 704 (S.D.N.Y. 1993).

22. *Morgan v. Kerrigan*, 509 F.2d 580, 598, n. 29 (1st Cir. 1974), cert. den., 421 U.S. 963 (1975); *Spangler v. Pasadena City Board of Education*, 311 F. Supp. 501, 524 (C.D. Cal. 1970).

23. 269 F. Supp. 40–41, 434 (D.D.C. 1967), affd. sub nom. *Smuck v. Hobson*, 408 F.2d 175 (D.C. Cir. 1969) (en banc).

24. *In re Skipwith*, 14 Misc. 2d 235, 338–39, 180 N.Y.S.2d 852, 866 (N.Y. Dom. Rel. Ct. 1958).

25. *Morgan v. Hennigan*, 379 F. Supp. 410, 426, affd., 509 F.2d 580, cert. den., 421 U.S. 963.

26. Leading cases include *Shofstall v. Hollins*, 515 P.2d 590 (Ariz. 1973) (en banc); *Dupree v. Alma School District*, 651 S.W.2d 90 (Ark. 1983); *Serrano v. Priest*, 487 P.2d 1241 (Cal. 1971); *Horton v. Meskill*, 376 A.2d 359 (Conn. 1977); *Rose v. Council for Better Education*, 790 S.W.2d 186 (Ky. 1989); *Robinson v. Cahill*, 303 A.2d 273 (N.J. 1973); *Edgewood ISD v. Kirby*, 777 S.W.2d (Tex. 1989); *Seattle School District No. 1 v. State*, 585 P.2d 71 (Wash.

1978); *Pauley v. Kelly,* 255 S.E.2d 859 (W. Va. 1979); *Washakie County School Dist. No. 1 v. Herschler,* 606 P.2d 310 (Wyo. 1980). One intradistrict case concluded that an 8 percent disparity in teacher expenditures would constitute a violation of federal equal protection even without reliance on the fundamentality of education. It did conclude that the district's efforts, which shrank the difference to 4 percent subsequent to the filing of the suit, precluded judicial intervention, since education was not fundamental under federal law. *Brown v. Board of Education of Chicago,* 386 F. Supp. 110 (D. Ill. 1974).

27. *Serrano v. Priest,* 487 P.2d at 1259, citing Coons, Clune, and Sugarman, "Educational Opportunity: A Workable Constitutional Test for State Financial Structures," *California Law Review* 57 (1969): 305, 388.

Chapter 4 More Than Equal:
New Jersey's Quality
Education Act

Thomas Corcoran and Nathan Scovronick

Policy makers in many states have been struggling to find more equitable methods to finance their public schools. They have been forced to address this difficult issue by state courts. Some of the recent court decisions have required more than the reduction of funding disparities among districts. They have demanded that legislatures act to ensure educational adequacy and improved school quality. In Alabama and Kentucky, entire systems of education, not just the funding formulas, were declared unconstitutional. Other states have been ordered to provide students with higher levels of skill or to give them the comprehensive education necessary to prepare them for a challenging economy. As we will see, the court in New Jersey required equalization and additional funding for special services to compensate for the disadvantages of children in poor districts and to equip them to compete with children from the wealthiest school districts in the state.

This demand for greater equity and quality has occurred in the context of a widespread loss of public confidence in the instruments of government and revolts against the taxes that support it. As of the spring of 1995, a number of states had reduced taxes; many had enacted, or had the public impose, expenditure limitations. The relation among these trends has become complicated and difficult for policy makers to manage.

Certainly this has been true in the case of New Jersey, the first state in the 1990s to face a court decision declaring its school funding law unconstitutional. Although one of the wealthiest states in the nation in 1990, New Jersey had huge disparities in the financial resources of its school districts. New Jersey was in many ways an excellent place to observe the interaction of the forces affecting the financing of public education in the 1990s. In this chapter we will examine the story of the Quality Education Act (QEA), an effort to provide a more equitable system of school funding for New Jersey.

SOCIAL AND ECONOMIC CONTEXT

In 1990 New Jersey was the second richest state in the union, measured by per capita income, yet it had four of the ten poorest cities in the country and several others that would have been the poorest cities in many states (Bradbury, Downs, and Small, 1984, p. 9). Most of its cities had grown poorer during the last two decades as the middle class moved to the suburbs. The cities had fewer new jobs and higher crime, fewer good housing choices and higher infant mortality, fewer services and higher property tax rates than the surrounding suburbs. Comparisons with the wealthier suburbs, at a slightly greater distance from the cities, were even more dramatic. The state's cities were mostly African American and Latino, and the suburbs were overwhelmingly white. This means that, from a statewide perspective, housing and schools were largely segregated (Orfield and Monfort, 1992, p. 10).

Of course, few people in New Jersey view these matters in this way, that is, from a statewide perspective. New Jersey is geographically among the smallest states in the nation, but it is extremely fragmented. There are 567 munici-palities and 614 school districts, and there is a strong tradition of local control. Each municipality, and each school district, is therefore functionally on its own when it comes to delivering services or educating children. For both munici-palities and school districts, the property tax is the primary source of funding; because of the enormous differences in wealth among the localities, there are wide disparities in spending on education.

Most New Jerseyans seem to accept these inequities as natural and just. Families move to the suburbs in part to find good schools for their children, and many believe that the relative advantage that their children gain is deserved, a consequence of their hard work and foresight.

The responsibility for protecting the rights of children, and for maintaining a statewide perspective, therefore rests with state officials. But no recent governor has been willing to address fundamental issues of the structure of public education beyond recommending voluntary school regionalization, because the racial politics are too volatile. The legislature is always too divided to take on these issues, with Democrats in general representing the cities and Republicans representing rural areas and wealthier suburbs. And despite their substantial statutory power, only one of the state's commissioners of education has tried to confront issues of educational equity and school reform, and he was driven from office soon after. In New Jersey, therefore, it has been left to the courts to act in these matters and for the political system to react.

HISTORY OF SCHOOL FINANCE LITIGATION
AND LEGISLATION

In 1975, the New Jersey Supreme Court had declared the state's old school funding law unconstitutional. The court found that the constitutional provision requiring a "thorough and efficient education" for all children had been violated because of inadequate school funding in the urban areas of the state. The court demanded that the school system prepare students to function as good citizens and as competitors in the labor market. It ordered the legislature to appropriate funds to assure this.

The legislative response, Chapter 212, required the state Board of Education to set goals and standards, established a planning process for school districts, increased state monitoring responsibilities, and substantially equalized the wealth supporting the education of each child. The new formula was financed largely by the state's first income tax, enacted one year later.

Although there was some initial progress toward fiscal equalization, time revealed that Chapter 212 was simply not powerful enough to overcome the enormous disparities in wealth among New Jersey school districts. The property wealth supporting each child in Princeton, for example, was ten times higher than in nearby Trenton. Under Chapter 212 more than half of the statewide cost of the schools continued to be financed by local property taxes, and property-rich school districts could raise more money per pupil with low tax rates than urban districts could raise with very high rates. The real estate boom of the 1980s, centered in the suburbs, increased these disparities in tax capacity and spending.

The poorest urban districts also served more children requiring additional assistance, including handicapped children, children with limited English proficiency, and children in remedial classes. The differences in spending levels between the suburbs and the cities led to enormous differences in class size, course offerings, teacher qualifications, support services, and facilities. In short, educational opportunities in the cities were curtailed by inadequate funding. By 1989–90, disparities across the state were worse than before the passage of Chapter 212 in 1975. The difference between spending in the twenty-eight urban districts later targeted by the court and the average spending in the wealthiest 108 suburbs ranged from $582 to $3,674 per pupil.

THE LEGAL, FISCAL, AND POLITICAL CONTEXT

By 1990, New Jersey was spending more per pupil than any other state (U.S. Department of Education, 1995, p. 157). Combined state and local budgets for public education during the 1980s more than doubled, from $4.0 billion in 1980–81 to $9.5 billion in 1990–91 (State of New Jersey, 1991, p. 16). In 1990, state aid for education comprised one-third of the state budget; the cost of the employer's share of teachers' pension and Social Security contributions, entirely borne by the state, had by then reached $1 billion.

The problems with Chapter 212 were apparent as early as 1981. In that year, the Education Law Center, a public-interest law firm, filed a complaint on behalf of children attending public schools in four of the poorest cities of the state. The plaintiffs in the case, *Abbott v. Burke,* wanted the court to declare Chapter 212 unconstitutional and require the legislature to enact a new school funding law. Throughout the 1980s, during the administration of Governor Thomas Kean, the state used a variety of stalling tactics to slow the progress of the case and avoid a school funding crisis.

When Governor Jim Florio took office in January 1990, almost all observers expected the New Jersey Supreme Court to find for the plaintiffs; the evidence on resource and program inequalities between the urban and suburban districts was viewed as too compelling for any other result. A decision in the case was expected by spring.

In the meantime, the new governor was facing a fiscal crisis of another sort. The boom of the 1980s had produced enormous benefits for the state's economy and had greatly increased state revenues. The size of the government had doubled under Governor Kean, and the budget had grown proportionately— from $7 billion to almost $14 billion. When the recession hit New Jersey, beginning in 1987, state revenues began to drop precipitously, however, and surpluses had to be used to balance the state budget.

In 1990, the new governor faced an immediate $600 million deficit and a projected $1 billion problem for the next year. He made huge budget reductions, but it was not enough to offset the effects of the recession on revenues. New revenues were needed.

In his first budget message, therefore, he proposed higher sales and nuisance taxes to balance the budget and a higher, more graduated income tax to finance property tax relief programs, including increased state aid to schools. The higher taxes were projected to bring in $2.8 billion, half from the income tax. Thus the new school formula was inexorably linked to the new taxes, providing part of the rationale for the increase. Democrats felt that the public would support more state aid for schools, especially if the vast majority of districts were "winners," and therefore would be more willing to swallow the bitter pill of higher state taxes.

The tax package also determined the timetable for the school formula. Democratic legislators wanted the tax package passed by June 1990 to keep it as far away as possible from the 1991 elections. This meant that a new school formula also had to be passed by June. Therefore, the governor established a working group to develop a new school formula shortly after determining that new taxes would be needed. (Both of the chapter authors served as members of this internal working group, which included representatives of the governor's office, the state treasury, and the Department of Education. The group began to meet in February, 1990, and completed its work in May when legislation for the new formula was introduced).

These were not the only issues before the governor and the legislature. Early in the session, there was a difficult and ultimately successful battle to tighten gun control laws. This celebrated victory over the National Rifle Association was later to play a key role in the struggle to reform school funding.

FLORIO'S EDUCATION REFORM AGENDA

The new governor wanted to improve the quality of the public schools. His predecessor's approach to school reform had been based on an attractive logic:

- Recruit better teachers through nontraditional routes and higher salaries, and improve existing teachers through in-service training and recognition;
- improve school management through training and new certification requirements;
- raise expectations through more demanding state tests of basic skills;

- use sanctions, including takeover of school districts, to force compliance when state requirements were not met. As a result of these actions,
- student performance would rise to meet the new expectations.

Members of the Florio administration did not reject these initiatives. Rather, they believed that their goals were too limited and that equity issues were not being addressed. Therefore, they hoped to broaden and deepen the state's approach to reform by adding:

- a more equitable school funding formula;
- state performance standards and assessment in the core academic subjects;
- a revision in accountability to give more weight to student performance and less to compliance with regulations;
- the expansion of early childhood programs to ensure that students enter school ready to learn; and
- a program of low-interest loans and grants for facilities repair and construction.

A new mechanism for funding public education was certainly central to their vision of reform, but they planned to combine new accountability standards, facilities funding, early childhood programs, and new school formula into a school reform package.

THE QEA

The governor's working group established four primary goals: an adequate spending level for each pupil, tax fairness for each school district, control over the rate of increase in spending, and financial stability for the system. To reach these goals, they agreed on a high foundation formula, a moderate local tax effort, and an annual limit on the total annual increase in state aid. The new formula was expected to distribute $4.6 billion in state aid in its first year, an increase of $1.1 billion over the amount distributed for the 1990–91 school year.

Unlike Chapter 212, the new formula would distribute almost three-quarters of the money on a wealth-equalized basis; the remainder would be distributed regardless of wealth in the form of transportation and categorical aid for handicapped children and others. The great majority of districts would receive additional state aid, with huge increases in the poorest districts and at least modest increases in the middle-class districts. More than 80 percent of the students in the state would be enrolled in districts scheduled to receive more aid. The wealthiest districts would lose funds because minimum aid would be eliminated. The formula provided a four-year transition fund to cushion the loss of aid in these districts.

To enable almost 75 percent of the aid to be equalized, state funding of $1 billion in teacher pension and Social Security costs had to end. These payments had to become a local responsibility, as they were for county and municipal employees. These state funds could then be shifted to foundation aid, increasing the amount available in the first year to $3 billion. All but the wealthiest districts would receive enough additional aid from this change to cover their pension costs. The state would continue to guarantee the integrity of the pension fund and assure sufficient payments to it. Nobody's pension would therefore be endangered by the change.

The pension shift was expected to be controversial. State payment gave a bargaining-table advantage to the New Jersey Education Association (NJEA), the state's major teacher's union, because it could negotiate with local school districts over salaries without regard to the impact of salary increases on a major fringe-benefit program. For these reasons, the NJEA, perhaps the state's most powerful lobbying organization, was expected to oppose the pension shift in spite of the state guarantee of pensions to its members and the potential benefit to them from the new money going to the schools. The working group considered dozens of alternatives. Faced with the necessity of making the pension shift, the group decided to avoid early private consultations with representatives of the education associations, who were expected to be unable to get past this issue to discuss larger issues of school finance.

Except for the categorical aid funds, the legislation to create the new formula did not prescribe how the money was to be used. Out of respect for the state's tradition of local control, responsibility for providing a quality education for every pupil would remain with the districts, but a companion bill called for revisions in the accountability system, replacing the process standards of Chapter 212 with higher, outcome-based standards in core subjects. In short, the state would provide the money and monitor the results.

The plan seemed to meet both the fiscal contingencies of the time and the requirements of financial equity, and it appeared to have the potential to stimulate local innovation and improvement of performance. In this form, the Quality Education Act was approved by the governor and introduced by Democratic legislators in both houses on May 1, 1990. The governor convened a large press conference at which he described a reform package that included the school formula, the new standards, funding for facilities, and a new early childhood initiative.

ABBOTT V. BURKE

One month later, on June 4, the New Jersey Supreme Court ruled in favor of the plaintiffs and declared Chapter 212 unconstitutional as it applied to twenty-nine urban districts. The court rejected the argument that meeting minimum state standards was a sufficient definition of a thorough and efficient education and dismissed the proposition that educational quality was unrelated to funding. In addition to emphasizing the need to improve substandard facilities in many poor districts, the court cited problems such as large class size and narrow course offerings. It demanded a high level of financial support for the poor districts to meet requirements that went beyond equal staffing and equal programs; the court specifically required that children in poor districts be given more services than those available in the wealthiest suburbs. If education had to be separate for the children in the cities, then it would have to be more than equal:

> It is clear . . . that in order to achieve the constitutional standard for the students from these poorer urban districts—the ability to function in that society entered by their relatively advantaged peers—the totality of the district's educational offering must contain elements over and above those found in the affluent suburban districts. If educational fare of the seriously disadvantaged student is the same as the "regular education" given to the advantaged student, those serious disadvantages will not be addressed, and the students in the poorer urban districts will simply not be able to compete. (*Abbott II* at 374)

The court ordered the legislature to design a new or revised funding system that would:

1. equalize spending for the regular education program between poor urban districts and the most affluent suburbs;
2. provide sufficient additional funds to redress the educational disadvantages of children in the poor urban districts;
3. assure that funding for poor urban districts would be certain every year, that is, not dependent on the budgeting or taxing decisions of the local school board;
4. take into consideration the municipal overburdening of the poor urban districts;
5. eliminate aid given specifically to wealthy districts that did not qualify for any other formula aid; and
6. implement or phase in a new formula starting in the 1991 school year (*Abbott II* at 342).

The court decision applied only to the twenty-nine poorest districts in the state, and its standard for parity in the regular education program was the average per-pupil spending in the state's richest districts. The court had no evidence before it, and it reached no conclusion, about education in the vast majority of districts in the middle.

Significantly, the court did not resolve the constitutionality of full state funding for the teacher's pension and Social Security contributions. Although the decision called such funding "constitutionally infirm," it left the issue unresolved.

LEGISLATIVE CHANGES TO THE QEA

After the court rendered its decision, frequent meetings were held between the governor's working group and the staff of the legislative leadership. Changes had to be made to the QEA to deal with the court's unexpected spending standard, tied not to program adequacy but to expenditures in the wealthiest districts. More money was clearly needed for the twenty-nine urban districts named by the court if they were to reach parity within a reasonable period.

The expanded group drafted amendments providing an additional 5 percent foundation aid payment each year to the twenty-nine "special-needs" districts and to one other similarly situated district. To avoid excessive expenditure increases in the wealthiest districts, which would then have to be matched with state aid increases for the much larger special-needs districts, the group also proposed modest spending caps for high-spending districts.

They decided to go forward with the pension shift. Without a court decision that clearly declared unconstitutional state funding for district pension and social security expenditures, it was obvious that the political debate would be dominated by opposition to the shift of responsibility for these payments from the state to local districts. Continued payment of these expenses by the state not only was disequalizing, however, but also reduced the amount of money available for foundation aid and therefore the capacity of the formula to provide increased support for middle-income districts.

All of these changes were incorporated in the bill during the legislative committee process. Brief hearings were held, all of which focused on the pension issue and on the caps on state and local spending, but no changes in the pension provisions were made. The bills were approved by several legislative committees in a party-line vote and were referred to the full Senate and General Assembly for consideration. The QEA legislation moved forward independent of the other pieces of the governor's reform agenda, and the issue of money was separated from the issues of higher standards and greater local discretion.

PASSING THE QEA

The political climate for legislative consideration of the QEA was greatly affected by the reaction to the tax proposals. Governor Florio had been elected by a substantial majority over a candidate who had pledged never to raise taxes. Although he refused to take the pledge, Governor Florio had during the campaign stated that he saw no need for new taxes. At that time the incumbent, Governor Kean, was maintaining that there would be a budget surplus, and the Democrats in the legislature were talking about a deficit of, at worst, $600 million. Governor Florio was clearly willing to (and did) cut much more than that, but many voters felt betrayed when he later recommended new taxes.

A citizens' group was organized to oppose the taxes. It was given a powerful forum by a new statewide talk-radio station looking for an audience and given substantial financial support by the NRA, which was infuriated by the passage of the ban on assault rifles. The NRA also promised to help finance an anti-Florio legislative campaign in 1991 centered on opposition to the taxes. The Republican legislative minority decided to conduct such a campaign and capitalize on the organized opposition.

The New Jersey Education Association decided to unconditionally oppose the QEA. For them, the proposed pension funding issue was the overriding concern. The NJEA leadership distributed misleading literature that implied that its members' pensions were threatened, and the reaction of its membership was immediate and emotional.

The School Boards Association, representing local school districts, was split. Leaders from wealthier districts, which expected to lose state aid and were opposed to the QEA, held a disproportionately strong voice in its delegate assembly. Those from middle-class districts, which were expected to benefit from the aid increases and property tax deductions, seemed confused by the arguments over the pension shift and spending caps, and with few exceptions, they failed to support the QEA. Support from the poorer districts, which stood to gain the most, was also weak both within the organization and in the wider political arena. Critics of the plan got by far the most attention in the press.

The Republican minority decided to capitalize on this opposition to the governor's proposals and to vote against the QEA. This stand was taken by all their members, even by those representing districts that stood to gain from the new formula. They unanimously attacked the QEA at the same time as they attacked the taxes; opposing the entire package seemed the most easily understood and effective strategy.

The income tax and the QEA, of course, could be legitimately linked; one would pay for the other. Because of this, the press had begun to characterize the governor as Robin Hood, taking from individuals with high income and giving to school districts serving poor and minority children. Some opponents took this further, encouraging the misimpression that the tax increases would hit everyone and that the aid increases would benefit only city schools; they protested not only the idea of taxing people hard-pressed by the recession but also the idea of sending money to urban districts where it would be wasted. The lack of program prescriptions in the bill made it easier to accept this argument (the standards bill was all but ignored). The tax issue and the school issue, taken together, proved to be explosive.

The Democrats moved ahead; the political and governmental cost of doing nothing was seen as too great. Between June 18 and June 21, 1990, the legislature passed the QEA and the tax package in a party-line vote. The governor held a press conference to thank the Democratic legislators and express his pleasure at the passage of his proposals; it was the last time he smiled for a very long time.

REACTION AND RETREAT: QEA II

Within a month, the governor's approval rating dropped dramatically. The radio stations stepped up their harangue, the protest groups grew larger, the NJEA got angrier, the NRA sent more money. Although neither the governor nor the legislators were on the ballot in 1990, the Republican party launched a strong antitax campaign. They tried to make state taxes the central issue in the reelection bid of Senator Bill Bradley, who had previously won by huge margins. Bradley tried to duck the issue, saying with some logic that it was not one for a federal official. Although he outspent his then-unknown opponent, Christine Todd Whitman, by a margin of twelve to one, he won by only a slim margin.

The election results sent shock waves across the state. Democratic legislators, all of whom were up for reelection in 1991, immediately announced that all aspects of the tax and school funding package were open for review. The governor appointed a blue-ribbon commission to look at school funding and the quality and efficiency of public education. The Democrats in the legislature developed a strategy for reelection based on delivering massive property tax relief before November. A new team from the administration began meeting with the education groups and negotiating with the legislature. As a result of these efforts, in March 1991, a revised version of the formula, popularly called QEA II, was passed. It made the following changes:

1. school aid was reduced by $360 million, and these funds were dedicated instead to municipal property tax relief;
2. stricter school spending caps were imposed;
3. the state's obligation to pay teachers' pension and social security costs was extended for two years while the governor's commission considered alternatives;
4. the annual cap on total state aid was tightened, and pension and other categorical obligations were required to be met each year before funds were allocated to foundation aid; and
5. the foundation level was reduced, at-risk aid was reduced, and save-harmless money was provided for compensatory education.

As a political strategy, this retreat did not work. The taxes, and to some extent the QEA, were the central issues in the legislative elections of 1991. The NJEA and the NRA supported Republican candidates. In a dramatic shift of political power, Republicans gained control of both houses of the legislature by margins large enough to override any gubernatorial veto. Neither the changes in the school formula nor the additional property tax relief secured political gain for anyone.

The second Quality Education Act was also bad education policy: it could not fulfill the court's legal requirements, meet the state's educational needs, or provide a workable framework for school finance in the long term. With the transfer of $360 million to property tax relief, it simply did not distribute enough money to achieve these goals. Continued state payment of district pension and Social Security costs meant that less than 50 percent of state aid was equalizing. The poor, urban districts lost almost half of their increased entitlement, and because of the tighter caps, some were not even permitted to spend up to the foundation level. In the first year of QEA II, their share of statewide school aid was the same as it had been under the old law. Between 1992 and 1993, under QEA II, the disparity in spending between rich and poor districts actually grew wider (Goertz, 1992, p. 22).

These changes also meant that there was not enough money in the foundation formula to assure reasonable levels of aid to middle-class districts. The new formula then lost its most important constituency. The enactment of QEA II, therefore, ensured a continuing school finance crisis in New Jersey.

CURRENT STATUS

In 1993, Christine Whitman ran for governor against Jim Florio; she promised a 30 percent reduction in income taxes. Although by then a majority of voters had decided that the 1990 tax increases had been necessary, the promise proved appealing, especially to voters undecided until the last minute. After taking office, she moved quickly to fulfill her campaign promise; the legislature supported her and lowered the tax; the change was financed by reducing state contributions to the teachers' pension fund.

The revised act was declared unconstitutional by the State Supreme Court on July 12, 1994. The state was ordered to enact by September 1996, and implement by September 1997, a new law that would guarantee parity in spending for regular education programs in the targeted urban districts as well as provide additional funds for meeting the special needs of their children. In all respects, the court repeated the reasoning and rhetoric of its 1990 decision. Significantly, the court retained jurisdiction over the case and said it would take action if its deadlines were not met.

CONCLUSIONS: NEW JERSEY

Clearly, QEA I was a missed opportunity. Most analysts have focused on the political mistakes that were made—the administration's haste to develop a new school formula, its failure to consult the education community, the lack of clear linkage between the formula and school reform, and the absence of an effective effort to develop public support for a solution prior to passing the Quality Education Act. These are all legitimate criticisms, but they ignore the political problems created by the court decision itself and the structural problems in public education that make it difficult for any redistributive law like QEA I to be passed and implemented.

By definition, courts only act on issues such as school equity when there is no political consensus. If the remedy chosen by a court in such circumstances is to be enacted and to last, the legislature and the governor have to be given tools that help them build that consensus. In *Abbott v. Burke*, these tools were denied to them.

By focusing only on twenty-eight urban districts, the court greatly limited the constituency for change. It is true that the plaintiffs' evidence in the case was restricted to comparisons between a handful of the poorest urban districts and the richest districts in the state, but the court substantially expanded the list of poor districts in its decision and could have gone further. A standard of need applicable to all districts, whether urban or not, would still have concentrated state aid in the poorer cities and at the same time could have greatly broadened support for the QEA. Instead, middle-income and rural districts felt left out of the decision, and the door was left open for future litigation by other classes of districts.

By setting a spending standard for the poor districts at the level of the wealthiest districts, the court required that resources be allocated for children in poor cities at levels to which the children in middle-income districts were not entitled. By going further and requiring that children in poor districts receive even more support than those in rich districts, the court produced a decision almost perfectly designed to foster resentment in the great majority of parents—and voters. The court standard necessitated a high level of additional tax support and led to the adoption of very restrictive spending caps on high-spending districts, both of which greatly intensified the opposition to the legislation.

The cost of the remedy was substantially increased by the court's preference for spending parity rather than program parity; every expenditure in the rich districts, whether for instruction or not, had to be matched. The court could have accomplished its fundamental purposes by requiring that all districts at least reach program parity with high-performing middle-class districts. Beyond the regular education program, special assistance to meet the needs of poor children might then have been both more affordable and more acceptable. Instead, the structure of the decision made it much easier for opponents to divide the state and much more difficult for proponents to establish and protect the required spending priorities or to raise and sustain the necessary taxes.

Finally, by failing to resolve the pension funding issue, the court set up a chain of events that turned the teacher's union into the leading opponent of the QEA. If state payment for teachers' pension payments had been declared unconstitutional, the NJEA would have had little choice but to support a new formula that produced so much new money and that could muster sufficient votes to pass both houses of the legislature. Despite any tactical mistakes that might have been made by the administration and the legislators, the strength of NJEA support might have been sufficient to force a political solution that overcame the other obstacles set by the court. Instead, a narrow-minded union leadership took its membership down the road of opposition and continuing fiscal crisis.

LESSONS FOR OTHER STATES

In 1990, New Jersey had a policy environment that was unique in many respects. Its supreme court was highly activist, its politics very partisan, its school system extremely fragmented, and the leaders of its NEA affiliate extraordinarily shortsighted. Nevertheless, there may be some lessons for other states.

There is a constituency for educational equity, as there is for higher standards and for cost control. Although there is some overlap among these groups, they are in many ways discrete and responsive only to their specific concerns. If a movement toward equity is to succeed at a time when confidence in government is so low, these constituencies must support it. This is especially true if the reform requires additional funding. Without the support of a broad coalition, the antitax and antigovernment rhetoric is too difficult to overcome. If there is a racial issue available for exploitation, securing equity becomes even more difficult.

A comprehensive and integrated package can best appeal to all the diverse constituencies. If it provides the promise of increased equity, quality, and efficiency, and if it is supported by a unified message, it has the best chance for success. If instead its pieces are separable, and the message fragmented, the coalition for reform can be split and its strength diluted, as it was in New Jersey.

As we have seen, QEA I would have provided the school districts of New Jersey with increased resources and a high degree of funding equity, and the state's taxpayers with stronger cost controls and property tax relief. It was accompanied by legislation on higher school standards, a bond proposal for school facilities construction, and appropriation for expanded preschool programs. Finally, it was proposed in the context of an existing state takeover law that provided a remedy for school district waste and corruption. Taken together, the proposals were comprehensive, but they were not presented as an integrated package, nor were they perceived as a package by the public. The takeover legislation in particular had been used so long as a rhetorical alternative to providing adequate funding that it was never effectively utilized to support it. Vital parts of the constituency for better schools were not mobilized or failed to understand how the Florio administration's initiative would affect them, and the coalition supporting the initiative was not broad enough to sustain the reform or the new taxes needed to support it.

A comprehensive and integrated reform proposal clearly has tremendous advantages, but there must also be sufficient time to explain it and sufficient time for a coalition to be built in support of it; QEA I moved from proposal to law too fast to do this. There was a good legislative strategy behind the tactics, but the public strategy was not nearly good enough. The right message has to be received for this kind of reform to succeed, and that takes time and effort.

The vast majority of households have no children in the public schools, and increasing numbers feel little or no obligation to support those schools. They will support reforms only if there is no additional cost or if they have confidence in cost controls. Of those with children in school, suburban parents form the majority in most states; many of them see public education solely as a means for personal advancement for their children, as a way to guarantee their future social status. They want schools good enough to make their children competitive with others like themselves, which means securing admission to competitive institutions of higher education. They will support reform only if the quality of their local system is maintained or advanced and they can maintain the advantages they seek for their children. For these reasons also, equity is not enough. Political leaders have to put together a comprehensive package and a message that is sensitive to these political realities and seeks to reconstitute a sense of community.

The problems that led to *Abbott v. Burke* will not disappear, and the need to resolve them will only become more urgent. In New Jersey, and in many other states, an increasing number of public school students are members of minority groups. With continued immigration, and with continued differential birth rates, this increase is likely to continue (New Jersey Department of Labor, 1992). By 2010, the first of the baby-boom generation will begin to retire, and the percentage of the population that is working will begin to shrink accordingly. As it ages, the baby-boom generation will begin making increased demands on scarce state resources and will have enormous political power to secure them.

At that point, the competition for resources between the aging and the poor (many of whom will be children) could result in an even more serious confrontation than what we have seen during the last few years. If, between now and then, another generation in the cities is neglected, the dilemma will be that much more serious. In the long run, we are all in this together.

REFERENCES

Katharine Bradbury, Anthony Downs, and Kenneth Small. 1984. *Urban Decline and the Future of American Cities.* Washington, D.C.: Brookings Institution.

Margaret Goertz. 1992. *The Development and Implementation of the Quality Education Act of 1990.* New Brunswick, N.J.: Center for Education Policy Analysis.

New Jersey Department of Labor. 1992. *Annual Report of the Division of Labor Market and Demographic Research* Trenton, N.J.: New Jersey Department of Labor.

Gary Orfield and Franklin Monfort. 1992. *Status of School Desegregation: The Next Generation.* Cambridge, Mass.: Harvard University Press.

State of New Jersey. 1991. *Budget in Brief, Fiscal Year 1991–1992.* Trenton, N.J.

United States Department of Education. 1995. *Digest of Education Statistics—1994.* Washington, D.C.: U.S. Government Printing Office.

APPENDIX TO PART ONE

The Courts and Equity: A State-by-State Overview

The following chart offers a state-by-state look at the history of funding equity litigation and its repercussions. The information is, to the best of our knowledge, up to date as of February 1997. The phrase "No known action" in the Notes column indicates that we are not aware of any litigation on the issue of school funding equity for that state. Updates and corrections to the chart are invited.

STATES	CASE(S)	RULING	NOTES
ALABAMA	1993 *Harper v. Hunt* Montgomery County Circuit Court 1997 State Supreme Court	Unconstitutional Unconstitutional	1993: Entire K–12 educational system ruled unconstitutional in both adequacy and equity. 1995: Circuit Court approved a remedy plan that includes student and educator performance standards, a core curriculum, and no academic tracking. 1997: State Supreme Court found reformed system unconstitutional and gave the legislature one year to offer a solution.
ALASKA			No known action.
ARIZONA	1973 *Shofstal v. Hollins* State Supreme Court 1994 *Roosevelt Elem. School Dist. #66 v. Bishop* State Supreme Court	Constitutional Unconstitutional	After *Shofstal*, state legislature added pupil weighting element to existing foundation program. The 1994 ruling found the system unconstitutional in a case based largely on facilities inequities. 1996: legislature agreed to provide $100 million in emergency funds for poorest districts' building needs, but a ruling by Maricopa County Superior Court ordered a totally new finance system by June 30, 1998, or the state must stop distributing state aid to schools.
ARKANSAS	1983 *Alma School Dist. #3 v. Dupree* State Supreme Court	Unconstitutional	After *Alma*, legislature raised state sales tax and created a new foundation program with weights for special education and vocational education students. Also created a second-tier

	1994 *Lakeview et al. v. Tucker et al.* Chancery Court	Unconstitutional	equalization mechanism which distributes an extra 1% of the total foundation amount to poorer districts. In-state disparities worsened after 1983. 1994: Chancery Court gave legislature two years to reform finance system. 1996: Voters approved a ballot measure making the property tax rate uniform and creating a redistribution program of tax money from wealthy to poor districts. A Chancery Court trial on the new system will be held in 1997.
CALIFORNIA	1971 *Serrano v. Priest* State Supreme Court	Unconstitutional	1972: Legislature increased foundation level and capped the growth of district expenditures. 1976: Court found state's efforts toward equity inadequate and ordered that disparities between districts be reduced to less that $100 per pupil. Legislature passed changes including higher inflation adjustment allowances for poor districts and a recapture provision to redirect property tax revenue from wealthy to poor districts. 1978: Proposition 13 enacted, a ballot measure which capped local property taxes and limited state's ability to raise taxes. By 1982, 95% of districts fell within (adjusted) maximum disparity of $200, mandated by *Serrano* (1976). Overall, California's ranking in per-pupil spending dropped from 5th highest in mid-1960s to 42nd highest in 1992–93.
	1976 *Serrano v. Priest II* State Supreme Court	Unconstitutional	
	1986 *Serrano v. Priest III* Appellate Court	Constitutional	
COLORADO	1982 *Lujan v. Colorado Board of Education* State Supreme Court	Constitutional	1988: Legislature revised funding formula from guaranteed yield to foundation program under threat of new lawsuit. 1992: Amendment 1 passed by voters, which limited increases in school spending to the rate of inflation. 1994: New finance act enacted based on cost of living, size, and number of at-risk students. 1996: Voters in fall election approved a 20% property tax cut, which

continued

The Courts and Equity: A State-by-State Overview (*Continued*)

STATES	CASE(S)	RULING	NOTES
			educators expect to have long-term negative effects on education funding.
CONNECTICUT	1977 *Horton v. Meskill* State Supreme Court	Unconstitutional	1979: Legislature passed a guaranteed tax base system (GTB) and a minimum expenditure requirement. In *Horton II*, plaintiffs challenged the new formula but it was upheld. In *Horton III*, the
	1982 *Horton v. Meskill II* State Supreme Court	Constitutional	formula was upheld but the court agreed that further amendments must meet certain guidelines. 1989: legislature increased education aid and replaced GTB with a foundation formula.
	1985 *Horton v. Meskill III* State Supreme Court	Constitutional	
DELAWARE			No known action.
FLORIDA			1994: 43 school districts and several students and parents filed a lawsuit in the state Circuit Court challenging the finance system and the use of state lottery revenues to offset cuts in general aid to schools. 1995: Circuit Court dismissed the case but plaintiffs plan to appeal.
GEORGIA	1981 *McDaniels v. Thomas* State Supreme Court	Constitutional	Although the system was upheld in *McDaniels*, the Court directed the legislature to take steps to increase equalization. 1985: legislature passed the Quality Basic Education law, which included funding equalization measures and greatly increased state and local education aid.

State	Case	Ruling	Action
HAWAII			No known action. Hawaii has the only statewide school district.
IDAHO	1975 *Thompson v. Engleking* State Supreme Court	Constitutional	1994: Legislature revised the state aid formula and approved a $92 million increase in funding for public schools. A state District Court dismissed a pending challenge to the state's finance system as a result of the changes. 1995: the plaintiffs filed a new case against the reformed system, focusing on adequacy instead of equity.
ILLINOIS			1992: Cook County Court dismissed a challenge to the funding system on the basis of separation of power. 1996: State Supreme Court dismissed appeal of the case, again citing the legislature's responsibility to fix school finance problems. Governor's 1996 efforts to revamp the formula died in the legislature.
INDIANA AND IOWA			No known action.
KANSAS	1976 *Knowles v. State Board of Education* Shawness County District Court	Unconstitutional	1981: changes made in formula after first *Knowles* ruling led to a ruling of constitutional. 1992: legislature passed a law for a statewide property tax level that redistributes some local revenues from wealthiest districts to poorer ones. Also provides controversial extra funding for districts with enrollment under 1,900, although 85% of the districts qualify for the supplement. 1995: U.S. Supreme Court declined without comment to hear an appeal of the 1992 law. 1996: Legislature cut the levy by 2 mills, with additional reduction by 2 mills next fiscal year.
	1981 *Knowles v. State Board of Education* Chatauqua County District Court	Constitutional	
	1994 *Unified School Dist.*	Constitutional	

continued

The Courts and Equity: A State-by-State Overview (*Continued*)

STATES	CASE(S)	RULING	NOTES
KENTUCKY	#229 v. State State Supreme Court	Unconstitutional	
	1989 *Council for Better Education v. Rose* State Supreme Court		1989: Sweeping decision found the entire K–12 system unconstitutional in curriculum, governance, and finance. 1990: Legislature passed KERA, the Kentucky Education Reform Act. Financial KERA measures include a guaranteed base of per-pupil funding, higher funding increases to poor districts, and a one-cent sales tax increase. By 1995, per-pupil spending had risen by 31% statewide, but disparities in some areas still exist due to property value growth in the wealthiest districts and the low minimum tax rate set by the 1990 law.
LOUISIANA	1988 *Louisiana Association of Educators v. Edwards* State Supreme Court	Constitutional	1992: A challenge was filed in state judicial district court by 26 school districts against the state's system, which included a minimum foundation program passed in 1992.
MAINE	1994 *MSAD #1 v. Martin* State Supreme Court	Constitutional	1995: Governor and legislature created a new funding formula which considers local income and cost of living as factors in determining a district's funding, to take effect in 1997.
MARYLAND	1983 *Somerset County Board of Education v. Hornbeck* State Court of Appeals	Constitutional	In *Somerset*, urban plaintiffs unsuccessfully argued that per-pupil funding should be equal across districts. 1994: The ACLU filed a suit charging that the Baltimore schools are inadequate and therefore unconstitutional. 1995: Baltimore filed its own suit for a greater share of state education aid.

State	Case	Ruling	Notes
MASSACHUSETTS	1993 *McDuffy v. Robertson* State Supreme Judicial Court	Unconstitutional	One week before the high court's ruling, legislature established a foundation budget for each district and a local contribution requirement, and required the state to make up the difference between the foundation budget and contribution requirement for low-wealth districts. Per-pupil spending must reach $5,600 (1994 dollars) by 2000.
MICHIGAN	1973 *Miliken v. Green* State Supreme Court	Constitutional	In 1984 case, the court ruled that the requirement to provide free public education does not demand equal funding. 1993: Voters approved Proposal A, which greatly reduced reliance on local property taxes to fund schools and raised the state's share of education costs through an increase in the sales tax. 1995: While spending gaps between districts have been closing somewhat, observers say that problems of equity and adequacy remain.
	1984 *East Jackson Public Schools v. State of Michigan* State Court of Appeals	Constitutional	
MINNESOTA	1992 *Skeen v. State* Wright County District Court	Unconstitutional	1993: State successfully appealed the 1992 ruling. 1995: NAACP filed suit for more funding for urban districts.
	1993 *Skeen v. State* State Supreme Court	Constitutional	
MISSISSIPPI			No action taken.
MISSOURI	1993 *Committee for Educational Equity v. State* Cole County Court	Unconstitutional	After the 1993 ruling, legislators rewrote the funding formula and raised taxes by $310 million. 1995: suit filed by 3 state legislators and others to block collection of the increased taxes. 1996: State Supreme Court found the 1993 finance law, and tax increase, constitutional.
	1996 State Supreme Court	Constitutional	

continued

The Courts and Equity: A State-by-State Overview (*Continued*)

STATES	CASE(S)	RULING	NOTES
MONTANA	1972 *Granger v. Cascade County School District* State Supreme Court	Constitutional	1989: Legislature passed a foundation program with a guaranteed tax base component, doubled overall levy mills, and added and reallocated other taxes. 1991: Under threat of new lawsuit, legislators strengthened the foundation program and placed caps on wealthier districts' spending, but also cut state education aid by $29 million overall.
	1989 *Helena Elem. School Dist #1 v. State of Montana* State Supreme Court	Unconstitutional	
NEBRASKA	1993 *Gould v. Orr* State Supreme Court	Constitutional	1993: State Supreme Court rejected a challenge to the finance system. 1996: Legislature voted to cap school share of local property taxes at $1.10 per $100, effective in fiscal 1999. Also approved an extra $50 million in state aid, based on property wealth.
NEVADA			No action taken.
NEW HAMPSHIRE	1993 *Claremont et al. v. State* State Supreme Court	Unconstitutional	New Hampshire relies more heavily on local tax revenues (90% of school income) for education funding than any other state. The state provides only 7% of school funding. 1993: State Supreme Court remanded the case to the Superior Court. 1996: Superior Court ruled that the system has problems but it is not the state's obligation to fix.
	1996 *Claremont et al. v. State* State Superior Court	Constitutional	
NEW JERSEY	1973 *Robinson v. Cahill* State Supreme Court	Unconstitutional	1975: State Supreme Court threatened to close N.J. schools unless legislature complied with *Robinson*. State income tax passed raising funding for all districts. In *Abbott*, Court found that funding

	1990 *Abbott v. Burke* State Supreme Court	Unconstitutional	disparities had increased under the revised system. It ordered the state to equalize per-pupil spending between the poorest and richest districts. It also mandated additional spending in poor districts above equalization levels to compensate for their "special needs." Legislature responded with the Quality Education Act (QEA), which raised sales and income taxes to fund increased aid. Some funds, originally intended for education, were diverted by the legislature to reduce local property taxes. The Court held in *Abbott II* that the QEA did not meet the mandate of its earlier decision and was unconstitutional. In *Abbott III*, the court set a deadline for adoption of yet another formula. 1996: The legislature adopted governor's plan to tie state funding to new core curriculum standards at levels well below the equity criteria of *Abbott.* A challenge was filed to the new plan immediately and was scheduled to be heard in March 1997.
	1993 *Abbott v. Burke II* State Superior Court	Unconstitutional	
	1994 *Abbott v. Burke III* State Supreme Court	Unconstitutional	
NEW MEXICO			1996: A case filed by 10 medium-sized districts was dismissed by a county court. Governor invited plaintiffs to join his school-funding task force to find a legislative solution instead of appealing the decision.
NEW YORK	1982 *Board of Education, Levittown v. Nyquist* State Court of Appeals	Constitutional	In *Levittown*, the court judged that the state had met its obligation to provide a "sound basic education." 1995: Two new suits were filed to challenge *Levittown*: one, filed by about 40 districts mostly from Long Island, asked the court to consider financial disparities which are causing inadequacy in some districts. The other, filed by the NYC-based Campaign for Fiscal Equity, argues that the city's

continued

The Courts and Equity: A State-by-State Overview (*Continued*)

STATES	CASE(S)	RULING	NOTES
			schools provide an inadequate education. The Long Island case was dismissed in 1995, but the NYC suit was allowed to proceed.
NORTH CAROLINA	1987 *Britt v. State Board of Education* State Supreme Court	Constitutional	1994: Five districts filed a suit in state Superior Court. 1996: Suit was dismissed: judges ruled that the state constitution requires "equal access," not "equal opportunities." The state Supreme Court has agreed to hear the case.
NORTH DAKOTA	1994 *Bismarck Public Schools et al. v. State et al.* State Supreme Court	Constitutional	1994: State Supreme Court voted the system unconstitutional by 3 to 2 but was one vote short of the supermajority needed to officially declare it so. 1995: Legislature passed a bill to reduce state aid to property-rich districts and give the extra money to poorer districts. Also created a $2.2 million supplemental fund to aid poorer districts.
OHIO	1979 *Board of Education of Cincinnati v. Walter* State Supreme Court	Constitutional	No changes resulted form 1979 case. 1995: Governor successfully appealed the 1994 ruling. Appeals Court said the legislature should decide finance matters, not the courts. 1996: Plaintiffs appealed the 1995 decision to the state Supreme Court. Decision was due in early 1997.
	1994 *DeRolph v. State of Ohio et al.* Perry County Common Pleas Court	Unconstitutional	
	1995 *DeRolph v. State of Ohio et al.* State Court of Appeals	Constitutional	

OKLAHOMA	1987 *Fair School Finance Council of Oklahoma v. State* State Supreme Court	Constitutional	Plaintiffs in *FSFCO v. State* charged that the constitutional limit on property tax levels kept poorer districts from raising adequate funds. In 1981, while case was moving through lower courts, legislature revised the system from a flat grant program to a foundation/guaranteed tax base formula with pupil weights. 1992: Voters approved an initiative that requires tax increases or new taxes to obtain a 3/4 vote in both houses or pass a statewide referendum.
OREGON	1976 *Olsen v. Oregon* State Supreme Court	Constitutional	In *Olsen,* court ruled that state's interest in local control outweighed its interest in equal opportunity. 1987: Voters approved a constitutional amendment to create a "safety net" that allows districts to operate at previous year's funding level, even if they are unable to raise additional funds through local levies. In *CEE v. Oregon,* court judged that by voting for the safety net, the public had approved the existence of funding disparity. 1996: Voters passed a constitutional amendment to require 3/5 of both houses to approve tax increases, and a measure to decrease property taxes by 20% statewide.
	1991 *Coalition for Education Equity v. Oregon* State Supreme Court	Constitutional	
PENNSYLVANIA	1978 *Danson v. Casey* Commonwealth Court	Constitutional	1990: A challenge was filed by nearly half of the state's districts saying poorer schools need more aid. 1995: A governor's task force charged with finding a legislative solution suggested no tax changes. 1996: State Supreme Court agreed to hear the 1990 suit. Decision was pending at press time.
	1979 *O'Donnell v. Casey* Commonwealth Court	Constitutional	
	1987 *Bensalem Twp. School Dist. v. the Commonwealth* Commonwealth Court	Constitutional	

continued

The Courts and Equity: A State-by-State Overview (*Continued*)

STATES	CASE(S)	RULING	NOTES
RHODE ISLAND	1994 *City of Pawtucket v. Sundlun* State Superior Court	Unconstitutional	1994: Court ordered massive funding reforms. 1995: State Supreme Court ruled that there are problems but they must be fixed by the legislature, not the courts. 1996: Legislature tied level of state aid to an assessment of districts' actual needs, instead of previous year's spending, a measure expected to benefit districts with a history of inadequate funding.
	1995 *City of Pawtucket v. Sundlun* State Supreme Court	Constitutional	
SOUTH CAROLINA	1988 *Richland County v. Campbell* State Supreme Court	Constitutional	
SOUTH DAKOTA	1994 *Bezdichek v. State* State Circuit Court	Constitutional	
TENNESSEE	1993 *Tenn. Small School Systems v. McWherter* State Supreme Court	Unconstitutional	1992: While case was moving through lower courts, legislature enacted the Basic Education Program to even out disparities. 1995: State Supreme Court ordered the state to equalize teacher salaries as well.
TEXAS	1973 *San Antonio v. Rodriguez*	Constitutional	In *Rodriguez*, The U.S. Court ruled that the right to education is not implicitly or explicitly protected by the U.S. Constitution.

	Court	Ruling	Description
	U.S. Supreme Court	Constitutional	1991: State legislature passed the "Robin Hood" plan creating new tax districts composed of rich and poor school districts with equal distribution of revenues within each tax district. 1992: "Robin Hood" plan overturned by state Supreme Court. 1993: Legislature passed law to cap property tax bases at $280,000 per pupil. Districts with more property wealth must adopt one of five methods for lowering its tax base, including taking in pupils from another district, combining with a poorer district, or detaching territory and annexing it to another district's tax rolls. Also added a guaranteed yield mechanism. 1995: Legislature voted to allow wealthy districts to maintain their 1992–93 funding levels through the 1997–98 school year.
	1989 *Edgewood Independent School Dist. v. Kirby* State Supreme Court	Unconstitutional	
	1995 *Edgewood Independent School Dist. v. State* State Supreme Court	Constitutional	
UTAH			No known action.
VERMONT			1995: After years of attempted legislation to achieve reform, ACLU of Vermont filed a suit in Superior Court charging that the state's system violates both the state and U.S. constitutions. 1996: Case was dismissed but both parties appealed to the state Supreme Court, whose ruling was pending at press time.
VIRGINIA	1994 *Reid Scott et al. v. Virginia et al.* State Supreme Court		1994: State Supreme Court ruled that the issue of school funding equity is for the legislature to decide, and specifically that there is no state constitutional mandate for equality in school spending or programs.

continued

The Courts and Equity: A State-by-State Overview (*Continued*)

STATES	CASE(S)	RULING	NOTES
WASHINGTON	1974 *Northshore School Dist. v. Kinnear* State Supreme Court	Constitutional	A very divided court in *Northshore* set the stage for 1978 case. In *Seattle v. State*, court agreed that many districts were hurt by dependence on funding approval by annual referenda. Basic Education Act of 1977 required a per capita education funding formula and a cap of 10% on the amount that could be raised above what was needed for "basic education" activities. 1987: The cap was raised to 20% and some districts, such as Seattle, were exempted from the cap for extracurricular activities.
	1978 *Seattle School Dist. # 1 of King County v. State* State Supreme Court	Unconstitutional	
WEST VIRGINIA	1979 *Pauley v. Kelly* State Supreme Court	Unconstitutional	In *Pauley*, state supreme court issued a set of broad guidelines describing the minimum level of education required by the state constitution. Case sent to circuit court to have guidelines fleshed out (*Pauley v. Bailey*, 1982), resulting in the painstakingly detailed Master Plan. Although some steps have been taken to equalize teacher salaries, modify the foundation program, provide school building funds, and develop new educational standards, the Master Plan has never been implemented, due to public resistance to the costs involved. 1995: A judge ruled that the requirements of the Master Plan have not been satisfied.

State	Case / Court	Ruling	Description
WISCONSIN	1976 *Buse v. Smith* State Supreme Court	Unconstitutional	In *Buse*, plaintiffs successfully challenged the recapture provision of the 1973 School Finance Act. In *Kukor*, there was no clear holding of the court. However, a plurality of the court held that the legislature is responsible for addressing funding disparities, not the court. A new constitutional challenge was due to be filed in February 1997 by a statewide coalition of school districts.
	1989 *Kukor v. Grover* State Supreme Court	Constitutional	
WYOMING	1980 *Washakie County School Dist. #1 v. Herschler* State Supreme Court	Unconstitutional	1982: Two constitutional amendments were passed: first, to increase the foundation aid and program income: second, to allow the state to recapture 75% of local property tax revenues above the state average and redistribute them to poorer districts. 1993:
	1995 *Campbell County School Dist. et al. v. State et al.* State Supreme Court	Unconstitutional	District judge ruled main formula constitutional but struck down three ancillary funding programs. 1995: Unanimous state supreme court ordered lawmakers to define a "proper education" and find a way to pay for it for every child by July 1997. Court struck down recapture scheme.

Reprinted with permission from *Funding for Justice*, Rethinking Schools, 1001 E. Keefe Ave., Milwaukee, Wis. 53212: (414) 964-9646.

Sources: *Fiscal Equity in Education: A Proposal for a Dialogic Remedy*, Michael A. Rebell, Robert L. Hughes, and Lisa F. Grumet (New York: Campaign for Fiscal Equity, 1995); *The State of Inequality*, Policy Information Center (Princeton, N.J.: Educational Testing Service, 1991); *School Finance Litigation: A Historical Summary*, Mary Fulton and David Long (Denver: Education Commission of the States, 1993); *State Investments in Education and Other Children's Services: Case Studies of Financing Innovations* (Washington, D.C.: The Finance Project, 1995); *Education Week*, articles from 1991–1997: NEA state affiliates in Ala., Ark., Colo., Miss., Okla., Nev., Va., Mass., Ga., N.D., Wis., Vt., Ky., and N.J.; state departments of education in Ala., Conn., Kan., La., Maine, Mich., Minn., Mo., N.H., N.C., Ohio, Penn., R.I., S.C., S.D., Texas, Wyo.; and the ACLU of Vermont. Research by Jennifer Morales.

Part Two The Political
Agenda of Education in the
States

Analysis of education reform necessarily must focus on state politics. The states ultimately are legally responsible for education and provide 50 percent or more of funding. A locally centered school district government structure also provides the additional cost of education from local property taxes. Historically, the federal government has never contributed more than 10 percent of the total funds for education, and those funds were directed to compensatory categorical programs. The states' central role in the legal structure of education results in litigation directed at state constitutional provisions.

Several legal scholars and activists believe that federal intervention is necessary to achieve state education reform. Bill Taylor and Marilyn Morheuser support establishing education as a national right so that state and local education programs would be subject to national review. I suggest in the introduction that the federal government should in fact concentrate on areas where it can uniquely contribute to American education, namely, in producing greater equity in funding and compensatory education. I note, however, that since the states are legally responsible for education, reformers must understand the nature of state politics, recognizing the differences in individual states and focusing their efforts for change on states.

Part II provides case studies of reform efforts in Michigan and New Jersey. The authors, Thomas Vitullo-Martin and Margaret Goertz, have been involved in state reform efforts and have a unique perspective on state-level politics. John Augenblick, a former staff member of Education Committee for the States, has for the past ten years worked as a consultant on school finance, primarily for state legislatures and their education commissions. His chapter, "The Role of State Legislatures in School Finance Reform," describes the political issues behind school finance reform and presents proposals for assuring successful legislative solutions to financial inequities.

Augenblick views cooperative state legislatures as the key to any effort to refinance school systems and as capable of reform without prodding from the courts. Even when court cases are won, the legislature remains the final arbiter of the state aid formula. When the legislature is ignored, he notes, policies are bound to fail. State legislatures have altered their state aid formulas without pressure from the courts in support of a genuine concern about fairness, in recognition of the fact that school restructuring requires additional funding, or as a result of tax restructuring plans.

State education policy involves a spectrum of politically sensitive issues related to taxes, the interests of teachers' unions, and the tension between suburban and urban areas. Reform of the educational system, therefore, requires responses to these various special interests. Education reform in New Jersey and Michigan was affected by attention to or neglect of these issues.

School reform often requires tax increases or a shift in emphasis from the property tax to a state income or sales tax. State politicians are hesitant to venture into this politically volatile area, especially during election years. Because education is funded largely through local property taxes, no discussion of equity and education can omit the issue of taxes. As related by Goertz, a taxpayers' revolt was an important factor in the flawed formulation of New Jersey's Quality Education Act and the defeat of Governor Florio.

The issue of taxes has been used a stimulus for reform, however, particularly when fueled by a strong resistance to the unpopular property tax. A showdown between the Michigan governor and the legislature over property tax issues has contributed to greater financial equity. Tax questions are always divisive and, despite Michigan's example, are more likely to deter than to promote comprehensive school reform. Although these issues are politically volatile, a restructuring of taxing and spending is essential to the discourse about and solution of comprehensive school reform.

Pressure from wealthy and suburban districts can also pose a significant political barrier to change. These districts oppose changes in the education system from which they already benefit. They protest attempts to cap their spending levels or in any way restrict their educational activities. New Jersey's cities are comprised of primarily poor and minority populations. Goertz points out that any formula designed to aid only the urban districts will fail politically. Because of population shifts, suburbs have greater representation in state legislatures, and the cities' needs have been undermined. My report to the Ford Foundation summarizing recent Howard Samuels Center research on the impact of state politics on school reform finds a conservative shift in the states that has resulted in an increasing anti-city agenda. Many noncity residents believe that increasing educational dollars for urban communities will not solve any of their problems.

Those working on New Jersey's QEA had to make many concessions to the wealthy and suburban districts to ensure that they would benefit as much as the urban districts from the new formula. Although the public perceived that the QEA directed most of the new state aid dollars into urban school districts, middle-wealth school districts received as much new aid for regular education as did the low-wealth communities. Goertz points out that reformers should have better informed these areas that they too would benefit from reform and that improving education in urban and poor areas is necessary. In addition, by expanding reform efforts beyond the finance issue to include reforms in curriculum and governance, other groups can also feel that they will benefit from reform efforts.

The primary objective of teachers' unions is to insure their members' jobs, salaries, pensions, and work rules. These goals often appear to be in conflict with the objective of improving education for all children, and this formidable state lobby can usually derail the most aggressive plans. Teachers' unions have opposed reform efforts in both New Jersey and Michigan. The Michigan teachers' union led political campaigns and a court case to challenge that state's charter school program and new finance plans. In New Jersey, the teachers' union led marches at the state legislature to protest QEA provisions to shift teacher pension and Social Security costs from the state to the local school districts and was influential in persuading the legislature to put QEA on hold.

Together with wealthy and suburban districts, the unions must be included in education reform discussions and coalitions. In New Jersey, legislators excluded education specialists from the reform debate. As a result, the closed-door development of the new formula led to much criticism revolving around the issue of teacher pensions. This approach to policy development had the advantage of getting a formula designed quickly but had the disadvantage of focusing subsequent debate on the development rather than on the substance of the act.

Successful education reform formulation at the state capital require gubernatorial support and legislative leadership. In the cases of New Jersey and Michigan, key representatives provided the necessary coordination, information, and influence. Augenblick believes that the leadership capacity of state legislators needs to be nurtured by organizing education conferences of legislators in different states, creating a legislative network to facilitate interaction across state lines, and arming legislators with critical data and expert assistance.

Governors play a key role in state education reform; this is evidenced in both Michigan and New Jersey. Vitullo-Martin ascribes great importance to the leadership of Governor Engler. Engler initiated extensive tax reforms that served as the basis for comprehensive school reform. Other governors have provided the impetus for reform for reasons including the crisis status of education in their state or an interest in changing the taxing policies of their state.

Potential roadblocks in achieving reform include controversies around taxes, the interests of the teachers' unions, the interest of wealthy and suburban districts in maintaining the status quo, and negative perceptions of the urban areas. Comprehensive school reform and broad coalition building may neutralize resistance from the teachers' unions and suburban districts. Increasing awareness of the need for a better education for all children and strong political leadership at the state capital are also necessary to deal with these challenges. Although the following chapters point out the difficult political issues affecting education, they also show that these factors need not paralyze reform efforts.

Chapter 5 The Role of State Legislatures in School Finance Reform: Looking Backward and Looking Ahead

John Augenblick

State legislatures play an important role in school finance. In part this is because, on average, states provide the largest share of all support for schools, about half of all current operating revenues. Also, regardless of what proportion of support is provided in a particular state (and there is some variation across states), legislatures are responsible for creating the procedures used to allocate state aid to school districts and for controlling, directly or indirectly, both the extent to which localities can generate funds for public schools and the ways school districts can spend their funds. In addition, it is the legislatures that have the responsibility for assuring that school finance systems fulfill state constitutional requirements, which typically require that education be provided in a "free," "uniform," "efficient," "thorough," "ample," or "basic" way (these are the specific words used in the constitutions of different states).

The role that state legislatures play in funding schools has evolved over a long period of time, beginning with the passage of statutes requiring that public schools be organized and giving local communities access to sources of revenue such as property taxes. The evolution of the state role in supporting education continues today, at an increasingly rapid pace, in response to changes in demography, public opinion, and litigation as well as to the availability of better research and the increasing knowledge of legislators and legislative staff.

Although some would argue that state legislatures have been recalcitrant in dealing with the broad spectrum of issues that surrounds school finance, significant improvements have been made since the late 1960s and, specifically, during the past decade. One indicator of improvement is that the level of funding for elementary and secondary education has grown enormously—between 1970 and 1992, per-pupil spending grew by 85 percent more than the rate of inflation. In addition, the equity of resource distribution has improved. Although equity is difficult to measure and the debate about equity continues to rage, some states have been able to resolve the issue; in the past couple of years, both Kansas and Maine have successfully defended their school finance systems. Finally, some states have fundamentally changed the structure of their state aid allocation formulas, some have attempted to link funding and systemic change, and a few have created procedures to evaluate how well they are doing.

This is not to say that legislatures do not need to be prodded to make changes in the ways schools are funded, that the situation could not be improved further in most states, or that there are not real problems in some places that are unlikely to be addressed in the near future. The purpose of this chapter is to briefly review where we are and to identify some activities that might be undertaken to increase the likelihood that school finance systems will continue to improve.

WHAT DO WE MEAN BY SCHOOL
FINANCE REFORM?

School finance reform means different things to different people. To most educators, it means the assurance of more money, primarily from the state, with as few restrictions as possible on the ways that money can be used; the words typically used to describe what educators want from school finance systems are *predictability* and *flexibility.* These are appropriate objectives—the first reflects the needs of those who organize how services are delivered, including the employment of people, and the second is consistent with generally accepted education improvement strategies that stress increasing the authority of people who are closest to the places where services are actually delivered.

For some school districts, school finance reform means improving equity and adequacy, particularly for pupils, by rectifying the long-standing pattern in which the availability of revenue has been linked with school district wealth despite the tax rates of low-wealth, low-revenue districts. These concerns have led to the litigation with which most people are familiar (*Serrano* in California, *Robinson* and *Abbott* in New Jersey, and, more recently, *Pawtucket* in Rhode Island). Of course, for other school districts, particularly wealthy districts that have had relatively high spending levels, school finance reform is something to be avoided at all costs (which may mean intervening with defendants in litigation brought by other school districts).

For some taxpayers school finance reform means reducing, if not eliminating, reliance on property taxes. A variety of approaches have been used to accomplish this objective, including controls on property taxes, property assessments, school spending, and the authority of government to make tax decisions. Experiences in California (Proposition 13), Colorado (Amendment 1), Oregon (Measure 5), Michigan (where most, but not all, residential property taxes were replaced with sales taxes), and other states have certainly demonstrated the need to respond to this concern.

To some interest groups, school finance reform means more federal support or the targeting of funds (from any source) toward particular pupils, functions, or services. Teachers' groups, in particular, have supported a larger federal role in order to improve fiscal stability (under the assumption that a three-legged stool, one supported by federal, state, and local funds in approximately equal proportions, is more stable than one relying on any two of those sources), and groups concerned about pupils with particular characteristics (such as handicapped or bilingual students) have supported requirements that funds be spent on services specifically provided to pupils.

To many legislators, school finance reform is something to avoid because it is difficult to win; a legislator may represent several districts, each of which may be affected differently by reform. Reform tends to require an influx of significant amounts of new state revenue, which may require either that new taxes be imposed or that funds be reallocated from other functions. Some legislators understand the issue of "fairness" associated with school finance, although typically more in terms of fairness for taxpayers than for pupils, and some legislators see school finance reform as a vehicle to obtain more accountability or to increase efficiency. A few legislators are particularly adept at manipulating school finance systems to direct funds in ways that benefit the districts they represent, which may be done without any regard for the overall impact on the system.

These words and phrases—*predictability, flexibility, equity, adequacy, preservation of the status quo, reducing reliance on property taxes, targeting funds, accountability, efficiency,* and *winning* (or *losing*)—are, for many people, what school finance reform is all about. Several problems arise in using these words: (1) some of them are not very well defined; (2) some of them do not describe objectives that can be measured easily; and (3) they can, and do, conflict with one another.

In general, school finance reform means changing the way state aid is allocated to school districts so that:

- the allocation of most state support is sensitive to the needs of school districts, which reflect the cost pressures caused by pupil, program, and district characteristics that are beyond their control;
- the allocation of most state aid is sensitive to the ability of school districts to provide their own support based on some commonly accepted way to measure fiscal capacity;
- school districts are permitted to generate funds on their own above whatever the state allocates, but the state controls the magnitude of such revenue and provides assistance to districts so that districts making similar tax efforts are able to generate similar funds;
- the state does not control the way school districts spend funds but does hold districts (and perhaps schools) accountable for improving pupil performance;
- the state considers district needs and fiscal capacity in providing support for transportation, special education (or other special programs), capital outlay and debt service, and personnel benefits (particularly retirement);
- the allocation of state aid is "neutral" in regard to pupil classification decisions (that is, there is no incentive to misclassify pupils in order to obtain revenue);
- taxes are collected fairly—meaning that property is assessed uniformly, the burden of taxation on individuals and businesses is appropriate, and low-income individuals are relieved of some of the burden;
- sufficient funds are available to meet state mandates;
- procedures for allocating funds directly to school sites exist;
- school districts are encouraged to develop new approaches to paying teachers that include factors beyond training and experience;

- schools pay attention to the issue of professional development, which many people consider to be the single most important place to spend money in order to promote systemic change; and
- there is some linkage between funding for education and social services.

In addition, school finance reform requires that the allocation system be evaluated periodically so that it keeps up with changes in the environment, it is continually modified to better meet its objectives, and the accuracy of the parameters that drive the flow of funds is maintained.

Although no state fulfills all of these objectives, there are some that do better than others in terms of particular components. For example, Florida's school finance system has long been considered to be very sensitive to the varying needs and fiscal capacities of its school districts; this responsiveness is accomplished through the use of pupil "weights" designed to reflect the relative cost of serving pupils with different characteristics. (Several states use pupil weights, rather than "categorical" programs, to recognize the costs associated with special education, vocational education, bilingual education, "at-risk" pupils, school district size, regional price differences, and so on. With pupil weights, a "regular" pupil, requiring no special services, may be counted as a single pupil (1.0) whereas a pupil requiring services estimated to cost two and a half times as much as a regular pupil is counted as 2.5 pupils.) Colorado and Washington are among the very few states that place limits on how much revenue school districts can choose to raise on their own. Louisiana and Minnesota match local funds (differentially, based on fiscal capacity) raised above the floor established in their foundation programs. (Under this approach, the state sets a revenue "target," usually in per-pupil terms, and deducts from that amount the yield of a particular tax, usually the property tax, at common tax rate in order to determine the amount of state aid a particular district may receive.) Nebraska returns a portion of its income taxes to school districts and then takes that revenue into consideration in the distribution of state aid. Kansas uses what amounts to a statewide property tax to assure taxpayer equity across the state, whereas Montana and Wyoming "recapture" funds to accomplish the same goal. South Carolina allocates some funds to recognize improvements in pupil performance. Missouri requires that a small portion of funds be used for professional development.

Among all the states, perhaps Kentucky comes closest to putting all the pieces together into a coherent package that (1) establishes a base level of revenue per pupil, common across all school districts; (2) adjusts that amount to consider a variety of cost factors; (3) allows districts to generate funds above the base and provides support to those with relatively low fiscal capacity; (4) limits how much money districts can generate beyond that point; (5) allocates some funds to schools in recognition of changes in pupil performance; (6) "equalizes" state aid for capital outlay (that is, makes the allocation of state aid for schools inversely sensitive to the fiscal capacity of school districts); (7) distributes monies for ancillary services that support families through school centers; and (8) evaluates how well the system is working so that changes can be made as necessary. The state is also considering the possibility of changing the structure of its statewide salary schedule to more appropriately compensate teachers.

THE ROLE OF LEGISLATORS IN REFORMING SCHOOL FINANCE

Given the different conceptions of school finance reform held by the variety of people who are involved, both those who build the systems and those affected by them, it is not surprising that changing a school finance system to accomplish all of the objectives identified above is not easy. Yet, some states have been able to adopt significant reform. It is clearly important for anyone interested in promoting school finance reform to understand what factors are responsible for its being accomplished in states. In this regard, the literature does not provide too much guidance. A great deal of the literature describes what happened, usually in one state, without analyzing why it happened. Because the situation in any state is so idiosyncratic, the literature makes for interesting reading but does not provide much insight concerning how to obtain particular results anywhere else.

No doubt, a variety of factors are responsible for creating a situation in which change can occur, and some of those factors are associated with state legislatures. First, it can be argued that a stimulus for reform outside of the legislature must be present; a legislature tends not to do things, particularly difficult things, unless it is required to do so or there is sufficient clamor for them. In Kentucky the stimulus was the 1989 decision of the state supreme court that declared the existing statute to be unconstitutional and required the development of new legislation. A similar stimulus has existed in Alabama, Arizona, Arkansas, California, Connecticut, Missouri, Montana, New Jersey, Rhode Island, Texas, Washington, West Virginia, and Wyoming. The substantial threat of such a decision can produce the same result, which appears to explain the behavior of legislatures in places such as Colorado, Kansas, and Massachusetts. Such a stimulus does not, however, necessarily produce the desired results, as shown by the continual struggle in places such as New Jersey and Texas, where multiple decisions finding the school finance system in violation of the state constitution have not produced results that people in general consider to be satisfactory. In fact, litigation can have a negative impact, unifying the legislature in defense of the status quo and interfering with attempts to undertake broader reform.

Interestingly, litigation has not been the major reason why some states have undertaken school finance reform. In states in which litigation played a tangential role at best, such as Colorado, Florida, Louisiana, Michigan, Nebraska, New Mexico, Oklahoma, and South Carolina, school finance systems have been modified in ways considered to be appropriate during the last twenty-five years (Florida in the early 1970s and Michigan most recently). A variety of stimuli appear to have been responsible for promoting change in those states, including (1) a genuine concern about the issue of fairness (Nebraska); (2) an uproar over property taxes (Michigan); (3) a desire to reform education linked with a perceived need for more funding (South Carolina); or (4) some combination of these things (Colorado).

A second requirement for legislative success in school finance reform is that new funds be available to cover the costs of operating a new system. Without exception, the implementation of a new school finance system incurs a substantial increase in state support. This is due to a variety of factors, including (1) a more precise specification of needs, which may incorporate costs associated with new programs and services or the full funding of services that have previously been underfunded; (2) a shift away from local support; and (3) a requirement that hold-harmless funds be paid to districts that would otherwise lose state support. Even if the legislature can agree on the structure of a new school finance system, the lack of new revenue to fund it is usually a sufficient reason to assure that it will not be enacted, which may explain the situation in Mississippi during the early 1990s. It is not unusual that sufficient funds are provided initially to support a significant change but several years later funding becomes an issue; the way the state distributed funds when less revenue was provided than the system required was the subject of recent litigation in Maine.

The third requirement to accomplish school finance reform is legislative leadership. Legislative leadership is not sufficient, by itself, to assure that reform occurs; however, it is a necessary element without which little is likely to happen. In every state in which substantial change has taken place, a small cadre of legislators, sometimes only a single person, recognized the problems with the existing system, became knowledgeable about alternative approaches, understood the political implications of the alternatives, pushed colleagues to embrace the change, and defended the change in public, sometimes to the detriment of their own constituents. It is not unusual that, absent this kind of leadership, within a few years after enactment a new system is picked over until it may not be recognizable.

People such as Rep. Norma Anderson in Colorado, Rep. Rick Bowden in Kansas, Rep. Jimmy Long in Louisiana, Sen. Mike Maloney in Kentucky, and Sen. Ron Withem in Nebraska are examples of individuals whose influence was critical in the development and passage of new school finance systems in recent years. Representative Ron Cowell in Pennsylvania and Sen. Ronnie Musgrove in Mississippi are instrumental in keeping school finance reform on the agendas of states where success has not yet been achieved. Legislative staff are also critical in school finance reform. People such as Ben Barrett in Kansas, Placido Garcia in New Mexico, Deb Godshall in Colorado, Larry Scherer in Nebraska, George Silbernagel in Louisiana, Ellen Still in South Carolina, and Tom Willis in Kentucky were responsible for the design and much of the technical support of new formulas.

This is not to say that governors and chief state school officers, and their staffs, are not important to the ultimate success of new school finance systems—in some states, such as New Jersey (particularly in light of Governor Florio's role in developing the Quality Education Act of 1990), South Carolina (in regard to Governor Riley's role in the implementation of the Education Improvement Act of 1984), and South Dakota (where two governors, Miller and Jankelow, pushed for reform despite a legal decision supporting the existing system), the executive branch has been instrumental in creating a funding approach and generating the support required to enact it. Department of education staff, such as Dale Dennis in Kansas, Tim Kemper in Nebraska, and Marilyn Langley in Louisiana, have also played key roles in developing and defending new school finance systems.

Fourth, it is important to improve the knowledge level of a wide range of people, particularly across the large number of special interest groups associated with education, which include teachers, school boards, administrators, parents in general, parents of pupils with special needs, public interest groups, the business community, and taxpayer groups—which rarely agree on anything having to do with money unless everyone obtains lots of new revenue. Too often, these groups do not understand the mechanics of school finance systems, the policy questions, or the alternative approaches that might be considered in addressing the issues. In states where such groups are knowledgeable about school finance and the political process, such as Indiana, they have been effective advocates of change.

Finally, the use of expert assistance is critical to successful school finance reform. Given the political nature of much of the debate that surrounds school finance, it is important to have access to an independent, objective perspective. Since almost everyone in a particular state has some stake in school finance—as employee, parent, or taxpayer—an objective viewpoint may need to come from outside of the state. In many of the states where progress has been made, the fingerprints of such an outside expert are evident. For example, in Kentucky, the task force charged with developing a response to the court's ruling received assistance from the Education Commission of the States (ECS) and the National Conference of State Legislatures; the subcommittees into which the task force divided each worked closely with an outside consultant, some of whom have maintained a relationship with the state ever since.

THE POLITICS OF SCHOOL FINANCE REFORM

It is not possible to discuss the relationship between legislatures and school finance without recognizing the political nature of the topic, which is among the most controversial legislators must face. This is true for several reasons. First, state support typically consumes a significant portion of a state's general fund budget (between 25 and 40 percent is not unusual); in most, support for elementary and secondary education is the largest single item in the general fund budget. This means that school finance receives a lot of attention, that changes are proposed almost every year, and that the issue is resolved after other, smaller fiscal issues have been addressed. Because of the magnitude of resources involved, changes in school finance systems tend to be made incrementally, modifying the total volume of funds based primarily on changes in enrollment and inflation; it is usually difficult to obtain new funds for programmatic changes unless state revenue is robust and attention is not focused on property tax reduction.

Second, decisions about school finance affect every legislator because school districts cover the entire state and every legislator represents one or more of them. To some extent this makes elementary and secondary schools different from other public institutions—such as hospitals, prisons, and colleges—which do not directly affect every legislator. It is almost impossible to enact new school finance legislation if key school districts would lose state aid, be required to raise their local taxes, or need to reduce expenditure levels; in Kansas, when a massive change was being considered, several school districts discussed the possibility of seceding from the state in light of the property tax increases and spending controls they faced.

Third, on average there are three hundred school districts in each state; although some states have fewer districts (Hawaii has only one) and others have far more (ten states have more than five hundred), the sheer number of districts results in wide variations in characteristics that affect the cost of providing education services, such as enrollment level, population density, and socioeconomic conditions. In order to minimize the politics of school finance, states use mathematical formulas to determine the allocation of state aid, and although the objective is to keep such formulas as simple as possible, it is difficult to do while making the distribution of funds sensitive to the different situations faced by school districts. In order to pass muster in the legislature, a school finance formula must be able to consider the needs of large urban centers and small, remote locations, which complicates formulas and subjects them to manipulation.

Fourth, most locally provided support is obtained from property taxes, perceived to be the least liked tax in almost every poll of people's attitudes toward taxes regardless of the magnitude of the tax relative to other taxes in a state or to property tax levels in other states. Property tax reduction, if not elimination, is often the strongest driving force behind school finance reform, as reflected in the actions taken in Michigan recently.

Fifth, lots of special interest groups have a concern about school finance, from the ones representing those who govern and administer the system to those representing employees, participants, or those who support the system; it is far easier not to change a school finance system than to run the risk of upsetting one or more of the interest groups that hover around the issue.

Finally, few people understand school finance and its complicated allocation mechanisms. Given the lack of knowledge, decisions are made in the simplest terms based on the fiscal impact of any proposed change and the extent to which particular districts are winners or losers. In this regard, modern technology has probably not served the interest of reform well; decision makers can see the fiscal impact of proposed changes instantly and can accept or reject a proposal for change without needing to understand its philosophical underpinnings or its objectives.

WHAT CAN BE DONE TO INCREASE
THE ODDS OF SUCCESS

If legislatures are critical to improving school finance systems, steps should be undertaken to assure their involvement. First, the leadership capacity of legislatures, including legislators and staff, needs to be nurtured. Activities that might be undertaken to accomplish this include conferences of people serving similar roles in different states, the creation of a legislative network to facilitate interaction across state lines, and the provision of useful information.

Second, state-specific catalysts for school finance reform must be identified. This requires a careful evaluation of a group of target states to understand the history, the politics, and the fiscal environment. It also would be appropriate to undertake an evaluation of the school finance system in order to determine its strengths and weaknesses; in particular, knowledge of weaknesses might serve as the basis of litigation, should that approach be considered the most appropriate stimulus for reform.

Third, research gaps need to be filled, particularly in the area of the relation between finance and systemic change. For example, although most states have adopted "foundation" formulas, they continue to use a political approach to determine the foundation level that drives the allocation of aid; research needs to be done that focuses on other, more rational ways to determine the foundation, or base, cost level. In addition, further research is needed to identify and quantify cost pressures that school districts with different characteristics face so that factors can be included in school finance systems; specifically, more research is needed to help policy makers properly recognize the fiscal impacts associated with different programs, such as special education, and different kinds of pupils, particularly those who are most at risk of failure.

Fourth, better ways must be found to disseminate information and expertise. Today there are fewer places to obtain good school finance information, and far fewer places from which to access expertise, than was the case a decade ago. National organizations such as ECS, which used to provide technical assistance to states on school finance, have less capacity to do so today. In addition, the university-based education policy centers that have been developing in recent years have done little work in the area of finance. Obviously, economics has something to do with this—states are reluctant to spend limited resources on expertise, and federal and foundation support that was available in the 1970s has for the most part evaporated.

It is difficult to specify which of these activities is the most important. In a sense they are all interconnected, so it may not matter where the process is started. In the long run, what is important is that whatever activities are undertaken be sustained over a long period of time and that systematic relationships across activities be developed. School finance systems—and linking finance to education reform—will require a significant commitment of resources, but that commitment will mean little if the activities supported are not state-specific, do not merge theoretical and practical concerns, and are not informed by the intensely political nature of school finance issues at the state level.

Chapter 6 Steady Work: The Courts and School Finance Reform in New Jersey

Margaret E. Goertz

On July 12, 1994, the New Jersey Supreme Court handed down its third decision in the school finance case *Abbott v. Burke.* This decision was the ninth state supreme court ruling in twenty-four years of school finance litigation in New Jersey.[1] In the intervening years, the state legislature enacted (and amended) two major school funding laws and increased state aid for education fivefold. Has intervention by the court made a difference? The answer to this question is both yes and no. The court has made four positive contributions to school finance policy in New Jersey. First, the court has established a definition of educational adequacy that is keyed to the educational programs, expenditures, and outcomes of the state's wealthiest communities. Second, the court decisions have driven the agenda for educational finance reform in New Jersey (Lehne, 1978) and provided political cover for administrations that strove to restructure the way the state raises revenues and distributes state aid (Byrne in 1975, Florio in 1990). Third, in the *Abbott* decisions, the court focused attention directly on the plight of poor, urban children and the state's responsibility to educate these children. Fourth, the funding laws and state aid appropriations that resulted from *Robinson v. Cahill* and *Abbott* ensured that the poorest school districts in New Jersey did not lose ground during the last twenty years. Between 1975 and 1992, the expenditure level of the lowest-spending districts increased from 73 percent to 78 percent of the state average. In addition, school tax rates of the poorest communities dropped nearly $1.00 (Goertz, 1978, 1994).

Court intervention has failed in three areas, however. First, although the poorest communities did not lose ground, the overall equity of the system has not improved since the days preceding the *Robinson* decision. Second, too few new funds were directed to the poor urban communities to enable them to provide a program that begins to approach a "thorough and efficient" education. Third, no political coalition has emerged in support of true school finance reform. In fact, attempts to provide additional resources to poor districts generated proposals to remove (or redefine) the state's constitutional guarantee of a "thorough and efficient" education.

The story of the Quality Education Act (QEA), legislation enacted in 1990 to respond to the court mandate in *Abbott v. Burke,* reveals the tradeoffs involved in developing school finance systems that are equitable, yet also fiscally sound and politically feasible. This chapter begins with a brief summary of the initial *Abbott v. Burke* decision. It then describes the political and fiscal context of the development of the QEA, political and structural problems with the law, and resulting changes to the formula. It ends with a discussion of the issues facing policy makers in New Jersey as they respond to the most recent court decision.

ABBOTT V. BURKE

In February 1981, the Education Law Center, a public-interest law firm in Newark, New Jersey, filed a complaint in New Jersey Superior Court on behalf of twenty children attending public schools in Camden, East Orange, Irvington, and Jersey City. The plaintiffs contended that New Jersey's system of funding education caused significant educational expenditure and program disparities between poor urban and wealthy suburban school districts, leaving poor urban districts unable to meet the educational needs of their students. They argued that the operation of the then-current funding law, the Public School Education Act of 1975 (Chapter 212), violated the "thorough and efficient" and the equal protection clauses of the state constitution and the law against discrimination.[2]

In June 1990, the court ruled in favor of the plaintiffs: Chapter 212 was unconstitutional as applied to poorer urban districts because the education delivered to the students was neither thorough nor efficient (*Abbott v. Burke II*). The justices found that "under the present system . . . the poorer the district and the greater its need, the less the money available, and the worse the education. . . . Education has failed there, for both the student and the State" (*Abbott II* at 295). The court then ordered the legislature to design a new or revised funding system that would meet the following criteria.

1. *Equalize spending for the regular education program between poorer urban districts[3] and property-rich districts.[4]* If the state allows the richer suburban districts to increase their spending, it must increase the funding of the poorer urban districts accordingly.

2. *Provide additional funds to meet the special education needs of the urban districts in order to redress their disadvantages.* Such assistance must be in addition to the funds needed to redress disparities in the regular education programs.

3. *Assure that funding for poor urban districts is certain every year and does not depend on the budgeting or taxing decisions of local school boards.* The legislature cannot meet the constitutional mandate simply by raising the guaranteed tax base under Chapter 212. The design of the funding plan should take into consideration the municipal overburden of the poorer urban districts.

4. *Eliminate minimum aid.*

5. *Implement a new formula starting in the 1991–92 school year.* The new system can be phased in. If the legislature provides for a phase-in of the new funding plan, minimum aid may be phased out in accordance with that timetable.

The court's decision applies only to poorer urban districts. The justices ruled that sufficient evidence was not submitted in this case to show that the constitutional mandate was violated in other school districts in the state.

THE QUALITY EDUCATION ACT OF 1990

On July 3, 1990, one month after the *Abbott v. Burke* decision, Governor Jim Florio signed into law a new school funding formula, the Quality Education Act of 1990. At the time of its passage, the QEA was heralded as a major step toward the reform of urban education and the achievement of school finance equity in New Jersey. Yet, over the next nine months the law was assaulted by citizens and major education interest groups throughout the state. In March 1991, four months before the QEA was to take effect, it was amended to provide greater property tax relief to taxpayers and less aid to the financially strapped urban school districts.

Critics of the QEA contend that the legislation was flawed because it was hastily conceived, was designed in secrecy, and had little educational substance. They argue that given more time and greater input from education interests, a "better" law would have emerged. Although more time and a more open decisionmaking process may have fostered greater political support for the new legislation, the substance of the law was shaped by the interaction of the court's mandate to equalize spending, the politics of taxation, and the politics of redistribution.

QEA I

Discussions of a new funding formula began in January 1990 (in the early days of the Florio administration) in anticipation of a ruling in *Abbott v. Burke.* Although members of the Florio administration were generally sympathetic with the claims of the plaintiffs in the *Abbott* litigation[5] and understood the programmatic and fiscal needs of urban districts, QEA I was developed as part of a larger fiscal reform. Governor Florio had three fiscal policy goals when he assumed office: (1) close an impending budget deficit of $600 million; (2) equalize tax burdens by assuming some of the costs of state-mandated county functions and by expanding and restructuring homestead rebates; and (3) increase state education aid and distribute it more equitably. The first goal would be met by raising the sales tax by a penny (from six to seven cents) and expanding coverage of the tax to telephone services, paper goods, soap products, and other household goods. The second and third goals would be met by increasing the income tax on the state's highest earners and by modifying the way in which state education aid was allocated to school districts.

The initial strategy was to separate the two tax changes. The sales tax would be considered first; this tax increase had to be enacted by June 1990 to balance the fiscal year 1991 budget. Deliberations about changes in the income tax and the state aid formula could continue during 1990. A court decision in the *Abbott v. Burke* litigation was expected in February 1990, too late to change the law for the 1990–91 school year, and the budget crisis had led to a decision to freeze state education aid for that year. Therefore, changes in the education aid formula and other tax reforms could wait for the fiscal year 1992 budget.

In late February 1990, the administration's strategy underwent a change when the Democratic leaders of the Assembly balked at voting separately on sales and income tax increases. They would vote only once on taxes, and that tax package had to generate property tax relief. This demand meant that the governor had to introduce a comprehensive tax package in his March 15 budget message that included measures to address the budget deficit, tax reform, and education finance reform. This situation made it even more difficult for policy makers to separate education policy from fiscal policy. It also increased the pace of policy development and the degree of secrecy imposed on the deliberations. The administration felt that the whole tax package would now rise or fall on the school aid formula. A lack of consensus on the school finance formula in the legislature would mean no support for the income tax, and no support for the income tax would mean no support for the sales tax increase.

A small working group was convened to develop ideas for a new school aid formula. The group rarely involved more than ten people; the core members were the state treasurer (and former campaign director for the governor), the treasurer's deputy for budget and finance, the governor's education policy advisor, and school finance experts from Treasury's Office of Management and Budget and the state Department of Education. Policy makers from the state Department of Education were not included. The governor was in the process of replacing the commissioner of education, Saul Cooperman, who had ruled against the plaintiffs in the *Abbott* litigation and was viewed as being insensitive to the needs of urban school districts. The working group was headquartered in the treasurer's office, another indicator of the strong fiscal focus of the state aid deliberations.

The working group started with a number of assumptions: (1) the court would rule in favor of the plaintiffs, throw out the old formula (a guaranteed-tax-base formula), and focus on program parity for all school districts; (2) a foundation aid formula was an appropriate way of bringing about finance reform; (3) minimum aid should be eliminated; (4) the new formula should maximize the number of districts eligible for equalization aid; and (5) the cost of state education aid must be kept in line with state revenues.

The group began by looking at a foundation aid formula with a foundation amount set at approximately the sixty-fifth percentile spending and more realistic cost factors for the categorical aid programs. This level of spending would, they felt, give districts parity in class size, curriculum, staffing, and course offerings—those factors that the middle class considered essential in a good educational program. They soon ran into fiscal constraints, however. The treasurer had set parameters on changes in the income tax that limited income tax revenue increases to about $1.1 to $1.3 billion.[6] Some of these new dollars were earmarked for other tax relief programs, such as a new homestead rebate program for low-income taxpayers and state assumption of some county costs. Therefore, the school finance group had to work with a revenue cap of about $1 billion. To meet this limit, the group had to reduce the foundation level to about the sixtieth percentile and make pension and Social Security costs the responsibility of the local districts, thereby increasing the proportion of state aid that was wealth-equalized.

In order to control the growth in state aid for education, the administration proposed tying increases in both the foundation level and overall state aid to growth in the state's per capita income (PCI), considered the best indicator of growth in income tax revenues, the primary source of revenue for school aid. (Use of the PCI was also intended to provide certainty in the level of revenue that would be available to fund school aid each year.)

The group also worked under a number of political constraints. Although the Democrats had a six-vote majority in both the Senate and the Assembly, some of the Democratic legislators represented wealthy communities. In addition, a number of "swing" districts included "middle middle-class" communities. Therefore, the new formula had to contain provisions that would help middle-income, as well as urban, school districts. These provisions included (1) incorporating an income factor in the wealth measure to help middle-income suburban communities where personal income had not kept pace with rapidly escalating property values; (2) providing transition aid to wealthy districts to ease the loss of minimum aid (and initially the loss of state pension aid); and (3) exempting low-spending, low-taxing districts (mostly districts in southern New Jersey) from the requirement that they tax at their required local effort as long as they met state criteria for providing a "thorough and efficient" education.

Education experts in the Senate and Assembly Democratic staff were not brought into the deliberations on the QEA until late April 1990, approximately one month before the bill was introduced in the legislature. They raised concerns about the equalization of state pension and social security funds, the lack of expenditure caps, and the structure of transition aid, but generally accepted the provisions of the proposed new law. They quickly recognized that shifting pension funding from the state to local districts was necessary to put more state aid into middle-wealth districts. In addition, all other local governments in New Jersey (for example, counties and municipalities) already paid the employer's share of public employee pensions, a fact not lost on the legislators who were also mayors. Education interest groups were shut out of all discussions of the proposed education finance reform because of the certain opposition of the

New Jersey Education Association (NJEA) and New Jersey School Boards Association (NJSBA) to local assumption of teacher retirement costs. The closed development of the new formula also reflected, in the words of one observer, the Florio administration's modus operandi—"put a plan on the table for discussion, rather than develop the plan at the table." This approach to policy development had the advantage of getting a formula designed quickly. It had the disadvantage, however, of focusing subsequent debate on *how* the QEA was developed, rather than on the substance of the Act.

The Quality Education Act was passed by the legislature with relatively few revisions in June 1990, shortly after the *Abbott* decision. The new law (1) changed the formula for distributing state education aid to local school districts from a guaranteed tax base to a foundation formula, (2) redefined the wealth measure used to allocate aid to include an income factor, (3) replaced the compensatory education categorical aid program with a program of aid for "at-risk" students, (4) eliminated the payment of minimum aid to wealthy school districts, (5) made the payment of teacher pension and Social Security costs the responsibility of local school districts, and (6) increased state aid to education by approximately $1.1 billion. Revenues for new state aid were generated by a $1.3 billion increase in the state's income tax.

Amending the QEA (QEA II)

Opposition to the tax package and the new school funding bill formed even before the governor signed the QEA into law on July 3, 1990, and revolved around the issues of the redistribution of state aid from wealthy to poor districts and higher taxes. On the day of the Assembly's passage of the QEA, members of the NJEA marched on the State House to protest the shift in teacher pension and social security costs from the state to local school districts. Whereas the teachers worried publicly that this shift would endanger the stability of the pension system, a private concern was that local assumption of the cost of the pensions would have a negative impact on the size of future salary contracts. In October 1990, the superintendents of twenty-five wealthy suburban school districts formed a coalition to oppose local assumption of teacher retirement costs and school spending caps. They argued that "the Quality Education Act goes beyond the mandate of the court . . . and includes provisions which will fundamentally weaken the most successful and highest-achieving public school districts in the state. . . . Weak schools should not be made strong by making strong schools weak" (*Position Paper*). They called for four changes to the QEA: return of the state's share of teacher retirement costs to the state, revisions in the criteria for at-risk aid, expansion of categorical aid, and reassessment of the cap formula.

Taxpayer concerns also undermined potential support for the new QEA. A grass-roots organization, Hands Across New Jersey, led a taxpayer revolt against increases in the state sales and income taxes.[7] The Republican party ran a strong anti-tax campaign in the November 1990 elections. The near-defeat of United States Senator Bill Bradley and the loss of Democratic seats in special state legislative elections led Governor Florio and the Democratic legislative leadership to announce that all aspects of the QEA were open for review.

Fearful about their fate in November 1991, when the entire state legislature would be up for election, Democrats in the state legislature amended the QEA in March 1991. The major amendments to the QEA (1) reduced the increase in state aid to education from $1.15 billion to $800 million and allocated the $350 million difference to municipalities for tax relief, (2) reduced the base foundation level by nearly $200 per student, (3) eliminated the provision that required districts to tax at their "fair share" in order to receive full foundation aid, (4) reduced "at-risk" pupil aid and created a compensatory education aid save-harmless provision, (5) reduced annual increases in total state education aid by 20 percent, (6) established more restrictive budget caps and applied them to a district's total budget, rather than to its budget for the regular education program, and (7) delayed the local assumption of teacher pension and social security costs for a two-year period. These changes were designed to force more dollars into local property tax relief and to address, on a temporary basis, the political backlash on the teacher pension issue.

Problems with the QEA

In its first two years (1991–92 and 1992–93), the QEA increased state aid by nearly $900 million, or 26 percent. Aid for the "regular education" program—foundation aid—increased almost $650 million, and aid for categorical programs—special education, bilingual education, at-risk aid, and transportation aid—grew another $450 million. These increases were offset by a reduction in state support for teacher retirement costs of $232 million due to the state revaluation of pensions. Aid to the thirty special needs districts increased $513 million, or 40 percent. As a result, their share of state aid increased from 37 percent in 1990–91 to 41 percent in 1992–93.

In spite of this infusion of aid, the QEA had a limited impact on the equity of the system. Statewide, there was no change in the expenditure disparity between the lowest- and highest-spending districts: it remained at around $3,800 per pupil for the regular education program. Other measures of equity—the coefficient of variation and the McLoone index, for example—also showed no change. The correlation between wealth and spending on the regular education program increased slightly. Looking at the thirty special needs districts, the focus of the *Abbott* decision, one finds little improvement as well. Spending differences between the special needs districts and the average expenditure of the state's wealthiest districts widened for fifteen of the thirty districts and exceeded $2,000 per pupil in ten of them (Goertz, 1994).

Several factors limited the impact of aid increases on equity (Goertz, 1993, 1994). First, although the public perception of the QEA is of a law that directed most of the new state aid dollars into the state's urban school districts, middle-wealth school districts received as much new aid for regular education (foundation aid) as did the low-wealth communities. The middle-wealth school districts received substantial increases in foundation aid because the foundation level for 1992–93 was well above the average spending of these districts, and districts educating 70 percent of the state's students were eligible for foundation aid.

Second, although most districts in the state were eligible for substantial new revenues under the QEA foundation formula, the amount of aid they actually received and then were allowed to spend was limited by the imposition of tight budget caps. Because the low-wealth districts were spending well below the foundation amount in 1990–91, the caps did not enable them to come up to the foundation level. Two years into the new law, half of the students were still living in districts spending below the foundation amount.

Third, although the highest-wealth districts in the state, on average, saw their total state aid reduced, they increased their net current expense budgets an average of 5 to 6 percent a year. When applied to their high spending base, these percentage increases translated into $1,000 to $1,200 per pupil. Although expenditures grew at a faster rate among the low-wealth districts, these communities saw increases of only $1,200 to $1,400 per pupil, on average, because of their lower base. As a result, little progress was made in narrowing the spending gap among districts or in reducing the relation between wealth and spending.

Finally, in order to keep the growth of state aid in line with the growth in state revenues, the QEA limited the amount that maximum school aid could increase each year. The law also required that obligations for nonfoundation aid programs be met before funding foundation aid. That is, the amount of money available for foundation aid is what remained after subtracting teacher retirement costs and all the major categorical programs (except debt service) from maximum school aid. In 1992–93, growth in the teacher retirement and categorical aid programs outstripped the permitted increase in maximum school aid. As a result, in the initial 1992–93 QEA budget, foundation aid was *reduced* by $34 million. The decision to revalue all state pension funds, including the teacher pension fund, lowered pension contributions for 1992–93 by $342 million, freeing up these dollars for foundation aid. This revaluation, however, was a "one-shot" adjustment.

Changes to the QEA

The threat of aid cuts to middle-income suburban districts in 1992–93 triggered several actions. First, the foundation aid districts began calling for changes to the QEA. Second, suburban Republican legislators introduced a constitutional amendment in June 1992 that would have replaced the current "thorough and efficient" clause with a funding formula that would limit the state's financial obligation to all school districts and would eliminate the requirement of substantial parity between poor urban and wealthy suburban districts. This amendment was opposed by all of the major education and advocacy groups. The Republicans dropped their plan to put the amendment on the November 1992 ballot but subsequently introduced a new funding law that incorporated many of the provisions of the proposed constitutional amendment.

   In response to the threat of the constitutional amendment and Republican funding plan, the major education interest groups (who are members of the New Jersey Association for Public Schools, or NJAPS)—groups representing urban districts, foundation aid districts, and wealthier suburban districts—and the Education Law Center proposed a compromise plan for the 1993–94 school year. This law, the Public School Reform Act of 1992, was enacted by the legislature in December 1992. It put the QEA "on hold," providing districts a limited percentage increase in their foundation aid, freezing the growth of categorical aid, and making the state responsible for funding teacher pensions and Social Security permanent once again.

ABBOTT III AND BEYOND

Abbott III

In response to the amendments made to the QEA in 1991 and the lack of progress toward parity for the special-needs districts, the Education Law Center returned to court in June 1991 to challenge the constitutionality of QEA II. In a per curiam decision issued in July 1994, the court reaffirmed its prior holding in

Abbott II and found the QEA unconstitutional because it failed to assure parity of regular education expenditures between the special-needs districts and the more affluent districts (*Abbott v. Burke III*). The court ordered the state to adopt a new funding formula by September 1996 that would yield substantial parity, "approximating 100%," and provide for the special education needs of the urban districts for the 1997–98 school year. It also charged the state to address the existing disparity in the upcoming school years of 1995–96 and 1996–97. The court retained jurisdiction over the case and found in May 1997 that the state had failed to meet its obligation. It once again ordered the state to assure expenditure parity by 1997–98.

Continuing Challenges in School Finance Reform

The short history of the QEA points out the difficulties of developing a school finance formula that enhances the equity of the system while meeting the fiscal and political needs of the state. Policy makers in New Jersey face similar challenges as they design a new finance program to replace the QEA.

It is estimated that meeting the court mandate will cost an additional $450 million. Yet, a formula designed to aid only the urban districts will fail politically. New Jersey's cities are poor, house most of the state's racial and language minority population, and are small. Because of their size, the cities have limited representation in the state legislature. They are also the target of racial and social bias in the state. Most citizens view urban school systems as "bottomless pits" where increasing expenditures have had little if any impact on student achievement and where more state aid will not make a difference.[8] This perception has been enhanced by the state takeover of three urban districts (Jersey City, Newark, and Paterson). In addition, any formula that provides parity for the special-needs districts but does not address the needs of the middle-wealth districts will result in a two-tier system: the special-needs districts and wealthy communities will be spending at one level, and all the other districts will have significantly fewer resources.

If its makers wish to garner support from the groups with influence in the legislature (high-wealth communities, other suburban communities with Republican legislators, and the major education interest groups), a formula cannot level down spending, take money away from wealthy communities (for example, reallocate categorical aid), add to the cost of doing business in school districts (for example, assign teacher retirement costs to districts), or harm middle-income communities. It is less clear how much financial aid must be given to the 450 low- and middle-income school districts to win their support for reform. These districts face growing enrollments, rising tax rates, and disgruntled voters. Although most benefited under the first year of the QEA, many were threatened with the loss of aid in the second year of the formula, and only a few received additional state aid dollars in the two subsequent years.

The members of the Education Funding Review Commission (EFRC), a bipartisan group created under the Public School Reform Act of 1992 to recommend changes to the QEA, debated what level of spending was necessary to provide a "thorough and efficient" education. The formula that received the support of all education groups in the state—poor, middle-income, and wealthy—set the foundation level of special-needs districts at the average spending of the state's wealthiest districts and that of the non–special-needs districts at 90 percent of that amount. A wealth-equalized add-on was available up to 100 percent of this spending level. Income was dropped from the definition of wealth, and teacher retirement costs remained the responsibility of the state. At-risk aid was retained and doubled for the special-needs districts. It was estimated that the plan would cost an additional $1.4 billion and would raise the state share of education spending from less than 40 percent to about 60 percent.

Thus, equity is expensive, particularly when it is politically infeasible to equalize categorical aid and pension costs, which account for nearly half of state aid. The NJAPS coalition must convince its members, the legislature, and the public that greater equity is needed (and wanted), that education spending should be increased and will lead to considerably higher levels of student achievement, and that increased state taxes *will* lead to reduced property taxes. This is a particularly difficult challenge because New Jersey is under extreme fiscal pressure, and the governor and legislature are committed to reducing state taxes and downsizing state government.

Governor Whitman has been faced with a recurring structural deficit (caused by several years of one-shot budget-balancing gimmicks), the school finance crisis, growing expenses in the state's Medicaid and corrections programs, and changes in federal aid. The legislature rolled back the one-cent increase in the sales tax in 1992, reducing state revenues by $600 million a year, and the governor cut the state's income tax by 30 percent, at an annual cost of approximately $1.3 billion. Although New Jersey has emerged from the 1990 recession, growth in employment has been limited. The situation at the state level has placed extreme pressure on local budgets and local property taxes. School tax rates rose 13 percent between 1992 and 1995.

Once again, school finance reform policy is linked to tax policy. While states across the nation are looking to reduce reliance on local property taxes for education (for example, Michigan, Wisconsin, and Vermont), New Jersey is moving in the other direction. State taxes are being reduced and costs shifted onto the local property tax. The state has cut taxes by nearly $2 billion a year, more than enough to address the *Abbott* mandate and cover the cost of the EFRC proposal. The tension in the forthcoming legislative session will be between the desire to maintain these state tax cuts (always a popular thing to do) at the same time as keeping local property taxes under control. There is no easy solution to this problem.

NOTES

1. The New Jersey Supreme Court handed down six decisions in an earlier school finance case, *Robinson v. Cahill.* The first decision declared the existing school finance system unconstitutional. The next three decisions concerned the legislative deadline for reforming the school finance formula. The fifth decision reviewed the constitutionality of the Public Education Act of 1975, while the sixth closed New Jersey schools until the state legislature voted the money necessary to fund fully the 1975 act. The first New Jersey Supreme Court decision in *Abbott v. Burke*, 100 N.J. 269 (1985) (*Abbott I*), remanded the case to the Office of Administrative Law rather than to the courts for the development of a complete record. The second decision rendered the state system of funding unconstitutional as applied to the state's twenty-nine poorest urban school districts (*Abbott v. Burke*, 119 N.J. 287 [1990]) (*Abbott II*).

2. Under art. 7 of the New Jersey Constitution, "the Legislature shall provide for the maintenance and support of a thorough and efficient system of free public schools for the instruction of all children in the State between the ages of five and eighteen years."

3. The court defined "poorer urban districts" as the twenty-eight districts that are classified by the Department of Education as "urban districts" *and* fall within District Factor Groups (DFG) A and B. These districts educate about 25 percent of the state's students. The DFGs are derived from a composite measure of community social and economic variables such as educational and occupational background of the population, per capita income of the district, and mobility. Districts are ranked from low to high on this measure and divided into ten approximately equal groups. The DFGs range from A (lowest socioeconomic status) to J (highest socioeconomic status). The court did not designate Atlantic City as a "poorer urban district" because of its high property wealth (*Abbott II* at 342, n. 18).

4. The court defined "property-rich districts" as the 108 districts in DFGs I and J, the two highest socioeconomic status groups.

5. For example, the governor's education policy advisor had testified for the plaintiffs in *Abbott*.

6. Rates would be raised only on the top 20 percent of taxpayers in the state—single

taxpayers earning more than $35,000 a year and households earning more than $70,000 a year. The top rate could not exceed 7 percent, in order to stay below the highest income tax rate in New York State.
7. For an excellent description of the taxpayer revolt, see Kehler (1992).
8. Research has shown, however, that the special-needs districts used new aid dollars to catch up on deferred programs and facilities, develop and expand social support programs, and strengthen their regular academic programs (Firestone, Goertz, and Natriello, 1997).

REFERENCES

Abbott v. Burke, OAL DKT. No. EDU 5581–85 (Aug. 24, 1988).
Abbott v. Burke, 100 N.J. 269 (1985) (*Abbott I*).
Abbott v. Burke, 119 N.J. 287 (1990) (*Abbott II*).
Abbott v. Burke, 136 N.J. 444 (1994) (*Abbott III*).
Firestone, W. A., Goertz, M. E., and Natriello, G. 1997. *From Cashbox to Classroom: The Struggle for Fiscal Reform and Educational Change in New Jersey* (New York: Teachers College Press).
Goertz, M. E. 1978. *Where Did the $400 Million Go? The Impact of the New Jersey Public School Education Act of 1975* (Princeton, N.J.: Educational Testing Service).
————. 1993. School Finance Reform in New Jersey: The Saga Continues. *Journal of Education Finance* 18(4): 346–65.
————. 1994. The Equity Impact of the Quality Education Act in New Jersey. Paper presented at the annual meeting of the American Education Finance Association, Nashville, Tenn.
Kehler, D. 1992. The Trenton Tea Party: The Story of New Jersey's Tax Revolt. *Policy Review* (spring 1992): 46–49.
Lehne, R. 1978. *The Quest for Justice: The Politics of School Finance Reform* (New York: Longman).
Position Paper on the Quality Education Act of 1990 by chief school administrators of twenty-five suburban districts, October 24, 1990.

Chapter 7 Charter Schools and Tax Reform in Michigan

Thomas Vitullo-Martin

The Michigan Public School Academy Act of 1993 (PA 362), when considered with the school finance reform passed as a companion bill, set in motion the most far-reaching, egalitarian restructuring of public education in any state in the latter half of the twentieth century. The magnitude of the change, not widely understood when the law was passed, is only gradually revealing itself as the law takes effect. It has astonished many observers that such a change could come from the nation's staunchest union state and could erupt seemingly from nowhere. The law passed in November and December 1993 had not been publicly discussed in September.

The setting for the reform was a Michigan legislature in which each house was evenly divided between Republicans and Democrats, with the governor's office held by John Engler, the former Republican Senate majority leader and a skilled legislative leader. The House split exactly, so that the speakership and committee chairs revolved be-

The author is indebted to Robert Wittmann of the Michigan Partnership for helpful comments on this chapter.

tween the two parties monthly. The Senate was Republican, but by a slim majority (twenty-two to sixteen) that was at best precarious on education issues. Reform legislation required bipartisan support. The most powerful single lobby in the state is the Michigan Education Association (MEA). The union has organized virtually every school district outside of Detroit (which is organized by the American Federation of Teachers [AFT]). The MEA political action committee, by a large margin the wealthiest Michigan PAC, is said to contribute $10,000 to the campaign of every legislator voting with it and to pledge $50,000 to an opponent of any legislator who has crossed it on a key vote. The MEA is a force in Democratic party politics and is vitally interested in school organization and finance reform.

The passage of these two conjoined reforms is an artful example of legislative compromise. Although the charter school and the tax reform laws both passed by wide margins, there was no majority for either taken alone. The many leaders—the governor, the Republican and Democratic leadership, and the MEA, important players among the business, tax, and education lobbies, and voucher proponents—believed they each had the advantage in the law.

The reforms passed in December 1993 were the compromise solutions to issues that had been contested for several years. The first was a movement seeking state aid for unrestricted education *choice* (including private schools); the second was a cluster of school *finance* issues, including the frequent failure of tax referenda, demands for property tax relief, and concern over escalating education spending.

Both parties wanted property tax reform. The governor and the Republican legislative leadership insisted that an organizational reform of the schools, to control costs and improve quality, would have to be considered first.

ORGANIZATIONAL REFORM AND SCHOOL CHOICE

Origins

In the late 1960s, Michigan passed legislation that provided a small per capita grant to private schools to support their basic instructional program—reading, math, and so on. Then, as now, private schools educated 12–14 percent of all students. The measure became a rallying point for the MEA and others making up today's powerful public education lobby.

The opponents launched a campaign against "parochiade," calling the modest grants an effort to "establish" Catholic parochial schools, since more than 90 percent of the private schools at the time were Catholic. Whatever their ideological concerns, the unions faced a bread-and-butter issue. At the time, 90 percent of the teachers in Catholic schools were members of religious teaching orders, had school site control, underpriced their labor, and would not be unionized.

The MEA proposed and, in a bitterly fought referendum, won passage of the strongest "Blaine Amendment" in any state. This Michigan constitutional amendment prohibits any aid, "direct or indirect," to any school that is not a public school or to help any student receive any education that is not provided by a public school. The amendment is directed against all private education, without even a pretense of a religious freedom rationale. Michigan cannot pay for private tutors unless they are employees of public schools, under a union contract.

Sentiment for state assistance to those using private schools has continued, but now the group assisted would be much different. Since 1970, Catholics have closed more than half of their Michigan schools and reduced enrollment proportionately. Catholic school teachers are now 95 percent lay, and many are unionized. Schools sponsored by other religious and secular groups have increased so that today Catholic schools comprise only about one-third of the more than one thousand Michigan private schools and enroll less than half of the private school students. There are, in addition, an estimated ten thousand home schoolers not included in these counts who provide an entirely new dimension to the issue.

Today neither the Catholics nor any other religious or secular sponsors of private schools desire direct funding, fearing loss of control over their own schools. Most seek state assistance to the families that choose their schools, in the form of state scholarships, matching grants, or tax offsets, arguing that the state should be more fair and neutral and should respect its citizens' educational choices. The general public agrees. For the past several years, Michigan polls have found a consistent majority of voters in favor of the state's assisting parents with the expenses of private schooling.

Over the past decade, business leaders—especially in the Chamber of Commerce—have began to work for state support of full educational choice. Business leaders expressed concern about the financial plight of the inner-city private schools; the failure of central city public schools to educate adequately the small portion of students they graduate; their evident indifference to that decades-long failure; the powerful influence of the MEA in the legislature; and the union's protection of waste, incompetence, and educationally damaging practices and privileges in the face of the schools' ineptitude.

The business community opposed proposals that would even hint at damaging public education, but, unlike public school leaders, they did not see competition as damaging. On the contrary, they spoke of school choice as a way of stimulating public schools to improve themselves, as a more practical approach to making the schools responsive, as a way of checking abusive practices, as a means of cleaning out deadwood. They linked choice and competition.

The Choice Movement and the Governor

In early 1993, a citizen's group and public policy organization, TEACH Michigan, began preparations for a constitutional referendum in 1994 to allow full choice. The group believed that in order to be successful, its policy and its constitutional amendment would have to appeal to the private school and business community, resonate with the various tax reform groups, appeal to groups seeking to improve public education, and be viewed as a positive and fair step by the general public.

Since only 20–25 percent of families in the state ever used a private school (only about 10 percent at any one time), the choice plan had to have benefits for families using public schools if it was to be politically practical.

In addition, TEACH recognized that it could not win by attacking public education, though some of its natural allies in the taxpayers' groups were vocal critics. It was itself, at core, an education reform group, strongly supportive of the highest quality education for everyone. Many of TEACH's supporters, including representatives of the leading providers of private education in the state—Catholic, Lutheran, and other Christian parishes—strongly supported public education.

Gradually, TEACH developed the position that choice was needed to individualize education to fit the diverse needs of children and that alternatives and competition would improve, not hurt, public education. An exercise of choice was not a finding that the public school was inadequate, only that it did not offer all that a particular student needed. The group's strategy was to emphasize in its policy proposal the needs of individual children and the family over those of the institutions.

"Individual education accounts," which held a student's share of all federal, state, and local education funds—a kind of individualized block grant—formed the center of TEACH's plan. Using a "debit card," families could allocate portions of those accounts to the public schools for basic instruction and for special areas of instruction but could also use a portion for services from private providers, such as Latin tutors or ice-skating trainers, to supplement the public school's offering. The public school would have to price its offerings, setting charges for basic instruction and for electives such as language and football. The idea is a powerful one. The policy would tend to equalize the opportunity of all students to cultivate their strongest interests and talents without having to equalize the resources of every school in the state—a needlessly duplicative goal beyond the state's capacity.

The TEACH plan was found to violate the Michigan constitution. Public education funds belonged to school organizations, not to individual students. Michigan could not assist education in any fashion except by funding public schools. In response, TEACH prepared to mount a drive to amend the constitution in 1994, coincident with the governor's reelection campaign.

Governor Engler and several key financial backers had encouraged the choice movement as well as TEACH. The governor's reelection campaign advisers believed, however, that a choice referendum would have a defining effect on the issues in the 1994 gubernatorial election and would draw funding and energy to his Democratic opposition. They preferred that the coming campaign focus on the broader issues of economic development and tax cuts, not the more narrow issue of full education choice.

The governor would head off TEACH's referendum if he could win passage of a school choice plan in the fall of 1993, before the referendum campaign would be organized. Since there could be no change in the constitution before then, the governor's plan had to be limited to choice of public schools. But giving parents the right to choose public schools was relatively pointless, since the schools themselves would not permit the choices to be exercised. The governor needed a plan that would encourage public schools to compete for students.

The governor first considered—and briefly proposed—a program of "individual education accounts" (IEAs) as a solution. An IEA would be set up in the name of each student, and the education funds available to that student—from the federal government, the state, and the district—would be credited to the account. The school would charge the account for each expenditure it made for services it provided to the student. The IEA would make it clear to parents how much the schools were "charging" for services they provided. The element of choice—and competition—would come into play because parents would have some ability to object to out-of-line expenditures or to propose purchasing services—noneducation services, for example—from alternative providers or to purchase services the student needed but was not receiving from the local school. As an extreme example, almost two-thirds of the school budgets in certain rural districts were spent on transportation; the governor thought that parents might make different arrangements and different allocations, given a choice.

Once it was determined that going outside the public schools would be unconstitutional, even for services the school was not providing, the best advantages of the IEA fell by the wayside. The governor turned to a simple approach: state grants that would follow the child to a chosen public school combined with public schools formed and funded by those choices.

The governor and the Republican leadership proposed a law under which new charter public schools (called public school academies) could be organized by any group (except a religious group) in any district, without the permission of the district. Each new school would have the legal status—but not the taxing authority—of a school district. Each would have its own board, a single campus, and a self-defined (though necessarily large) attendance district. Each would define its own size, grade span, educational focus, and educational program, would devise its own evaluation scheme, and would be measured by certain state-wide tests. Each would be funded solely on the basis of enrollment (receiving the same per-pupil grant as the district in which the charter school was physically located, that is, between $4,200 and a cap of $5,500). Any student could attend any charter school; no permission from the "home district" was required, and no entrance testing was permitted. Charter schools would use a lottery to select students if applications exceeded available space.

The new school became an operational public school only when an authorizing body (of which the law identified 663—all university, college, or school boards) approved the application and agreed to oversee operations. Approval made the proposed school legally a public corporation, similar to a public hospital, sports authority, or utility district and subject to the laws governing public corporations.

A charter school would receive its state per-pupil funds quarterly. When the plan was introduced (before the finance reform), those less certain about the merits of public school competition were heartened by this requirement, since the state provided no operational funding to about one-third of the districts, and therefore would have to make special appropriations for the charter schools. The education lobbies believed they could kill any such appropriation.

PROPERTY TAX AND FINANCE REFORM

The property tax was a strong political issue in its own right, one that would influence the outcome of the 1994 gubernatorial election. It also posed a problem for the design for independent, competitive charter schools in the governor's plan.

Origins

Like every other state save Hawaii, Michigan divided itself into relatively small taxing jurisdictions, each granted limited taxing powers by the state and charged with providing free elementary and secondary education to the jurisdiction's residents. Michigan had 559 such jurisdictions, the largest coterminous with Detroit and enrolling about 10 percent of the state's students, but others exceedingly small, including five school districts that were comprised of only a single one-room schoolhouse each.

This arrangement helps create a sense of ownership among a district's residents—for good or ill. Local public schools belong to local residents, have the exclusive franchise on free schooling within their territory, and have no obligations to outsiders—that is, residents of other jurisdictions of the state. Virtually all school districts exclude nonresidents from free services, and most exclude nonresidents from any services at all. When they permit any enrollment of outsiders, school districts invariably charge tuition (generally equal to the per-pupil cost of education). With the exception of schools that recruit athletes from other districts, no public schools provide scholarships to out-of-district students, not even to further integration. The property tax, with its suggestion that local schools are the product of the efforts of people living in a defined geographic area, helps justify these policies.

To many, it was important to preserve the claim of local ownership of local schools that is rooted in the property tax. But the tax is not adequate to its purpose. And whether adequate or not, it has caused political problems that politicians, if they would be successful, are forced to address.

However well it worked in the nineteenth century, for much of the past forty years the property tax has been inadequate for funding schools in Michigan and in most other states. Real estate does not evenly reflect industrial and postindustrial wealth. Property wealth tends to cluster within economic regions, so that some sections have very high values and others very low, producing difference in school funding related neither to need nor to effort. Some undeveloped areas have such low property values that no practical rate of property taxation could support the needs of their public schools.

At similar tax rates, Michigan's school districts received per-student operating revenues from local taxes ranging from less than $1,000 in poorer areas to more than $10,000 in wealthy Detroit suburbs. The property tax base serves the wealthiest 20 to 30 percent of districts well but not the rest. Many districts, including Detroit, could not support adequate local schools by taxing local property wealth.

In order to overcome this problem (while preserving the property tax), most states make up some of the difference in revenues generated by local taxes through state "equalizing" funds. Michigan applied a complicated formula that guaranteed that a community taxing itself at a given millage rate would raise a certain number of dollars per student. The local tax revenues would be collected, and then the state would make up the difference. Michigan provided about 33 percent of the *average* local district's budget, most of it as equalizing aid. In fact, the state provided no general support to 30 percent of the districts, the "out-of-formula" districts, so named because they were too wealthy to receive aid. Most of the state aid went to about 70 percent of the districts, with some poorer districts receiving up to 70 percent of their local school budget from the state.

The state equalization aid only slightly reduced the distance between rich and poor districts. If the state were to provide enough revenues to bring every school up to the expenditure level of the wealthiest districts, it would require an additional $7 billion, as much again as it was spending.

The Problem of Financing Competitive Charter Schools

For the proposed charter school reform, it was important whether the state was providing money to the local district. The state can spend its own funds on charter grants; in political reality, it could not direct local school districts to spend local education tax dollars on charter schools that were not controlled by local authorities, nor require local taxpayers to pay the costs of out-of-district students to those schools. Since the state did not provide general aid to the wealthiest 30 percent of the districts, these districts would not be involved in any voucher-based charter school plan unless it was directly funded by a separate state appropriation, a politically impractical path.

The financing problem was not quite as severe as it seemed. Michigan in fact provided a substantial amount of aid to the out-of-formula districts. The state paid for the Social Security and retirement benefits of most school district employees and paid the health insurance premiums of retired teachers; it simply failed to count this aid as part of the local school budget, thus understating the cost of expenditures—and the amount of state support—in each district.

The value of the hidden aid to each district was in the range of 20 to 25 percent of salaries, and salaries accounted for 75 to 80 percent of expenditures in most districts. Generally speaking, higher-spending districts had more staff and paid much higher average salaries than poorer districts, so this hidden state aid was greatest for the wealthiest districts. For example, in 1993–94, the poorest districts in the state had operating budgets of about $2,200 per student, with higher-than-average class size and teacher salaries averaging in the low $20,000s. The wealthiest districts had operating budgets in the range of $12,500 per student, with lower-than-average class size and teacher salaries averaging in the middle $60,000s. The state's unacknowledged contribution of salary benefits amounted to about $400 per student for the lowest-spending district but $2,400 per student for the highest-spending district. The state gave almost as much in salary benefits to the wealthy district as the poorer district had to spend from all sources. The state's unacknowledged aid to the wealthy district was greater than its total aid, including equalization aid, to the poor district.

Beginning in the early 1990s, when many teachers retired and health insurance costs increased by large amounts annually, the state saw 25 percent annual increases in these costs, equal to hundreds of millions of dollars. The unexpected increases had repeatedly unbalanced the state budget and forced the legislature to reconvene and cut appropriations—an unpopular task. The problem contributed to the demand in the legislature for school finance reform.

In the finance reform, the state turned this unacknowledged aid into part of its basic grant for every school. Now the wealthiest 30 percent of districts are seen to be receiving substantial amounts of state aid, paving the way for a plan for funding competitive charter schools that could operate throughout the state.

Beginning in the mid-1970s, Michigan saw a dramatic appreciation in property values, particularly in its vacation and retirement areas. At the same time, the fixed-income and retirement populations swelled, and wage-earners faced, at best, stagnant incomes. Property values increased by an average of 250 percent for the state, more than tenfold in some communities. Although property tax rates did not greatly increase, tax collections per family increased in proportion to the property values, stressing family budgets. During a period in which school enrollments dropped by 20 percent, school budgets—and school tax revenues—increased by an average of 250 percent.

This pattern forged a taxpayers' revolt against school budgets and local tax referenda. In 1976, the voters passed the Headley amendment to the state constitution, which required that school districts refund to the taxpayers any tax revenues due to property value increases in excess of inflation or submit their budget to the voters in an annual "tax override" referendum, which allowed the districts to keep their windfall. The amendment made school budgets an annual taxpayers' issue.

Through the early 1980s, communities rarely turned down tax override referenda, but by the early 1990s, referenda were turned down frequently and repeatedly. As schools lost bond and budget referenda, public education leaders began to cut programs and to search for a more secure source of tax income, one less subject to frequent public votes.

To substitute for local property taxes, the teachers' unions and the education lobby wanted a dedicated statewide tax, not annual appropriations from the legislature. They preferred a dedicated portion of the state income tax, a source that would be permanent and would automatically increase with inflation and the economy.

Property tax relief was especially important to Governor Engler because he had been elected in 1990 on the promise to deliver it, and he had twice sponsored referenda to cut property taxes that failed, in part because of MEA opposition. He did manage to get a moratorium passed that stopped reassessments for one year, but that was expiring, and he faced reelection just as much higher property tax notices would be mailed in 1994.

In the summer of 1993, both Republicans and Democrats were jockeying for leadership in the 1994 gubernatorial elections. With his promise of property tax reform, Governor Engler had taken the center ground on the popular issue. But he could not deliver any reform without Democratic help.

A leading Senate Democrat, Debbie Stabenow (D.-Lansing), was positioning herself to be the centrist Democratic candidate for governor in 1994 and lead candidate for MEA support. In July 1993, Senator Stabenow made a preemptive strike—a bold move to take the tax issue from the governor while satisfying the education lobby's concerns for a stronger tax base. The senator introduced a bill abolishing the property tax for schools. Some thought it was a political gambit to embarrass the Republicans, who would normally have voted against a bill introduced by the Democratic minority leadership.

In the ensuing roll call, two Republican senators unexpectedly voted for the measure, causing an apparent tie. The Republican majority caucused (with the governor participating) and decided to support the Democratic bill. The measure passed the divided Senate 30 to 4 and sailed through the House with the governor's backing. The dramatic new law cut taxes without defining replacement revenue, one of the requirements that Democrats had previously imposed.

The two sets of legislative leaders met in relative secrecy to work out a plan for replacement funding that met all legal requirements. Eventually the two sides agreed to a mix of statewide property taxes, local business taxes and overrides, block granting of the existing state funds, and a replacement tax that was either a sales tax and cigarette tax or an income tax, the choice to be made by the voters in a referendum. They agreed that the charter school and school finance bills would be approved in tandem as they had been in December 1993.

The MEA, to oppose Governor Engler, mounted an expensive campaign against the sales tax option he supported, effectively casting him as the architect of the sales tax. But the campaign, ironically, was equally effective in establishing the governor as the principal "property tax cutter," and Senator Stabenow's role was forgotten. At the same time, the tobacco lobby heavily funded a campaign to defeat the 75 cents-per-pack cigarette tax increase, part of the sales tax package. The large tobacco spending backfired. The sales tax choice won.

Senator Stabenow promised to be strongest opponent of Governor Engler in the general election in November 1994. But by the time the gubernatorial primary candidates had to be selected, the MEA had become firmly opposed to the charter schools and refused to back Stabenow, who was associated with their passage. The strongest critic of charter schools in the primary campaign, a redistricted congressman named Howard Wolpe, ran on a platform that included repeal of the charter school law. With MEA backing, he won the primary but lost the general election by a large margin.

The New Tax Reform: Sales Tax Replaces Property Tax

The new school finance law replaced local property taxes with a statewide sales tax increase of 2 cents (for a total of 6 cents) dedicated to the education fund.

The legislature intended to remove all local property taxes for schools but was unable to because of still another constitutional amendment that put a ceiling on its own ability to tax. State taxes could not rise above a certain percentage of state gross economic activity, and therefore the state could not fully assume funding for local education expenditures without making draconian cuts in its programs in order to stay within its constitutional limits. Instead, it eliminated all *local* property taxes for *primary residences* and imposed in their place, in addition to the sales or income tax, a 6 mill state-collected property tax. It required local school districts to impose a property tax on businesses and second homes (non-homestead residences) of 18 mills, for a total of 24 mills on businesses. In return, it gave districts a per-pupil grant ranging from $4,200 to $6,660. Districts that failed to enact the 18 mill levy did not receive the state grant. The state grants were scheduled to increase yearly, with a higher percentage increase for the smaller-grant districts than for the higher until parity is reached.

Districts that had previously spent more per pupil than the new state grant could enact a tax override to make up the shortfall. These districts had to bring the tax on residential property up to the full 24 mills business was paying, however, before any additional taxes could be imposed on all property. The authority to levy additional taxes was capped at the previous per-student expenditure. Thus, wealthier districts became relatively overtaxed.

Districts also had the right, for three years, to increase their local tax revenues by 3 mills for program improvements by a local referendum. After three years, this increase had to be voted on at the intermediate school district level, which on average serves ten school districts. The effect of enlarging the taxing and benefit area was to reduce further local differences between districts in property and school revenue wealth.

As a result of the reform, for practical purposes all districts became funded on their enrollment, not their local tax collection. Thus the introduction of school choice would potentially affect every district's enrollment and therefore its budget.

Districts that previously had high millage rates but low property wealth did well. Homeowners in Detroit, for example, reported saving several thousand dollars in property taxes per year. Districts with high property wealth per pupil already exceeded the state's guarantees, so they received little by way of state grants. In effect, they lost some of their local tax base to the state, and the costs to them of their high-end spending increased. Overall, the financing reform reduced some of the inequities of the property tax, shifted taxes onto individuals in a relatively progressive fashion, and increased the per-pupil resources of the lowest 20 percent of school districts.

For the charter school legislation, the change in school finances meant that the state could fund the charter public school *just as it now funded every public school,* on a grant-per-student basis. Charter schools did not require any special allocation or any additional funds. As a child switched from a district public school to a charter public school, the dollars would follow. If a new charter school could attract enrollment, it would automatically have a budget. No politically controlled approvals would be involved.

CHARTER SCHOOL GROWTH IN MICHIGAN

In the first year (1994–95), 10 charter schools began operating, and 30 more were in development. In the fall of 1995, 25 schools had begun operating; by 1996, 76; by 1997, 104. The numbers are projected to continue increasing for a decade, until they reach an equilibrium point of about 1,000 charters in 2007—assuming the legislation holds.

Charter schools start small and increase their enrollment gradually over several years. At full size, on average, they will be smaller than today's public schools. By 2007, there should be about 300,000 students in one thousand charter schools. This number will equal only about 15 percent of all enrolled students, and it is less than the student population increase (due to increased births) in the same years. These projections also assume transfers from some existing private schools (and the closing of those schools) and a reduced rate of formation of new private schools in favor of charter schools.

These projections, however, are also based on the assumption that existing public schools will reform their operations to increase satisfaction among minority families and will then be able to hold students in the face of competitive opportunities. If the public schools do not significantly increase the worth of their offerings to minority communities, the charter school enrollments will be greater.

Finally, these projections also assume that the charter law will not be adversely changed. Each legislative session, beginning in 1994, has seen some modifications that have both strengthened and weakened the law.

In 1994, responding to a court decision that found the law unconstitutional on technical grounds that had to do with the definition of *public school* under the Michigan constitution, the legislature corrected the problems. But the court challenge had come in response to the actions of a one-room school district in central Michigan that approved the first school to be chartered in the state, the Noah Webster. That school was a "virtual school," enrolling and networking children who were being home schooled across the state. It had an enrollment of two thousand students within the first month, giving it a $10 million budget. The legislature changed the rules and took the authority to approve charter schools away from small school districts.

By 1995, one university, Central Michigan, had taken the lead in chartering—so much so that it became the dominant charterer of the five hundred or so boards authorized to charter. The legislature imposed a cap on the number of charters that could be approved by universities—a figure that was to increase

each year through 1999 and that had reached 150 by 1997—and further prohibited any one university from authorizing more than half of the charters.

By 1996, much larger charter schools began to appear. Two new schools
serving the inner city of Lansing opened, attracting almost sixteen hundred
students from the Lansing public schools—an $8 million budget impact. One
of the charter schools contracted with the Edison Project, a private corporation
that provides education and management services, to operate its school. The
Lansing public school district, stung, in turn contracted with Edison to operate
its own charter school, beginning in 1997. Edison will, in effect, be competing
with itself in inner-city Lansing.

The first set of public school academies has enrolled higher proportions of
minorities and low-income students than the districts in their areas. This
pattern is not surprising since the students most likely to seek out charter
schools at the first opportunity are those most unhappy with their present
education. Minority and special needs students are more likely to be in that
group.

Because charter schools have no neighborhood bounds, they will on average
be more integrated along racial and income lines than the average public school
in Michigan, which is highly segregated. In fact, if these schools were segregated, they would be highly vulnerable to civil rights enforcement actions; they
would not have the immunity most school districts now enjoy based on the fact
that racial exclusion is an unintended effect of the district boundaries.

In the end, the small reform of charter schools will transform Michigan
public education, ending the exclusionary patterning of districts, empowering
those with the poorest educational options, and equalizing educational opportunity. The charter schools will be the source of entirely new kinds of private-
public cooperative ventures that will be statewide in their appeal and therefore
can be highly specialized. As charter schools become more numerous, and their
competitive pressure on districted schools stronger, the districts will have to
change the way their manage their own schools, making them more freestand-
ing entities responsible for their own success or failure. The fact that children
are not simply assigned to the district school but have the power of choice, and
alternatives to choose from, will help the districts free up their schools.

Teachers will be advantaged because they will become more valuable to
schools, and more of the budget will be given to attract and hold them. But the
unions will no longer be able to protect wasteful work rules and incompetence,
because their schools and incomes will decline if they do. In other words, the
teachers' union will move in the direction of the UAW.

FUTURE FINANCE REFORM

By creating a centralized state funding source for all of local education, Michigan has virtually guaranteed that substantial interdistrict differences in levels of per-pupil funding will disappear over time, for constitutional reasons if not for political ones. Both state and federal constitutions appear to prohibit inequitable treatment before the law. In the past, the Supreme Court has refused to apply this standard to the school financing issue, in deference to the states' long-standing practice of using the property tax to finance schools—a kind of grandfathering exclusion. But a new central state tax that allocates differing amounts to children solely on the basis of their residence, without rational justification, is very unlikely to withstand state or federal constitutional scrutiny.

The most surprising change in Michigan is that the wealthiest districts appeared to lose so much in the financing restructuring, given the reasonable assumption that they were powers in the legislature. It is too soon to know the actual effect of these changes. That research needs to be done now.

Part Three Stakeholders
in Equity Reform

There are many stakeholders in the education process; all have a vested interest in education policy outcomes. They include state and local professionals, such as superintendents, commissioners, and school administrators; teachers and their unions; mayors; governors and other elected state and city officials, especially legislative committee and budget chairs; civic-style education interest groups; parents and their associations; students and community activists; the media; business leaders; and foundations. All of these groups have an interests in the reform process, and cooperation among them is essential to achieving change. The business community in most cities and states has been an important collaborator in school reform; it also maintains an interest in school accountability and in property taxation.

In Chapter 8, Martha Darling of The Boeing Company explains that the business community's interest in education derives from serious concerns about its need for an educated workforce and an educated citizenry for the future. The Boeing Company's involvement grew out of increased international competition, the technological transformation of American manufacturing, and an interest in creating a better quality of life for its people.

Clarence N. Stone, a professor at the University of Maryland and a longtime scholar of urban politics, believes that various segments of the community must recognize that they have a shared interest in a common objective; society in general will benefit from a well-run school system that enhances human and social capital. According to Stone, a community exhibits civic capacity when groups and individuals, including business executives, work together toward a strategy for improving education. A common vision and effort are necessary, Stone argues, because human capital development requires involvement from a wide spectrum of stakeholders and because the quality of education students receive sooner or later will affect the broader community.

There are obvious strategic advantages to coalitions involving education professionals, politicians, community groups, and the business community. In my chapter, "School Reform in New York and Chicago: Revisiting the Ecology of Local Games," I explain how education reform in Chicago was a product of a sustained coalition of stakeholders resulting in longer-lasting and broader reform than New York's. In Chicago, community organizations were active in initiating and sustaining coalition politics and engaging traditional civic groups, political officials, and the business establishment as activist partners in the reform agenda. Community groups worked with the business community, which has a tradition of civic responsibility in Chicago. In addition, foundations in Chicago played a critical role in sustaining reform. Chicago's successful decentralization efforts can be attributed to coalition-building.

In New York, owing to a lack of coalition-building, the 1969 decentralization legislation failed to redistribute power and maintained the professional and centralized bureaucratic control of the school system. Many potentially interested groups, including the business community, remained on the sidelines. As a result, the legislation reflected the teachers' union's priorities. Citywide civic action in New York is dominated by a more traditional progressive reform style that gives prominence to professional and middle-class groups lacking in grassroots or neighborhood ties.

Involvement of a wide segment of the community in discussions about education is also necessary because a large share of education occurs outside the classroom. Stone's initial findings on civic capacity and urban education in eleven cities, as well as his continuing research, points out that schools cannot provide a basic education for urban populations without the involvement of the entire community. "Human capital formation," or cognitive and social skills gained from the community as a whole, contribute to a student's academic performance, which is affected not only by classroom education but also by early childhood development, work, sports, mentoring, post-school expectations, and social and health supports.

Early on, Stone found weak parent involvement and weak engagement of teacher associations in almost all of the eleven cities studied. Those cities showed the varying influence of the federal courts, state governments, foundations, mayors, and businesses. Most significant, his report concludes that the scope of reform activity corresponded to the scope of civic capacity mobilized.

A significant amount of research on the business community has pointed to its major influence on education reform principles including professionalization of the school bureaucracy at the turn of the century, building a productive and efficient bureaucracy, and, currently, stressing the importance of school performance and accountability. As Darling explains, the business community tends to minimize finance equity reform, placing greater emphasis on curriculum and school structure.

Continuing dissatisfaction with student performance, despite finance reforms in the 1970s, led to proposals for comprehensive reform of Washington schools in early 1990s. The business community was an active participant in these efforts. In 1983, the Washington Roundtable, a group composed of the CEOs of the major companies in the state, established an education committee chaired by T. Wilson of The Boeing Company to oversee a major study of the state's K–12 school system. The Roundtable has provided continuity of business attention and the opportunity for growing numbers of business leaders to become knowledgeable about the issues. Not only did the Roundtable become, over the period, the prime voice for the business community in state education policy discussions, but it also initiated or helped to initiate collaborative activities with various education professionals and politicians.

Although the Washington Roundtable was actively involved in education policy discussions, the business community has not always understood the benefits of participating in an education coalition, as is evident in my comparison of New York and Chicago. The business sector in New York has never been an open and active partner in the political life of the city, perhaps because of the dominant role of real estate interests. In contrast with Chicago business leaders, New York corporate leaders identify with national and international issues. They do not see themselves as citizens of the city. It is not surprising, therefore, that they do not share an active concern for the city schools. Although business leaders in New York may be critical of the system, they have not participated in any coalition politics or joint efforts with other city actors in defining and seeking solutions to school problems. The abdication of the business community from involvement in reform in New York City schools creates an imbalance of stakeholders.

Achieving school reform requires involvement from a wide spectrum of stakeholders, including the business community. The examples of Washington State, New York City, and Chicago all point to strategic benefits of forming broad coalitions. Communitywide participation in education in turn strengthens society through human capital development; this is most evident in areas with high levels of civic capacity, according to Stone. By increasing the number of voices involved in education policy, political democracy is reinforced through a broadening of political participation.

Chapter 8 Necessary but Not Sufficient: Moving from School Finance Reform to Education Reform in Washington State

Martha Darling

Since the 1970s, school finance reform has been an important component of state-level efforts to achieve educational equity for children. Legal challenges to state school financing systems have largely focused on substantial district-to-district disparities in per-pupil aggregate expenditures, and court-ordered remedies have had the limited goals of increasing the state's share of local school funding and equalizing its contribution statewide.

It should not be surprising that the narrow pursuit of enhanced revenues for schools in the name of interdistrict equity does not always find favor in the business community. For business leaders, finance reform does not automatically suggest qualitative improvement in student results. Their interest in school reform efforts derives from serious concerns about the quality of the educational experience and about the ability of school systems to ensure an educated work force and an educated citizenry for the future. Their continuing engagement as valuable and valued members of any education reform coalition will increasingly depend on targeting opportunities for systemic change that will produce dramatic improvements in student, teacher, and school performance.

The experience of education reform in the state of Washington supports this conclusion. School finance reform entered the policy arena following constitutionally related court challenges in the mid-1970s. Reforms have entailed the rearrangement of inputs and elements of the educational delivery system. Although funding equalization may have been necessary, the numbers demonstrate that it was not sufficient; the performance of the state's students was not significantly affected.

Comprehensive systemic reform of Washington's schools began in earnest in the early 1990s and will certainly continue past the century mark. Results—dramatic improvement in what students know and are able to demonstrate—will be the yardstick against which the success of Washington's efforts will be assessed over the next decade. Only when all students achieve at high levels will the sufficiency test of education reform be met.

WASHINGTON'S K–12 FINANCE REFORM

In 1976, voters in the Seattle School District twice rejected the district's property-tax-based school levy proposal, resulting in a budget reduction of approximately 40 percent. Seattle, joined by a few other large districts, then brought a lawsuit against the state claiming that the degree of levy dependency violated the state constitution's charge that the common schools be the state's "paramount duty." The courts concurred, and the legislature was assigned the task of defining, and then funding, "basic education."

This court decision led to the Basic Education Act of 1977. That legislation committed the state to full funding for "basic education," which was defined primarily in terms of enrollment-linked inputs such as student-teacher ratios, contact hours, Carnegie units, and the like. A key component of the funding formula was a statewide salary allocation schedule for certified instructional staff based on years of service and education. This de facto statewide salary schedule, with the salary equalization that resulted, has played a dominant role in state funding equalization.

The legislature also passed a companion measure that capped at 10 percent the amount school districts could raise from local operational levies. Initial grandfathering of high-levy districts and later modifications, including raising the limit to 20 percent, have left in place a small number of districts in excess of the legislated cap. The overall effect of the funding formula adopted in 1977, however, has been a substantial increase in state funding of the K–12 schools and substantial equalization statewide of dollars supporting the schools.

Thus the finance equalization concerns that have landed a number of states in court in recent years were addressed in Washington State more than fifteen years ago. But what appears as a story with a satisfactory ending from a constitutional perspective has turned out to be only a preface. The main body of Washington's story is concerned with a more fundamental question about the state's school system: its performance in terms of student achievement. A focus on results that began in the early 1980s has increasingly come to dominate state and local policy discussion.

A DECADE OF PREPARATION

The year 1983 was an important one for educational policy in Washington. The phase-in of the equalized state funding approach had been completed, with percentage shares reaching levels that have remained relatively stable since: state, 82 percent; local, 12 percent; federal, 6 percent. Prompted in part by the fact that more than 45 percent of the state budget flowed to the public schools under the Basic Education Act formula, and anticipating national questioning of the results this money was producing, the legislature in 1982 created a broadly representative Temporary Committee on Educational Policies, Structure, and Management. By 1983 the Temporary Committee was fully operational and thoroughly scrutinizing virtually every facet of the state's education system, from pre-kindergarten to post-secondary. In response to similar state budget concerns, the newly formed Washington Roundtable, a group composed of the CEOs of the major companies in the state, established an education committee chaired by T. Wilson of The Boeing Company to oversee its initial study of the state's K–12 school system. In the midst of this heightened state activity came the publication of *A Nation at Risk,* which dramatically altered the national debate over the schools, attracting massive publicity with its alarming rhetoric about a "rising tide of mediocrity" and "unilateral educational disarmament."

The Temporary Committee made its recommendation-laden final report in 1985 and then disbanded. The Washington Roundtable has continued to promote education reform with reports, recommendations, and lobbying activities at the legislature. It would be difficult to overestimate the importance of the Roundtable in providing continuity of business attention and the opportunity for growing numbers of business leaders to become knowledgeable about the K–12 school system. Not only did the Roundtable become, over this period, the prime voice for the business community in state education policy discussions; it also initiated or helped initiate collaborative activities with the various education stakeholder groups. Greater communication and understanding of perspectives and positions among these policy players were critically important benefits of these activities. First, the Education Vision Team (1989–92) brought together leaders from the Roundtable, the Office of the Superintendent of Public Instruction, the governor's office, legislative leaders, the Washington Education Association, the Washington State School Directors Association, the state PTA, and other education groups to develop a common vision of the direction the school system should pursue in the years ahead.

Moving from the vision to the implementation stage, Roundtable member businesses provided the funding and framework for the creation of the Education Renewal Institute, or ERI (1990–94). The ERI gave financial and technical support to four school districts undertaking significant restructuring initiatives aimed at improving student performance. Its policy board again brought together business leaders with their counterparts in various education groups and the state teachers' union. Finally, during the annual legislative sessions the Roundtable became well known to legislators, legislative staffs, and the governor's office, as well as to the various education group leaders and lobbyists. Working together across organizational lines, although not always in full accord on every policy issue, was crucial to the legislative achievements of 1993.

In the late 1980s and early 1990s, a shift in understanding began to emerge within the business community and the education groups about the kinds of state policies needed to support increased student academic achievement. Both the Temporary Committee and the Roundtable echoed in their early pronouncements some of the national panel recommendations to require more academic seat-time, with more course time devoted to core subjects and fewer diversions during the school day. A longer school day or school year also found some advocates. The assumption was that results would improve if all students took four years of the science, math, history, and English then offered in high school. Little attention was focused on the content and instructional quality of existing courses or on how student learning would be measured.

Several indications of less conventional thinking were evident, however. First, both the Roundtable and the Temporary Committee gave top priority to state-funded expansion of early childhood education programs modeled on Head Start, which then newly elected governor Booth Gardner made his only "request" legislation in education in 1985. Though initially modest, the program was approved and has been expanded each biennium. Washington now leads the country in the coverage of early childhood education for at-risk four-year-olds. Second, the Roundtable refused to support a state minimum competency test for high-school graduation. In the course of its study of student assessment, the Roundtable confronted the reality that states with such exams tended to "dumb down" the test so that a low, politically tolerable level of failures (1–3 percent) was attained. Moreover, the Roundtable found that significant resources were diverted from mainline instruction for the vast majority of students to satisfy the legal requirements for denying a diploma to a few. The CEOs concluded that Washington did not have the problem for which a minimum competency test was the solution. Although the Roundtable's concern with student achievement remained, more sophisticated approaches involving higher standards and evidence of their attainment by all students became the focus, as evidenced in a 1989 Roundtable report, "Creating Exceptional Public Schools for the Next Century."

During this same period several multiyear studies by education groups were also completed. The resulting reports, based on substantial member participation, projected some bold directions for schools in the future. The Washington Education Association's "Restructuring Public Education: Building a Learning Community," issued in 1989, paralleled the Roundtable's recommendations. "Schools in the Year 2000: A Futurescape" was the Washington State School Directors' 1990 contribution to a vision of a restructured learning system from a local leadership perspective.

THE PERFORMANCE-BASED EDUCATION ACT
OF 1993

Despite significant movement in state education policy during the 1980s, incrementalism was running out of time. The magnitude of the challenge schools were facing in providing students with the knowledge and skills necessary for the twenty-first century was becoming clearer to leaders in business and in government. Several international comparisons of student mastery of mathematics and science placed American students well behind their counterparts overseas. The sustainability of Americans' quality of life, democratic institutions, and economic competitiveness came into question. Both at the state level and nationally, more and more groups concerned about public education were starting to frame the issue as one of standards-driven systemic change.

In 1989 President George Bush and the nation's governors met at the Education Summit in Charlottesville, Virginia, and later adopted six national education goals, to be accomplished by the overly optimistic target date of 2000. These goals were a call for high standards. And the National Council of Teachers of Mathematics was ready, having completed a ten-year effort with the publication of the Math *Standards,* a document that offered a comprehensive restatement of the math knowledge and skills students should be capable of at different developmental stages. Subsequent standards development work has proceeded in other areas of the curriculum at both state and national levels.

In another development critical to Washington's legislation, the national Business Roundtable in 1990 launched its education initiative, linking CEOs with state governors to concentrate on state-level policy in support of the six national education goals. In Washington this partnership brought together Frank Shrontz, CEO of The Boeing Company, with Governor Gardner, who already had accumulated a record of interest and activism on behalf of school reform. In addition, five years of legislative attention to education reform issues in cooperation with the governor provided a knowledgeable group of legislative leaders of both parties who were essential to the 1993 results.

The catalyst for bringing together all these elements to generate comprehensive education reform in Washington was the Governor's Council for Education Reform and Funding, which met from mid-1991 to December 1992. Although the council was created in the immediate aftermath of a statewide teachers' strike over the legislature's failure to fund a salary increase, the charge to the panel reflected a much larger agenda. The executive order establishing the twenty-one-member group, which was chaired by the governor, posed three specific challenges:

- to create a flexible educational system that would allow each student to achieve at high levels;
- to create a performance-oriented system that would emphasize results rather than the maintenance of existing policies and procedures; and
- to review existing funding, prioritize those funds, and determine methods to obtain any necessary additional funds.

The membership of the council merits an additional observation. Intentionally, members held positions of great influence. They included three Roundtable CEOs, including Boeing's Shrontz; the legislative leadership from both parties; leaders from the major education groups, including the teachers' union; several prominent elected officials; and a newspaper publisher. If real change were to come about, it would require a council this weighty. Equally, failure to produce dramatic changes in the ways schools functioned and students learned would have serious consequences. As the governor stated at the council's initial meeting, the group represented "our last, best chance" to shift the focus, energy, and resources of Washington's public K–12 system to student performance.

Thus student learning soon became the focus for the Governor's Council. The challenge was twofold: to establish what individual students should know and be able to do; and, based on an understanding of the factors driving the current school system, to find ways of changing them to improve student results. To address the students, the council embarked on a broad public process to define what became four student learning goals for the state. To address the system, members undertook a comprehensive analysis of the gaps between the functioning of the state's largely input-driven system—based on salaries, staffing ratios, class size, and contact-hour requirements—and a prospective outcomes-driven system based on expected student results and student demonstrations of what they know and are able to do. Committees tackled issues related to management and governance, professional development, school readiness, school-to-work transitions, and funding, all from the student learning angle.

The final report of the Governor's Council became the main education item on the state legislature's agenda when it convened in January 1993. And in a record four months, the report's recommendations were converted into concrete form in House Bill 1209, also called the Performance Based Education Act of 1993.

The legislature's intent language reveals the commitment to student results:

> The legislature finds that student achievement in Washington must be improved to keep pace with societal changes, changes in the workplace, and an increasingly competitive international economy. . . . To increase student achievement, the legislature finds that the state of Washington needs to develop a public school system that focuses more on the educational performance of students, that includes high expectations for all students, and that provides more flexibility for school boards and educators in how instruction is provided.

To bring about such results, the legislation directed a fundamental reorientation of the K–12 system from one based on "seat time"—sitting through twelve years and a certain number of Carnegie units earns a diploma—to one focused on the educational performance of students. Thus the legislature placed in the statutes, for the first time, four student learning goals. Because schools must

> provide students with the opportunity to become responsible citizens, to contribute to their own economic well-being and to that of their families and communities, and

to enjoy productive and satisfying lives . . . the goals of each school district, with the involvement of parents and community members, shall be to provide opportunities for all students to develop the knowledge and skills essential to:

(1) Read with comprehension, write with skill, and communicate effectively and responsibly in a variety of ways and settings;

(2) Know and apply the core concepts and principles of mathematics; social, physical, and life sciences; civics and history; geography; arts; and health and fitness;

(3) Think analytically, logically, and creatively, and to integrate experience and knowledge to form reasoned judgments and solve problems; and

(4) Understand the importance of work and how performance, effort, and decisions directly affect future career and educational opportunities.

To translate these goals into guidance for schools and educators, the legislature specified that "essential academic learning requirements" (content standards), student performance standards, and a performance-based assessment system be developed by a state Commission on Student Learning. These linked elements were to be available for voluntary implementation by 1997–98 and universally in use by 2000. In addition, a Certificate of Mastery was to be developed for students at about age sixteen.

Although the state's intent was clear about the "what" of student learning, the legislature recognized that the "how"—the way each school would reach a successful result with its student population—would require much greater local flexibility in terms of both instructional approaches and materials and the organization of the school day, week, and year. In addition, it recognized that educators would have to take on new roles and responsibilities for a performance-based system to come into existence. Thus, to enable educators to assess their local requirements and develop appropriate local strategies and plans, the legislation provided grants to schools beginning in the 1994–95 school year for school-based planning and professional development. Additional assistance was available in the form of funding for local programs matching mentor teachers with first-year teachers and veteran teachers experiencing difficulties, as well as for principal and administrator internships. Another provision anticipated development of an educator performance assessment system for initial certification a few years down the road. The principle is that if students are expected to demonstrate what they know and are able to do, teachers should also be expected to demonstrate mastery of their field.

For the longer term, the legislature recognized the need to scrutinize its own responsibility for inflexibility in school operations and organization. Decentralizing more decision-making to school districts and individual schools would require a serious review of the compliance procedures and mechanisms with which Washington, like other states, had responded to decades of incremental federal and state mandates. The Joint Select Committee on Education Restructuring, formed to review this accumulation of law and regulation, was charged with repealing or modifying the provisions and mandates that are not necessary to the functioning of a performance-based K–12 school system.

Such decentralization and deregulation could only occur, however, with the development of a statewide accountability system. Because this system is to be based on student performance, its design and implementation necessarily await the development of the state's "essential academic learning requirements" and performance-based student assessments by the Commission on Student Learning. Once that work is completed, the legislation anticipates a combination of awards for high-performance districts, assistance for underperforming districts, and intervention for persistently underperforming districts. The task of designing these responses has also been assigned to the Commission on Student Learning and is to be completed by 2000.

Several other provisions of the legislation are noteworthy. A state technology plan is under development. To address student readiness to learn, pilot grants have been made to community-based consortia to implement comprehensive plans for coordinated school and human services. A limited number of school-to-work transition grants have also been made to model programs integrating academic and vocational curricula and involving partnerships with employers for work-based learning.

Finally, the legislation posed the funding question again, not in terms of equalization but, intriguingly, in terms of the continued appropriateness of the overwhelming bias toward input equalization in light of the move to a school system based on student outcomes. Thus, a legislative fiscal study committee was charged with the review and potential revision of the state's approach to K–12 funding to ensure consistency with the new emphasis on student performance.

As this account of legislative provisions and subsequent activities shows, a substantial amount of reform and restructuring work is under way in Washington. Not only has the new state policy framework commanded action by the Commission on Student Learning, the Office of the Superintendent of Public Instruction, the state Board of Education, and others at the state level, but it has also motivated a number of local districts and schools to move ahead of the legislated timetable in rethinking and reorienting local policy and practice to support increased student achievement. The pace of change, though uneven, is accelerating.

This leads to some concluding thoughts about business involvement—in particular, why business came to the education reform table and what it has the potential to contribute.

BUSINESS INVOLVEMENT

Increasing competition—regional, national, and global—has been the business reality of the last decade. The fact of vastly altered operating environments is as true for local banks as it is for The Boeing Company. In companies that have recognized the competitive challenge for what it is, major organizational restructuring has followed, aimed at fundamentally changing the ways businesses accomplish their work and deal with people. (The vocabulary used to describe this process includes *systemic change, reengineering, reinventing, customer focus, culture change,* and *high-performance organization,* all terms now at risk of overuse.) The effort of continuously improving quality while restraining cost increases involves a long-term perspective and a long-term commitment, but corporate leaders have concluded that the alternatives of incremental improvements and short-term thinking will put them out of business.

A second reality business leaders face is the technological transformation of American manufacturing and service companies. There was a time when the majority of jobs could be filled by people with limited formal education. At one point, Henry Ford bragged that every job on his assembly line could be filled by a worker with just ten minutes of training; his production lines were designed to accommodate such employees. As automation has entered both the manufacturing process and the service sector, jobs have become increasingly more complicated. Whereas work has usually become less taxing physically, the intellectual and educational demands on workers have grown. This is certainly true for technology-driven industries such as aerospace and electronics; it is equally true in banking and insurance. Because more and more business leaders recognize that their products and processes require employees educated to much higher standards than in the past, it is not surprising that they see education as a key to corporate success in an increasingly competitive global marketplace.

A third perspective many business leaders bring to policy discussions around the K–12 schools extends well beyond the narrow focus on employee knowledge and skills. The leaders of The Boeing Company, like their corporate counterparts in the Pacific Northwest and in other regions of the country, recognize that the quality of life in communities where Boeing is located and the functioning of America's democratic institutions are absolutely dependent on effective public school systems. Business leaders also see their commitment to supporting improved public schools as an investment in and commitment to their communities. Taken together, these factors—competition, technological change in the workplace, the quality of life and our democratic system—help to explain the increasing amount of time and resources companies such as Boeing are expending in working with educators, schools, and education policy makers.

As described earlier in this chapter, business leaders have played a key and increasingly sophisticated role in Washington's education reform story. From the creation of the Washington Roundtable in 1983, through the passage of the state's comprehensive reform legislation a decade later, to late 1990s implementation efforts, corporate leaders have become knowledgeable about education policy and practice. Externally, they have worked with the traditional education groups and state policy makers to shape policy agendas, move policy discussions along, fashion compromises, and, in the end, bring their substantial influence to bear. Finally, many have marshaled company resources to support local implementation efforts by schools districts and schools in the communities where they are located.

To all of these activities they have brought certain "business" perspectives to questions of education policy and organization strategic planning, a focus on the customer(s), a willingness to challenge current organizational arrangements and practices, and a concern for identifying key performance indicators and measuring results. Many of these approaches have been novel to the education setting. And many, in modified form, are proving to be highly useful tools in the effort to dramatically improve the educational experience and outcomes of America's children.

Business also has the potential to provide the consistency of purpose and communications necessary during the phased implementation of performance-based K–12 school systems. Whether situated within individual companies such as Boeing or through business organizations such as the Washington Roundtable, an institutionalized corporate capacity to track the course of reform implementation is essential. Once legislation is passed, the attention of legislators, advocates, and interested citizens can wane. Moreover, legislative turnover, even before the era of term limits, has always put multiyear programs at risk of diversionary "fine tuning" or unintended disabling. Outright reversal by legislators never party to the original problem identification and policy deliberations is also a long-term hazard.

In addition, most school reforms legislated in state capitals are almost invisible to citizens in their home communities. Since the transition to performance-based schools will be played out at the local level and will involve different roles and responsibilities for students, teachers, administrators, and parents, it is vital to communicate with these constituencies about the changes under way and the need for them. In Washington, as in Kentucky, the business community, drawing on its own experiences in corporate restructuring, has recognized the need for such communications and is, in the absence of other volunteers, stepping up to this vital task with a multiyear support commitment.

Lest this chapter end on too optimistic a note, it should be observed that business is not always the "perfect" partner in education reform activities. Where the agenda is only "more money," business will most likely be in opposition. An occasional overreliance on business tools and experience may grate on nonbusiness sensibilities. If proposals for change must await consensus among all interested parties, business may, after a time, either strike out on its own or seek strategic alliances with a few parties. Controlled impatience—reflecting a desire to cut through the process and get to the action—may characterize businesspersons' behavior in meetings.

Business involvement will not be sufficient for comprehensive school reform. If the difficult but essential transformation of our public education system into one in which schools both expect and enable the achievement of high standards by all of America's students is to be successful, however, business will be a necessary collaborator. The challenge is too big for any one sector of society to tackle alone. Many businesses in Washington and nationwide increasingly believe that there is no real alternative but to work in a partnership of efforts. A rich collaboration involving the private, the nonprofit, and the public sectors will make possible the schools that will ensure that America's children will enjoy a rich quality of life and plentiful economic opportunities in the twenty-first century.

Chapter 9 School Reform
in New York and Chicago:
Revisiting the Ecology
of Local Games

Marilyn Gittell

School reform efforts in New York City in 1967 and in Chicago in 1989 provide a laboratory for the comparative study of regime politics in education. Using Long's local game theory, this analysis reveals significant differences in the two city cultures. Differences in the outcomes of the reform efforts can be explained as a product of the ability of city stakeholders to coalesce and advance their interests at the state level.

For two decades, studies of power in American cities have focused on the issue of economic growth. Macroeconomic analysis was substituted for micropolitical and policy analysis, and cities, not unexpectedly, were characterized as *dependent,* with little or no control over their own destinies. This was, in part, a consequence of the very narrow definition of economic growth, which excluded human-capital outcomes. City economic elites, according to these analyses, reigned unchallenged in their growth management of cities. In addition, national and international economic policies of capital formation predetermined the important economic outcomes in cities, particularly the decline in manufacturing industries and the growth of service-sector employment. Traditional political and policy issues, considered secondary to these broader concerns, were virtually ignored.

Underestimating the relevance of policy issues has provided reinforcement for labeling cities as dependent and further discouraged active concern with the formulation of political solutions to city problems. There has been a visible lack of interest in structural and process reform of cities. The vitality of the grass-roots reform efforts of the 1970s, which looked to expansion of citizen partici-pation and the role of neighborhood and community organizations, was depre-ciated by the pessimism of growth politics. This change in the emphasis of urban scholarship took its toll on the political and intellectual status of the city in American political life. The limiting effect of urban research that concen-trates solely on economic growth is in sharp contrast to the work of the previous decade. Clearly, it represents the waning influence of Norton Long's emphasis on the ecology of local games, which focused attention on the centrality of American cities and political reform (Long, 1958).

THE ECOLOGY OF LOCAL GAMES:
COMPARATIVE POLITICS
OF SCHOOL REFORM

This comparison of school reform in New York and Chicago represents a return to the ecology of local games. I pursue an analysis of the stakeholders to inform and increase the understanding of the political process and institutional change. I also describe how city political culture affects political outcomes.

Political reform of school systems, since the Progressive movement at the turn of the century, has stressed professionalization and centralization of the school system under a unified bureaucratic structure. Maintaining an insulated school system independent of city politics was a stated goal, and it served the emerging professional cadres well for several generations. In contrast, 1960s movement politics, which was primarily concerned with broadening participa-tion and creating a responsive political system, shifted the thrust of governance reform. The essential elements of the new school-reform movement of the 1960s and 1970s were increased parent and community participation and re-duced professional and bureaucratic controls through decentralized decision-making at the school or neighborhood district level. The motivation for these political and governance reforms was to make the system more responsive to excluded and underserved populations whose needs were greater but whose power in the system was negligible.

In comparing the experiences of two of the largest city school systems in the country, New York's and Chicago's, and their attempts to achieve significant political reform of their schools, one can discern the differential role of city and state stakeholders and the character of coalition politics. Although these city efforts to achieve institutional and social change were undertaken twenty-two years apart (New York in 1967 and Chicago in 1989), they provide a laboratory for the comparative study of regime politics in education. Definitions of growth politics exclude education and human-capital development, thus ignoring a major area of city initiative. This comparative analysis of city school reform reveals significant differences in the two cultures. One can explain differences in the outcomes of the reform efforts in the two cities as a product of the ability of local stakeholders to coalesce and advance their interests at the state level.

There are consistent stakeholders in every city who are engaged in the struggle for control of city schools: state and local school professionals, including superintendents, commissioners, and school administrators; teachers and their unions; mayors; governors and other elected state and city officials, especially legislative committee and budget chairs; civic-style education interest groups; parents and their associations; students and community activists; the media; business leaders; and foundations (Fuhrman and Rosenthal, 1981). The differing roles of these stakeholders—their strengths and weaknesses and their ability to form coalitions and mobilize support and resources—affect outputs, both educationally and politically; their successes or failures vary accordingly. No single elite necessarily controls educational policy; however, school professionals and bureaucrats are, as Weber (1958) predicted, in a prime position to dominate the arena and control the game. The determination of any effort to achieve school reform is affected by which stakeholders become engaged, the inclusiveness of their strategies, and the strength of their commitment and leadership.

An important determination to be made from this analysis is how and under what circumstances the strongest of elite players, the business leaders of the city, elect to participate in the politics of school reform. According to Logan and Molotch (1987), it should be nonmobile classes of business that have an incentive to intervene in local politics. In fact, that was not the case in Chicago or New York school reform efforts. In Chicago, it was the enlistment of both mobile and nonmobile business—as well as support by other stakeholders—and their willingness to build a strong and diverse coalition of interests that was important to their success.

Because of the legal structure that shapes state-local relations, cities and city school districts are ultimately dependent on state legislatures and governors to change the structure of city schools. The final battleground for institutional change is, therefore, always at the state capital. Accordingly, the consistency and demonstrated strengths of a city coalition are important determinants of success in achieving reform. State political actors, governors, legislative chairs of finance and education committees, and education bureaucrats, as well as state-level interest groups, are important players in city school reform. Access to these state actors depends in part on the structure of the state's party politics, on the cohesiveness of the city interests, and on lobbying effectively.

The state arena is shaped by similar conditions in Illinois and New York. School professionals have a long tradition of successfully pleading their cause at the state level and have excellent access to state political and bureaucratic officials. Strong teachers' unions and school professional associations are powerful stakeholders on both the city and the state level in New York and Illinois. State legislators and governors rely on these groups for financial aid and election support. The ideological tradition of anti–large city politics in both states is reflected especially in state legislative politics (Gittell and Hollander, 1971).

There are, however, significant differences in the way city stakeholders in New York City and Chicago confront state politics. Fuchs (1992) describes political behavioral differences between New York City and Chicago as a product of strong party control and weak interest-group politics under Mayor Daley, as compared with weak party control and strong interest-group politics under Mayor Lindsay. She concludes that community-based organizations in Chicago increased their autonomy as a direct result of the reduced strength of the Democratic party organization and the encouragement of Mayor Washington. Squires et al. (1987) argue that the power of the machine already had declined under Daley from 1971 to 1975 and that blacks and community-based organizations exhibited power before Washington was elected mayor. In comparison, Mayor Lindsay's support for a stronger role for community-based organizations was undermined, according to Fuchs (1992), by the fragmented nature of New York City political institutions. She explains that Mayor Washington was able to use his office to achieve citywide goals. Her analysis would, therefore, suggest that the success of Chicago school reform was a result of that tradition in Chicago. The lack of success of Lindsay's school-reform program, according to Fuchs's analysis, could be attributed to the combination of a comparatively weak mayoral system, decentralized party structure, and the strength of highly organized interest groups—in this case, the United Federation of Teachers (UFT), which opposed the plan. Squires et al. (1987) describe the historical ability of Chicago mayors, including Daley, to work with Illinois governors and the private sector. New York City has not had that tradition; on the contrary, conflict between the city and the state is demonstrated by the periodic creation of state agencies to supersede the city's governance structure.

THE CHICAGO STORY

In 1988, the Illinois State Legislature and the governor responded to a strong coalition of city interests' demands for fundamental change in the Chicago schools (Chicago School Reform Act 1987, 85–1418). The state approved an extensive plan for school decentralization that shifted decision-making from the city school bureaucracy to local school councils (LSCs) in each school. The legislation called for a devolution of power from the superintendent's office to the local school. Local school councils composed of parents and teachers were given decisionmaking power over personnel, budgeting, and curriculum matters, as well as the hiring of school principals, the allocation of school monies, and the development of education improvement plans.

Given the radical character of the plan, it was surprising how little opposition arose to challenge the legislative action. Coalition politics in Chicago was the key to the school-reform effort. All the major stakeholders in education politics in the city participated in the effort to reorder priorities in education and change the structure of power in Chicago schools.

Chicago's success in achieving such a thorough school reform goes beyond the conclusion that community organizations only deter elite action (Mollenkopf, 1983; Browning, Marshall, and Tabb, 1984). It suggests that strong grassroots groups can have a decisive role in structuring broader city coalitions and participating in redirecting city priorities. Chicago school reform is a story of the leadership role of community organizations in initiating and sustaining coalition politics and in engaging traditional civic groups, political officials, and the business establishment as activist partners in the reform agenda. School reform in Chicago reflects coalition politics in its classic democratic conceptualization.

The political culture in Chicago was seemingly amenable to the widely representative coalition. Community activists initiated, understood, and supported a coalition structure. Perhaps they learned from earlier failures, or perhaps the 1980s was a time of coalition politics. Chicago, however, has a long history of support for, and responsiveness to, community organizations; it is, after all, the city of the Alinsky tradition (Horwitt, 1989).

Another element of Chicago's political culture is the business community's tradition of civic works. It is well known for its involvement in the maintenance not only of a high standard of architecture and planning of the physical character of the city but also of its economic and social life. Although not necessarily an agent of social change, the business community has demonstrated strong political-civic concern. It supports a variety of public agendas and has a tradition of working with diverse city groups. This style of business is integral to any characterization of Chicago's political culture and is as important as the city's history of supporting activist local and neighborhood groups.

These community groups also recognized that real school reform would only be achieved with wide support in the city and with business leaders playing a dominant and supportive role. They actively pursued business leaders in the reform process, encouraging them to be activist partners from the beginning. The Chicago United (CU), a long-standing, influential organization of Chicago businessmen, was a major stakeholder that worked directly with local neighborhood and activist groups. It hired an Alinsky organizer who had been a union organizer and an experienced activist in the Latino community to give CU a leadership role in the reform effort and to guarantee their ties to community groups. Chicago United and other business leaders provided substantial financial support to hire established and well-regarded lobbyists to carry the school reform campaign to the state level. Business stakeholders' political sophistication and strong ties to political leaders supported the efforts of the activist groups in the state capital.

Another factor in Chicago's success was Mayor Harold Washington's willingness to make school reform a priority and to invest his leadership in the effort. A well-thought-out plan for the engagement of the stakeholders in a city education summit planning group assured the mayor of a leadership role. This united front of political, economic, and community interests gave the governor and the legislature little room for denial.

The Chicago reform is directed at the redistribution of power in an urban school system. The reform calls for changes in who makes the decisions in important areas of school policy. Teacher, parent, and community roles are broadened through the creation of school-governance structures.

The centerpiece of the Chicago plan was the emphasis on the individual school as a unit of governance and education policy. This provided a stronger basis for arguing the purpose of governance reform and its relation to educational change. It recognized that school districts, even at the neighborhood level, could be disconnected from the parents and teachers in the school. The plan restructured its districts to reflect the creation of LSCs; it reduced the total number of districts to ten and included one high school in each district. District councils in Chicago are composed of one parent or community member elected from each LSC, totaling forty-five to fifty members (each district includes forty-five to fifty schools). Principals were most immediately affected by the changes because they became employees of the LSCs. They are now dependent on the school decision makers for contract renewal and are no longer responsible to central school headquarters. The Chicago reformers stated clearly their intention that principals should be given as much power over staff, budget, and curriculum as it takes to produce results; they are then to be held directly accountable for the outcomes.

The powers of the professional bureaucrats at school headquarters were also changed by the emphasis on school decision-making. The Chicago superintendent, in fact, attempted for two years to delay the devolution of power to the school level, seeking tight control over the allocation of funds. His efforts proved unsuccessful, and he resigned at the end of the school year in 1992. The selection of the new superintendent was an important next step in ensuring the integrity of the school reform. The central bureaucracy and supervisory staff continue to assert their power. Surprisingly, the city coalition that was responsible for the passage of the legislation resisted early efforts toward centralization. In addition, a state financial oversight agency was charged with guaranteeing implementation of the decentralization plan.

The ability of the city coalition to weather the opposition to school reform in Chicago has some important political implications. The centralized party structure may influence the status and the development of community groups as a countervailing force in city politics. Several long-standing, active Chicago organizations were primary actors in the school reform. United Neighborhood Organization (UNO), Designs for Social Change, the Urban League, Chicago Panel on Public Schools, and myriad other neighborhood groups provided the basis for the coalition that saw the business community as an important ally.

Chicago United, representing largely mobile business interests and historically concerned with education and other city issues, understood that the highly bureaucratized Chicago school system was responsible for the underprepared labor force that made up their hiring pool. For several decades, the business community had expressed its concerns but had never joined the effort for fundamental political reform. The business community was invited to participate in Mayor Harold Washington's Education Summit group, which prepared early city school reform plans and was later a part of the broader effort to pass state legislation. In their earlier roles, CU members came into direct contact with activist reformers; that contact was instrumental in encouraging their participation in the reform coalition and also explained their willingness to support a radical plan for reform, as well as their continuing commitment to it.

The Chicago school decentralization is most notable for getting off the ground with a sense of immediacy of purpose. In its first months of implementation, a transitional Board of Education decided it had to make the decentralization "real" in the eighteen months of its legislative life and that it had to send that message to everyone concerned. All of their actions were measured against that purpose. Within weeks, they transferred seven hundred central-headquarters staff to the local districts and schools to announce the diminishing importance of central staff. They transferred budget and budgetary discretion to the schools and encouraged local curriculum development and change. The legislation provided for the immediate scheduling of school board nominations, elections, organization, and support to ensure the transition. Soon after the initial effort to reduce the size of the central staff, resistance increased and prevented further transfers of personnel.

Not enough attention has been paid to the role of foundations in city politics and particularly in city school-reform efforts. Chicago foundations were unified and strong supporters of the school reform, staying the course to completion in the state capital and into the implementation phase. There are many who would say that the Chicago school reform could not have happened without the support and encouragement of the MacArthur Foundation in particular.

The Chicago school reform was achieved not under the umbrella of movement politics but, rather, as a product of old-style pluralist coalition-building. The school-reform plan includes most of the elements embodied in the concept of community control that emerged in the 1960s but that New York City failed to achieve—because the plan was too radical, most assumed. The coalition that made the reform possible in the 1980s in Chicago was composed primarily of community and civic organizations, with a prominent role played by the business community and political leaders. State and city officials who supported the effort served as instruments of these groups, guiding their plan through the legislature. The majority leader of the state legislature invited all interested parties to hammer out the legislation in his office over a twenty-one-hour period. The political leadership of the city, first under Mayor Washington and then under Mayor Daley, worked with the strong coalition that dug in its heels to produce political decentralization of the school system. A strong governor, although a Republican, added his leadership and support because of the consistent role of the city stakeholders. The media and major city newspapers were fair in their reporting or were supportive of the reform effort.

Chicago school reformers surveyed other large-city school systems in the country, including New York City's, before they made their school-reform plan final. Coalition leaders did not want Chicago to emulate New York City's failure to achieve a devolution of power; their plan reflected a recognition of the need to act decisively. Even now, maintaining their vigilance, the coalition members are attentive to the constant threats to the integrity of the reform. They are particularly sensitive to the need for support mechanisms and have also recognized the need for training of school councils. There is talk of providing the boards with more information on education options and broader goals for their improvement plans. They have also encouraged principals to take on more imaginative education programs.

In 1996, the state transferred full school budget control to the mayor of Chicago. This centralization of financial power outside the school district was viewed by some of the stakeholders as a departure from the decentralization. Other analysts saw the action as a way to engage the mayor as an important stakeholder in school outcomes. The new law did not take away any of the powers granted to the LSCs. The mayor appointed as the head of the school system his highly regarded budget director, who immediately changed the school budget processes and restructured the central office. Chicago school reform now seems to have successfully achieved central reform with a devolution of power to the schools.

Recent evaluation reports conclude that the 1988 reforms have resulted in substantial changes in the schools and their programs. The most active participatory schools produce the most significant change. Test results show important improvements in reading and math scores in more than half of the schools. More than twenty school improvement networks have been created in the districts, and many are working to reshape curriculum and school programs.

The Chicago school reform, because it embodies political decentralization and the potential for a redistribution of power, offers the opportunity to observe what happens when decisionmaking power is transferred to the community and to parents. Theories of citizen participation will be informed by the more than 30 percent participation rate in the first election of LSCs (as compared to national school board election participation rates of about 10 percent), the nomination and participation of 17,000 candidates, and the election of 5,420 LSC members. This represents a significant opening of the school system to new participants.

NEW YORK CITY: A FAILED REFORM

The history of the movement for community control of the schools and decentralization in New York City in the late 1960s is a story of failed politics, a lack of a common stakeholder vision and coalition for change, and the strength of professional resistance to change. The decentralization plan, enacted by the state legislature in 1969 after two years of struggle, provided for the creation of thirty-three elected school boards in districts having only the power to select a community superintendent. The UFT and the Council of Supervisory Associations (CSA)—the school professional groups that had a historical presence in state regime politics—directed and controlled the legislative agenda. Mayoral and gubernatorial support of the reform was weakened by the legislative response to vested professional interests. The reform mayor (Lindsay) and Republican governor (Rockefeller), joined by the Ford Foundation's president (Bundy), were unable together to achieve the school reforms.

Although Lindsay supported decentralization and created a panel (headed by Bundy and known as the Bundy Panel) to present a plan for action, there was no effort to expand the stakeholders or to organize a city coalition; many potentially interested groups in the city remained on the sidelines, and some actively opposed what they considered to be a minimal devolution of power to the community. The UFT and the CSA, experienced and major actors in New York State politics, easily derailed state legislation that would have produced some devolution of power in the city school system.

An outgrowth of the civil rights movement, the school-reform campaign and plan in New York City embodied the concept of community control. The community organizations that shaped and initiated the school reform were abandoning a failed school-integration agenda. They had been actively engaged in that struggle from the time of the *Brown* decision in 1954 (*Brown v. Board of Education of Topeka*, 347 U.S. 483) and were frustrated by the school system's resistance to change (Rogers, 1968).

Citywide civic action in New York is dominated by a more traditional Progressive reform style. That tradition gives prominence to professional and middle-class groups that lack grassroots or neighborhood ties. Those groups, including the Citizens Union, the Citizens Committee for Children, and the

Citizens Budget Commission, support centralization and professional control. A weak citywide party organization meant stronger district or precinct party organizations as mediating agencies for lower-income and working-class populations. Activism in community organizations is centered in particular neighborhoods. Sayre and Kaufman (1960) described the veto power of activist interests in the city, but in fact, community organizations in most neighborhoods were not active until the 1960s.

According to Mollenkopf's (1992) review of the Lindsay administration, there was a planned expansion of community-based activities funded by the city to blunt the movement toward community control by school reformers. The fragmentation of community organizations and their shift in roles from advocacy to service during the Lindsay years also undermined their role as coalition builders (Gittell, 1980). Mollenkopf (1992, p. 91) concluded that "the extra-party mechanisms that promoted 'poor-reform' politics in other cities thus failed to have the same effect in New York."

The 1969 New York decentralization legislation reflected the teachers' union's priorities. It called for district board elections in New York City in May during off years by a complicated system of proportional representation designed, it seemed, to discourage participation. All personnel powers, except the appointment of the community superintendent, were retained centrally. Teacher and principal examinations, strongly criticized in every study of the school system but strongly supported by the professional groups, were retained under a central Board of Examiners. Curriculum remained centrally supervised and controlled. Limited budget discretion was given to the district boards. None of the devolution of power recommended by the Bundy Panel was included in the legislation. Interestingly, a 1991 New York State legislative commission report evaluating the impact of the 1969 law recommended an increase in community power in the districts and schools along the lines of the original recommendations. In 1995 the city reverted to a strong chancellor who was selected to recentralize the city school system. Among his early efforts was a legislative push to take powers away from the districts and assert his power to remove local district board members.

A fortuitous 1970 court decision, *Louis C. Mercado and Boston M. Chance v. The Board of Examiners and the Board of Education of the City of New York, et al.* (Civil Action 70 civ 4141, 1970), had eliminated the principal's examination, declaring it unrelated to the competencies needed by principals in their job. This gave the elected community boards an opportunity to appoint principals with state credentials until a new exam could be devised. This was a devolution of local power that reformers had sought but had been denied by the state legislation. The new appointment power was used effectively to diversify the administrative staffs in the more active local school districts in minority neighborhoods until a new exam was adopted.

In presenting the Bundy plan, elite groups failed to engage directly the activist local school organizations, parent groups, or teachers. An elite group of city leaders assumed it could exercise the clout necessary for legislative action. Significantly, no effort was made to enlist the support of any segment of the business community in New York in the school-reform effort. There was a total lack of appreciation for the potential power of a coalition with business interests. This reflected New York City's history of limited engagement of mobile business in the needs of the city.

The battle for school decentralization had been engaged in New York since 1967 as a result of the initiatives taken by demonstration districts. These districts (espousing community control of local schools) were created in 1967 by the Board of Education, with Ford Foundation funding and Mayor Lindsay's support, prior to the decision to proceed with a citywide decentralization plan. The Oceanhill Brownsville Demonstration District Board acted immediately on its election to appoint a community superintendent and challenge the power of the central board by firing (or, as they claimed, transferring) fourteen teachers whom they judged to be unqualified. A six-week strike was called by the UFT, which claimed that the district had violated the contract by initiating personnel actions and ignoring the contract and due process (Berube and Gittell, 1969). The crippling strike and the union's demand to abolish the demonstration districts suggested its strong opposition to school decentralization. The strike was a clear declaration to the public and to state and city political leaders that the union would not tolerate reduction of their powers or any adjustment in their negotiated contract. Elected state legislators could not ignore the fact that the UFT was the major lobbyist in the state, funded more state legislators in their electoral campaigns than any other organization, and spent more on lobbying than any other organization in the state.

The UFT did not relent even after it won its battle to abolish the demonstration community school districts. This was to be a lesson for the future: the union would not relinquish power over the school system to anyone. Several legislators who supported the reformers were defeated in their subsequent campaigns by UFT-funded and -supported candidates. (For a full discussion of the politics in the legislative arena, see Gittell and Hollander, 1971.) After the defeat of the demonstration districts, the several foundations that initially supported the community-control movement also withdrew from the battle. They were responding, at least in part, to the power demonstrated by Albert Shanker, the UFT president, in convincing a congressional committee (the Patman Committee) to tighten restrictions on foundation finances.

The New York City school-decentralization plan adopted in 1969 by the New York State legislature reflected an already defeated community agenda for political decentralization. Movement politics itself was insufficient to achieve social change, although it should be credited with developing the content of the reform. Limited coalition politics, the limited number of school groups backed by the city's political leadership, the governor, the mayor, and a newly appointed foundation leader with strong commitments to social change were unable to sustain the battle or achieve a shift in power.

CITY POWER AND POLITICS

This tale of school reform reflects significant differences in the two cities' political cultures, particularly in the role of the business community. Elite analysis either assumes monolithic behavior on the part of business elites in American cities or distinguishes between mobile and nonmobile business behavior. The traditional role of a city's business community can determine its activism, its commitment to minorities and to social change, and its interaction with groups and political leaders. The willingness of other stakeholders, however, to engage segments of the business community in reform is also significant. Corporations in Minneapolis, Chicago, and San Francisco have historically been more participatory and interactive than those in New York and in cities such as St. Louis, Cincinnati, and Atlanta, where paternalistic and authoritarian styles are more common (Gittell, 1980).

The business sector in New York has never been an open and active partner in the political life of the city, perhaps because of the dominant role of banking and real estate interests. Some observers have noted an emphasis on development promoted by the powerful real estate interests in the city at a cost to overall economic development (Moss and O'Neill, 1991). Brecher and Horton (1993) suggest that investment bankers in New York are in a special position among business interests because they have a very direct interest in increasing city debt. Often they find themselves allied with city unions to increase expenditures. The Progressive movement enlisted the business elites in New York City at the turn of the century; at that time, they were committed to professional reform of the political system. The business community in New York

City has demonstrated little interest in marginalized groups in the city. In contrast to Chicago business leaders, New York corporate leaders identify with national and international issues. They do not see themselves as citizens of the city. It is not surprising, therefore, that they do not share a concern for the city's schools. Business leaders in New York may be critical of the system, but they have not participated in any coalition politics or joint efforts with other city actors in defining and seeking solutions to city school problems.

The attitude of foundations in New York City can be compared to the corporations that are located there. The large foundations—Ford, Carnegie, and Rockefeller—view themselves as national or international organizations; thus they avoid responsibility as city citizens. This is in sharp contrast to the foundations in Chicago, most of which are active participants in the city's life. The MacArthur Foundation sets aside a large budget for its work in Chicago, largely in support of community organizations. The foundation also established a $40,000,000 fund for support of the schools under the reform program over the next decade.

The failure of school reform in New York City is a reflection of the same political and cultural limitations. New York City lacks the strong base of community organizations that played such a dominant role in the Chicago school reform. The three demonstration community school districts were created in 1967 as a response to community activism; they became the strongest advocates of citywide school reform, emphasizing the need for a redistribution of power in school decision-making. The ease with which the school professionals were able to undermine the districts (they were discredited within three months of their creation and dissolved within a year) speaks to the overwhelming power of the professionals. The failure of any other organizations in the city—including business and the independent sector—to become engaged in reform, and the lack of viability of community organizations in New York City, especially in low-income areas, can be explained only in part by the mediating role of decentralized party organizations.

The continued maintenance of a Progressive reform agenda, professionally controlled and unsympathetic to neighborhood power, is also a significant aspect of New York political culture. The structure of regime politics in New York City is best characterized as top-down, lacking the pressure to broaden inclusion and to deal with coalitions. The failure of city stakeholders to act as a cohesive force at the state level is historic and also in sharp contrast to the Chicago experience. The New York City delegation to the state legislature, largely Democrats, has rarely acted as an organized force to promote city interests. Nor have Democratic governors and mayors exercised leadership to build broader coalitions to advance the cause of reform.

The goal of political democracy is the broadening of political participation, increasing the power of a wider variety of stakeholders and guaranteeing their engagement in the policy process at all levels by restructuring political institutions to accommodate them. Strong local organizations are a vital element in that effort. As Putnam's (1993) seminal study of Italian regional politics demonstrates, strong community and civic organizations developed over long periods of time contribute to a culture of civic virtue that makes government more inclusive and more responsive. Ross Gittell (1992), in his study of four medium-sized American cities, also demonstrates that more viable and constructive economic development takes place in cities with strong community organizations that can participate in the policy process. Cities with a strong tradition of grassroots groups are in a better position to develop broader coalitions that will be more responsive to the needs of a larger population.

This comparison of two cities' efforts at school-system reform suggests the importance of building grassroots organizations and broad-based reform coalitions; it also suggests, however, that city traditions die hard. Until reformers in New York City recognize the difference between relying on professional, top-down reform and building stronger community-based organizations and constituencies, success at changing institutions and broadening participation is likely to be unachievable.

REFERENCES

Berube, M., and M. Gittell, eds. 1969. *Confrontation at Ocean Hill Brownsville*. New York: Praeger.

Brecher, C., and R. Horton. 1993. *Power Failure*. Oxford: Oxford University Press.

Browning, R. P., D. R. Marshall, and D. H. Tabb. 1984. *Protest Is Not Enough: The Struggle of Blacks and Hispanics for Equality in Urban Politics*. Berkeley: University of California Press.

Fuchs, E. R. 1992. *Mayors and Money: Fiscal Policy in New York and Chicago*. Chicago: University of Chicago Press.

Fuhrman, S., and A. Rosenthal. 1981. *Shaping Education Policy in the States*. New Brunswick, N.J.: Rutgers University Press.

Gittell, M. 1980. *Limits to Citizen Participation: The Decline of Community Organizations*. Beverly Hills, Calif.: Sage.

Gittell, M., and E. Hollander. 1971. Education: The Decentralization-Community Control Controversy. In *Race and Politics in New York City: Five Studies in Policy Making*, edited by J. Bellush and S. David. New York: Praeger.

Gittell, R. 1992. *Renewing Cities.* Princeton, N.J.: Princeton University Press.

Horwitt, S. D. 1989. *Let Them Call Me Rebel: Saul Alinsky, His Life and Legacy.* New York: Knopf.

Logan, J., and H. Molotch, eds. 1987. *Urban Fortunes: The Political Economy of Place.* Berkeley: University of California Press.

Long, N. 1958. The Local Community as an Ecology of Games. *American Journal of Sociology* 64:251–61.

Mollenkopf, J. H. 1983. *The Contested City.* Princeton, N.J.: Princeton University Press.

———. 1992. *A Phoenix in the Ashes: The Rise and Fall of the Koch Coalition in New York City Politics.* Princeton, N.J.: Princeton University Press.

Moss, M., and H. O'Neill. 1991. *Reinventing New York.* New York: New York University Press.

Putnam, R. D. 1993. *Making Democracy Work: Civic Traditions in Modern Italy.* Princeton, N.J.: Princeton University Press.

Rogers, D. 1968. *110 Livingston Street Revisited: Politics and Bureaucracy in the New York City Schools.* New York: Random House.

Sayre, W. S., and H. Kaufman. 1960. *Governing New York City: Politics in the Metropolis.* New York: Russell Sage Foundation.

Squires, G. D., L. Bennett, K. McCourt, and P. Nyden. 1987. *Chicago: Race, Class, and the Response to Urban Decline.* Philadelphia, Pa.: Temple University Press.

Temporary State Commission on the New York City School Governance. 1991. *Governing for Results: Decentralization with Accountability.* New York: Author.

Weber, M. 1958. Essay on Bureaucracy. In *From Max Weber: Essays on Sociology,* edited by H. Gerth and C. W. Mills. New York: Oxford University Press.

Chapter 10 Linking Civic
Capacity and Human
Capital Formation

Clarence N. Stone

This chapter reports on an ongoing study of "civic capacity and urban education" in eleven cities.[1] It first explains why the focus of the study is human capital rather than schooling more narrowly understood. Next, it explores the meaning of civic capacity and its aptness as a core concept in an examination of the contemporary politics of urban educational reform. Finally, it presents some preliminary findings.

TOWARD A BROAD VIEW OF EDUCATION:
HUMAN CAPITAL FORMATION

Schools cannot do it alone. This is the growing consensus among those concerned with improving urban education in America. Schools, of course, have the front-line responsibility for enabling their students to assume a productive and rewarding place in modern society. Yet in actuality schools have limited control over many of the conditions that offer opportunities to, contribute to the skills of, and shape the aspirations of their students.

Measures of academic performance, drop-out rates, levels of college attendance, and related indicators correlate strongly with the socioeconomic background of students. The great unmet challenge for urban schools is to break that link between social background and student performance—and break it in such a way as to assure that all students have the level of educational attainment needed in a technologically advanced society. Though there are scattered successes, the overall pattern remains one in which a background of disadvantage is a predictor of a weak academic showing. Although the classroom experience is undeniably important, there are nonetheless limitations on what formal schooling can accomplish by itself. Reformer John Goodlad (1984, p. 343) argues that "schools alone are neither sufficiently powerful to guide young people through the turbulent adolescent years nor sufficiently cosmopolitan to effectively link the worlds of school and work."

Because schools have the official responsibility for educating students, the easy temptation is to hold schools wholly responsible for student performance. If, however, instead of thinking about schooling, we think about the total process of acquiring cognitive and social skills, we get a different perspective. This is a more diffuse process that comes about through accumulated experiences with a variety of social institutions. It is this process that can be termed "human capital formation." Families, neighborhoods, peer groups, the mass media, and workplaces all provide individuals with opportunities to acquire knowledge, social skills, insights, and various forms of information that can enhance the desire and ability of students to achieve academically and find a place in the mainstream labor market, as well as enter into a variety of noneconomic activities.

That student test scores, grades, drop-out rates, and levels of college attendance correlate with socioeconomic status should be no surprise. After all, the personal and private opportunities available to individuals vary enormously according to social background, especially such factors as family income, level of parent education, race, ethnicity, and place of residence. Accordingly, some students are advantaged in the process of human capital formation, others disadvantaged. What schools are able to accomplish can be either facilitated or constrained by the nonschool experiences of students. If personal and private experiences contribute little in a positive way to the process of human capital formation, then schools face a much greater challenge.

For contemporary urban education—that is, for systems in which a high proportion of students come from a disadvantaged background—the challenge of academic performance is especially severe. Indeed, the prospects of a poor showing by students are so strong that urban school systems sometimes gravitate toward defensive postures, seeking to protect themselves against criticism by holding the larger community at arm's length instead of seeking to enlist help. For schools that serve largely disadvantaged students, there is no self-correcting process to be triggered. The students cannot be expected to come forward and acknowledge that they are disadvantaged in the process of human capital formation. Their parents cannot do it without calling attention to what others may regard as parental deficiencies. Administrators and teachers are not likely to take the initiative in acknowledging the limitations of what they can achieve in their professional capacities.

By all accounts, the connection between socioeconomic disadvantage and academic performance is a difficult matter for public discussion. Words such as *disadvantage* and *deficiencies* carry enormous ideological baggage and often give rise to debates that contribute little to problem-solving but lead instead to doctrinal scorekeeping. Some analysts are even wary of the concept of human capital, fearing that it is a way of blaming poor children and their parents for their lack of success (Williams, 1994). This perspective fails, however, to confront the full workings of the system of stratification and the ways in which it underinvests in those in the lower strata. Information about opportunities and the inculcation of aspirations, expectations, and motivations vary among social strata.[2] Though not easy to document, these differences are at least as pervasive as differences in school spending and in all likelihood more telling.

By directing attention to the diffuse process of human capital formation, we can appreciate that education in the broad sense involves much more than acquiring diplomas and credentials. The following help shape human capital formation:

- early childhood development—including both family and childcare experiences that can contribute to learning readiness (note that a larger proportion of middle-class than lower-class children are enrolled in preschool programs, and the gap may widen with scheduled decreases in Head Start funding);
- in-school experiences—with a reminder that what happens in the classroom is affected by family and peer group influences (for this reason, some have advocated the development of "youth charters" to bring into line the various influences on students);[3]
- extraschool experiences—which can range from work to sports and other extracurricular activities but can also include school-reinforcing experiences such as mentoring and tutoring (there are more organized extraschool youth-

development activities in middle-class areas than in lower-class neighbor-hoods);

- post-school transition to work or college—which can take a form that heightens aspirations, focuses on the worth of schooling, and furthers human capital formation or that falls short on each of these counts; and
- social and health supports, from preschool on—which can come from within the family or can be provided by various programs, but in any case contribute to the individual's capacity for human capital development.

Overall, then, although formal education is clearly important,[4] in-school experiences are just part of the picture. Because formal schooling is embedded in the larger process of human capital formation, schools, *standing alone*, have limited leverage. Time spent in the classroom is, after all, quite limited—by one calculation (assuming steady school attendance) school occupies one-third of a child's waking life (Damon, 1994, p. 31).

Education broadly understood thus has a large nonschool component. No matter how politically delicate the matter may be, there is a stubborn reality that will not go away: social background stratifies opportunities for individuals in ways that create advantages and disadvantages in human capital formation, and this is a fact that affects education in a profound way.

CIVIC CAPACITY

The heavy dependence of human capital formation on student background could be lessened if the larger community made a compensatory contribution to the process. Such a contribution, however, would not be a "natural" action; that is, it would be unlikely to happen spontaneously. Instead it would have to be generated politically, that is, by different elements of the community coming together to make a deliberate effort to do what otherwise would not be done.

Because the word *political* has acquired a negative connotation, the eleven-city study uses the less tarnished phrase *civic capacity* to refer to bringing together diverse groups in pursuit of community problem-solving. Regardless of the terminology used, the underlying concept stands in need of renewed appreciation. Philosopher Hannah Arendt (1963) describes politics as the activity by which a people change an established course of events; they alter, by their collective and deliberate action, what might otherwise be an inevitable outcome. Thus an acknowledgment that "the schools cannot do it alone" invites a political initiative—coming together to remedy a problem. Because the jurisdiction and capacity of the schools are limited, only a conscious and broad-based effort can enrich the otherwise diffuse, deficient, but seemingly "natural" process of human capital formation as it works for disadvantaged students.

Once we realize that student performance is linked to a broad and informal human capital formation process, a case can be made for realigning the school-community relationship. In order for the performance of disadvantaged students to be improved, the community needs to contribute to the process, devising specific efforts to enhance the informal development of human capital and facilitate the official educational process. Schools need to reciprocate by enlisting the efforts and contributions of various elements of the community.

A new vocabulary has grown up around the struggle to end the isolation of the schools and to rethink the relation of the community to education. *Restructuring, collaboration,* and *partnerships* are among the major terms that have come into use to foster greater cooperation between schools and their communities. The struggle is not one that is always fully understood, and the participants in it don't necessarily see it the same way. Education professionals and, in some instances, even parents may fear intrusion into what they see as their bailiwick.

Community participants, especially business executives, may see their role in education as quite limited in both time and scope. Indeed, they sometimes operate with the explicit assumption that *the* problem is one of making schools accountable. The diffuse process of human capital formation is not necessarily one to which most business leaders are attuned—hence, they may acknowledge no duty to contribute to the process of human capital formation for the disadvantaged.

A broad community responsibility for education is not something toward which most people routinely gravitate. More likely they see the normal state of affairs as one in which professional educators are responsible for the academic performance of students, businesses strive to protect their individual profit margins, and other community entities pursue their own individual agendas. This is the classic American pattern of pluralism and what many regard as the natural social order.

Poised against this conventional view is an awareness, variously felt, that community involvement is needed; that a broad and intentional coalition of "stakeholders" would be a highly useful means for pursuing much-needed educational improvement. The emergence of the term *stakeholder* is significant in itself. It implies that various segments of the community recognize that they have a shared interest in a common objective. To become conscious of the role of stakeholder is thus to display a form of community-mindedness.[5] In the case of education, the obvious candidates for active roles as stakeholders (aside from professional educators) are parents and businesses and other employers. And the concept of human capital formation points to a potentially longer list of participants that includes racial, ethnic, and religious groups, as well as a range of nonprofit organizations and governmental agencies concerned with youth development and various issues of child welfare.

This project uses *civic capacity* to denote the extent to which major sectors of the community come together with a shared concern, in this case educational improvement. Thus, if we think of the usual state of affairs as one in which participants are focused only on their immediate connections and their particular occupational roles, then civic capacity is marked by a move beyond this stage toward embracing a *community* role and accepting a *civic* obligation. Using the rhetoric of community roles and civic obligations is, of course, not the test of civic capacity. Instead, the real test is the ability to *build and maintain* alliances among representatives from the school system, city hall, other public agencies, the nonprofit sector, the business sector, and parent and community-based groups—alliances that are able to work together on a shared problem-solving agenda.

To act in a community-minded way involves much more than entertaining a noble sentiment. Action has a social context. Civic cooperation requires trust that each participant will fulfill her or his obligations. Participation in a collective effort is increased by the extent to which each participant feels assured that others will honor their responsibilities.

Some observers use the term *social capital* to describe the degree of trust that surrounds efforts to promote cooperation (Putnam, 1995). It does not spring up full-grown but develops over time with accumulating experience and reinforcing interactions. Civic alliances can, of course, be built around purposes other than educational improvement. Economic development, historic preservation, acquiring a major-league sports team, and welfare reform are among the diverse aims that could be and have been pursued.

Civic cooperation in one policy domain (economic development, for example) might or might not facilitate cooperation in another (education, for instance). The transferability of cooperation is one of the issues with which this project is concerned, and the preliminary results of the present study suggest that cooperation transfer is far from automatic.

Education poses a special challenge as a sphere of civic cooperation. Educational improvement is a long-term and largely open-ended process. It is not neatly bounded, like building a new sports stadium. Cohesion and being able to sustain cohesion over time are therefore particularly valuable. Moreover, because educational improvement is such an open-ended process, a broad base of resources is especially useful. Hence, a widely inclusive coalition is highly valuable. Inclusiveness and cohesion, however, are in tension with one another. The wider the coalition, the more difficult it is to achieve and maintain cohesion. The special challenge in the education arena is, then, one of how to overcome the natural tension between wide inclusiveness and high cohesion in order to achieve both.

Of course, building civic capacity is not the only approach that can be taken to improve education. An alternative might be to accept pluralism and simply concentrate on strategic opportunities to promote incremental improvements (cf. Marris and Rein, 1973, 1982). Small steps are easier to take, and, if a misstep is made, it is easier to recover (Martz, 1992). But one might question whether incrementalism provides enough leverage, especially sustained leverage, to bring about the kind of restructuring needed to make a substantial and cumulative impact (Hochschild, 1984). John Goodlad, for example, calls for a set of interconnected moves—"improvement will come about not by tackling . . . problem areas one by one, but by addressing all or most of them as a system" (1984, p. 271). Systemic reform has become the watchword of those concerned about the need to improve education (Smith and O'Day, 1990), and if reform is to be truly systemic, then tinkering with such matters as graduation requirements or even teacher training is not enough. Successful educational reform will require the mobilization of civic capacity, perhaps locality by locality, and a restructuring of the way in which schools and communities are related to one another.

FINDINGS

Spinning out an academic vision of systemic reform is one thing. Mobilizing a community around it is a different matter. "Stakeholding" is not yet widely practiced. When we turn to the eleven-city study, the picture is not encouraging. The accumulated research for this project shows that, among the cities studied, there is no case of a comprehensive program of reform and educational improvement backed by an active coalition representing all sectors of the community. At the same time, there is no instance of a school system devoid of reform activity and efforts to improve education. And there is no example of a school system operating without significant involvement from other sectors of the community. The picture is a mixed one, with much activity and a variety of bridge-building efforts under way, but activity and efforts that fall short of a comprehensive approach.

Table 10.1 gives an overview of the involvement of selected actors in education reform.[6] The weakness of parent involvement offers itself as the most imposing fact about urban education, this despite the wide recognition of the importance of parental participation for improving education and the strong urging of the U.S. Department of Education (1994). Significantly, city school systems are not heavily populated by the middle class. Only two of the eleven cities have less than a majority of their students eligible for federally assisted meals, with the rest ranging up to 85 percent eligibility.[7] Their great stake in urban school reform notwithstanding, poor and other nonaffluent parents are immensely underrepresented.

A second prominent fact in the eleven-city study is the weak engagement of teacher associations in the promotion of reform. Although they are part of the reform coalition in three cities, in another three they are active and vocal resisters, and in the remainder they are nonplayers. Superintendents also play a surprisingly modest role in the cross-city picture. Though perhaps key actors in as many as four cities (Boston could become a fifth), the intense cross-pressures surrounding the office foster high turnover and work against a central leadership role (Jackson and Cibulka, 1991). As the D.C. case illustrates, even when the superintendent is willing to initiate reforms, the weakness of constituent support can limit his or her ability to do so.

A number of other actors play varying parts in the eleven cities. The federal courts, state governments, foundations, and, in three cities, the mayor emerge as major actors in educational reform. But none of these represents a grassroots constituency. In that category, community-based organizations and various racial and other advocacy groups play a significant part in about half the cities but not in the remainder.

The role of business is also quite varied. In some, it plays a broad and institutionalized part, but in others, given how much the quality of education affects business, its place is extremely modest, including little more than organized support for an occasional reform-minded slate of school board contenders. In light of the big part that business has played in educational reform at the state and the national level, this limited role at the city level calls for explanation. At higher levels of government, reform activism often consists mainly of an endorsement of broad and general principles. The policy aim is legislative enactment. At the local level, educational reform calls for concrete and particular steps. Costs become an immediate factor. Actual implementa-

Table 10.1. Civic Capacity by City: Involvement of Selected Actors in Educational Reform

City	Business	Parent	Teacher	Superintendent	Other
Pittsburgh	Broad and institutionalized	Some, but not among the top actors	Included in reform coalition	Active promoter	Foundations, state governments, and community-based organizations (CBOs)
Boston	Broad and institutionalized	Varied but not a cohesive force	Included in reform coalition	In transition to active promoter	Foundations, mayor, state government, and CBOs
Los Angeles	Broad and institutionalized	Very little	Included in reform coalition	Active promoter	Foundations and advocacy groups
Baltimore	Somewhat broad and institutionalized	Very little	Very little	Highly selective promoter	Foundations, mayor, state government, and CBOs
Houston	Rising and institutionalized	Very little	Very little to minor	New, but with reform support	Foundations and CBOs
Washington, D.C.	Institutionalized but guarded	Narrowly based	Resistant to reform	Lacks firm political base	U.S. Congress
Detroit	Institutionalized but contested	Mixed, but quite small	Resistant to reform	Reform superintendent ousted	Foundations and state government
Atlanta	Small	Small	Very little	New appointee, following a nonleader	State government, CBOs, and J. Carter's Atlanta Project
Denver	Small	Very little	Resistant to reform	New and selective promoter	Foundations, nonprofits, state government, and federal court
St. Louis	Small	Very little	Very little	Very little	Foundations, federal court and mayor
San Francisco	Very little	Very little	Very little	Active promoter	Federal court and advocacy groups

tion is not only more contentious, it is also a more drawn-out process, and it entails working with a specialized set of actors and procedures that are remote from the day-to-day activities of most business executives.

Educational reform is thus unfamiliar territory to many in the corporate world, and as one St. Louis businessman explained, "It would take an incredible amount of time to deal with that bureaucracy." In today's competitive business world, he offered, "working in one election was enough of a commitment for me" (quoted in Stein, 1994, p. 17). Contrary to what might have been expected, business involvement in other areas, such as redevelopment, or in specific projects, such as building a new sports stadium, has not smoothed the way for involvement in education.

In the eleven cities, the scope of reform activity generally corresponds to the scope of civic capacity mobilized. Cities such as Atlanta and St. Louis, where business involvement was limited, are also cities in which there is little reform activity. Pittsburgh, Los Angeles, and Boston, by contrast, have wide and institutionalized business involvement and an extensive amount of reform activity.

The most conspicuous exception to this pattern is San Francisco.[8] In most cities with substantial reform activity, business has played the role of legitimizer of change. In San Francisco, the authority of the court met that need. In a desegregation case, the federal judge used a consent decree to constitute a panel of outside education experts, and they devised a program of academic improvement as well as measures to achieve racial balance. The consent decree has also enabled the superintendent to work closely with the panel, disregard union rules, and disregard potential resistance as he reconstituted key schools and provided accompanying staff development. The advantage of the consent decree is that it connects goals to concrete action at the school level. The disadvantage is that the highly focused program of academic improvement is confined to a few targeted schools.

Systemwide improvement is to be found among few of the eleven cities. Instead there are numerous special initiatives, pilot projects, and innovative programs at one or a few schools, and there is little effort to expand these limited activities into citywide programs. Site-based management, for example, is extensively discussed and endorsed in principle in most of the eleven cities, but, with the possible exception of Pittsburgh, a comprehensive program of implementation is not in evidence. The key to Pittsburgh's success may be that both the superintendent and the teachers' union are an integral part of the reform coalition *and have been for some time.*[9]

Most of the reform activity seeks to change school structure and practice. Only Houston's reform focuses on building networks to strengthen neighborhood and parent supports. In general, noneducators perceive the barriers to academic achievement as being internal to schools. Educators, on the other hand, see family and community problems as the key obstacles.[10] Fragmented and partial efforts instead of systemic change stem from a lack of consensus about the basic character of the situation. Issue definitions diverge too sharply to bring disparate parties together around a comprehensive program of educational change. In most cities, aspirations to improve education come in a faint second to anxieties about jobs, opportunities for professional advancement, and loss of turf. And in some cities the search for educational improvement is further hampered by past racial practices and by earlier battles over urban renewal and school desegregation.

CONCLUSIONS

Educational reform has to contend with the stubborn fact that, since the publication of the Coleman report three decades ago, research has sustained its finding that family and community background is the most consistent predictor of student performance.[11] Various attempted alterations in school practice, including recent experiments with vouchers, have not dislodged the pattern (*Washington Post*, July 16, 1995). Moreover, there is a long history of unrealized reforms that has left many people doubtful about the ability of schools to actually implement and sustain major innovations (Cuban, 1988).

This chapter has suggested a need to look beyond the reform of school practice itself to the larger issue of human capital formation. Family and community influences are important. Information and expectations about jobs and economic opportunities are vital. Hence, educational improvement may well ride on a broad-based effort to enhance human capital formation for disadvantaged youngsters and thus on linking school reform to community change. If so, the needed reform is indeed systemic and requires a corresponding form of mobilization.

In the eleven-city study reported here, "civic capacity" serves as the indicator of the extent to which various segments of the community have been mobilized to foster educational improvement. Although no city scores at the top of the scale, and some score quite low, there is variation in the strength of civic capacity around educational improvement. Business involvement is especially uneven, and parent participation is disappointingly low. The African proverb that it takes the whole village to educate a child is widely quoted but little practiced. Therein lies a major political challenge in the path to the systemic reform of urban education.

Experience in the eleven cities suggests that the natural drift in urban communities is away from civic capacity. Various sectors of community life tend to operate in isolation from one another, producing no shared understanding of the city's problems and how to respond to them. Yet there are various efforts to build bridges and promote greater communication. The Pittsburgh experience suggests that this is a long-term process and that the business sector can play a key facilitative role if it is willing to take a broad community-building view of its civic responsibility and institutionalize its involvement in community problem-solving. At the same time, business must tread softly. Past involvements in narrow programs of economic development leave behind a heritage of distrust not easily turned around.

NOTES

1. This project is funded by the Education and Human Resources Directorate of the National Science Foundation, NSF grant no. RED 9350139. The eleven cities included in the study are Atlanta, Baltimore, Boston, Denver, Detroit, Houston, Los Angeles, Pittsburgh, St. Louis, San Francisco, and Washington, D.C.

2. See Ogbu (1978); Matute-Bianchi (1986). But note also the argument by Damon (1994) about a society-wide foundation for declining expectations, particularly in today's youth culture.

3. In his monumental evaluation of contemporary schooling, John Goodlad (1984) emphasizes the need to come to terms with an autonomous youth culture often radically at odds with the educational goal of the school system. On youth charters, see Ianni (1989); Damon (1994).

4. My observations are in no way intended to suggest that formal education is unimportant. They are about how the experience of formal education is related to other influences. For interesting research on the impact of formal education, see Scribner and Cole (1973); Saxe (1988).

5. If the term *stakeholder* is already in use, one might ask, why use the term *civic capacity?* The answer is that it suggests a deeper involvement than *stakeholder*. To be a stakeholder only implies that various actors have a stake in (in this case) education. *Capacity* suggests something more: that various actors can contribute to educational improvement by their active involvement. The term *civic capacity* is thus intended to accent the importance of a broad base of involvement. The scarcity of parent involvement among our eleven cities, discussed below, is therefore a serious deficiency in civic capacity. It isn't just a matter of missing political clout, narrowly understood. It is that a potentially important contributor to educational improvement is missing in most cities. This point is derived from my

understanding of how urban regimes, and opportunity-expanding regimes in particular, operate (see Stone, 1993).

6. This table is based on case study accounts done for the project and completed in early 1995. The table, it should be remembered, represents only one point in time, whereas reform is a dynamic process. Thus the picture in all cities is subject to change as the process continues to unfold.

7. Council of the Great City Schools (1994).

8. The discussion below is based on Fraga and Anhalt (1995).

9. On the importance of insider participation, see Goodlad (1984); Grant (1988); and Hawley (1988).

10. See the recent surveys by the Public Agenda Foundation: Farkas (1992) and Immerwahr (1994).

11. Coleman (1966). See also Jencks et al. (1973).

REFERENCES

Arendt, Hannah. 1963. *Between Past and Future.* Cleveland: Meridian.

Coleman, James S. 1966. *Equality of Educational Opportunity.* Washington, D.C.: Government Printing Office.

Council of the Great City Schools. 1994. *National Urban Education Goals: 1992–93 Indicators Report.* Washington, D.C.: Council of the Great City Schools.

Cuban, Larry. 1988. *The Managerial Imperative.* Albany: State University of New York Press.

Damon, William. 1994. *Greater Expectations.* New York: Free Press.

Farkas, Steve. 1992. "Educational Reform: The Players and the Politics." Report from the Public Agenda Foundation prepared for the Charles F. Kettering Foundation.

Fraga, Luis R., and Bari E. Anhalt. 1995. "The Politics of Educational Reform in San Francisco." Field site report for the Project on Civic Capacity and Urban Education.

Goodlad, John I. 1984. *A Place Called School.* New York: McGraw-Hill.

Grant, Gerald. 1988. *The World We Created at Hamilton High.* Cambridge, Mass.: Harvard University Press.

Hawley, Willis D. 1988. Missing Pieces of the Educational Reform Agenda. *Educational Administration Quarterly* 24 (November):416–37.

Hochschild, Jennifer L. 1984. *The New American Dilemma.* New Haven: Yale University Press.

Ianni, Francis A. J. 1989. *The Search for Structure.* New York: Free Press.

Immerwahr, John, with Jill Boese and Will Friedman. 1994. "The Broken Contract." Report from Public Agenda prepared for the William Caspar Graustein Memorial Fund.

Jackson, Barbara L., and James G. Cibulka. 1991. "Leadership Turnover and Business Mobilization," in *Politics of Education Association Yearbook,* 71–86. Washington, D.C.: Falmer.

Jencks, Christopher, et al. 1973. *Inequality.* New York: Harper & Row.

Marris, Peter, and Martin Rein. 1973, 1982. *Dilemmas of Social Reform.* Chicago: University of Chicago Press.

Martz, Larry. 1992. *Making School Better.* New York: Times Books.

Matute-Bianchi, Maria Eugenia. 1986. Ethnic Identities and Patterns of School Success and

Failure Among Mexican-Descent and Japanese-American Students in a California High School. *American Journal of Education* (November):233–55.

Ogbu, John. 1978. *Minority Education and Caste.* New York: Academic.

Putnam, Robert D. 1995. Bowling Alone: America's Declining Social Capital. *Journal of Democracy* 6 (January):65–78.

Saxe, G. B. 1988. The Mathematics of Child Street Vendors. *Child Development* 59:1415–25.

Scribner, Sylvia, and Michael Cole. 1973. Cognitive Consequences of Formal and Informal Education. *Science* 182 (November):553–59.

Smith, Marshall S., and Jennifer O'Day. 1990. "Systemic School Reform," in *Politics of Education Association Yearbook,* 233–67. Washington, D.C.: Falmer.

Stein, Lana. 1994. "Education and Civic Capacity." Report for the Project on Civic Capacity and Urban Education.

Stone, Clarence N. 1993. Urban Regimes and the Capacity to Govern. *Journal of Urban Affairs* 15(1):1–28.

United States Department of Education. 1994. *Strong Families, Strong Schools.* Washington, D.C.: U.S. Department of Education.

Williams, Rhonda M. 1994. "Culture as Human Capital," in *African Americans and the New Policy Consensus,* edited by Marilyn E. Lashley and Melanie Njeri Jackson. Westport, Conn.: Greenwood.

Part Four Engaging
the Community

Community organizations have played a key role in education reform in recent years, not only in broadening participation in this area of public policy but also in providing strategic advantages for reformers. Part IV describes the significant efforts of particular community organizations that have been instrumental in state education reform, including the Prichard Committee in Kentucky, Designs for Change (DFC) in Chicago, and the Intercultural Development Research Association in Texas. The authors, all leaders in these organizations, have actively participated in reform efforts in their states. Their experiences point to the importance of community groups in educating the public, organizing effective coalitions, providing continuity, maintaining reform efforts, and ensuring accountability.

Local participation in education has been limited since the Progressive movement in the twenties, which shifted emphasis from localism and lay participation in decision-making toward centralized bureaucracies and boards. Professionalism insulated the schools from the public. In the sixties, the school reform movement attempted to reengage the public in public education and to include new groups in the process. Public discourse was encouraged by the activism of the civil rights movement and the new populist goal of a more participatory political system. Decision-making became more democratic through governance reforms, as well as through the proliferation and activism of citizen interest groups. These groups have been effective in sparking and sustaining reform throughout the country.

Community organizations have made a major impact on state court litigation and on the implementation of reform efforts in state legislatures. Community groups have affected the outcomes of litigation in a variety of ways. In Texas, these groups identified prospective litigation-oriented groups to take the lead; educated legal experts in the workings of the Texas funding system; provided collaborative analyses of legal strategies as well as data collection and analysis to strengthen the case; and contributed financial support. In Kentucky, the Prichard Committee served as amici curiae in the court case, influencing the court to go beyond a strictly financial analysis and declare the entire school system unconstitutional.

These groups have also played a key role in lobbying state legislatures and governors to produce satisfactory legislation by educating constituents or by directly lobbying politicians. The Prichard Committee maintains aggressive behind-the-scenes negotiations with state officials, urging them, on one hand, to take credit for bold action and, on the other, providing political cover when needed. In Chicago, the strategy of the ABC's Coalition, which was instrumental in passing the 1988 reform legislation, was to convince legislators from outside Chicago that the bill would improve Chicago's schools without affecting their own. In Chapter 11, Albert Cortez stresses the continuing importance of these groups as links between the community and political representatives.

One of the most important lobbying strategies these groups employ is educating the public about the need for reform. They hold public meetings and collect and disseminate critical data on the schools. In Texas, community groups convened conferences, symposia, meetings, discussion groups, and other gatherings in order to develop networks of proponents of school reform. Cortez points out that the lack of available information about financial disparities was one of the major stumbling blocks in early reform efforts in Texas. In Chicago, DFC organized low-income and minority parents in South Side and West Side schools and publicized findings of low reading achievement, high dropout rates, and the school system's substandard programs for children with disabilities. Robert F. Sexton of the Prichard Committee points to the key role that community groups can play in informing the media in order to increase coverage of the issues.

These authors point to the need for community organizations to form creative alliances not only with other such groups but also with other stakeholders, including the business community. Kentucky's Prichard Committee has formed important coalitions that bring together groups such as the Kentucky Youth Advocates, the Kentucky League of Cities, the Kentucky Education Association, and the Kentucky Chamber of Commerce. In Chicago, the ABC's coalition—composed of parents, advocates, and business leaders—was an important player in the reform process. The loose-knit coalitions in Texas have worked together successfully despite varying agendas and varying levels of participation, resources, and expertise. Forming and maintaining such networks of organizations is not always easy, but it is crucial for effecting successful bottom-up reform.

Community groups have brought continuity to the reform process in many states. These groups have often existed for many years, overseeing the reform from beginning to end, whereas state politicians and educational professionals are not always in office for the duration of the process. The longevity of these groups serves as a critical link between officials, prevents policy from veering off course, and establishes a long-term, reliable source of information for the public.

The continuity of these groups has also served to assure the maintenance of reform and to ensure accountability. Advocacy groups in Chicago that were established to lobby the state legislature for change have continued to play a major role in sustaining reform by aggressively monitoring the central board and administration, analyzing its budget, advocating the restructuring of the central administration to support reform, and opposing board of education rules that threaten local school councils and principal autonomy. Since the Kentucky Education Reform Act was passed in 1990, the Prichard Committee has persistently worked toward ensuring that the act is implemented in a consistent manner and has prevented politics from derailing or diverting attention from reform. It is considered a model of interest group organization for school reform.

Involvement of community organizations has clearly been a factor in producing and maintaining successful school reform throughout the country. These groups not only provide a voice for the public in the political process but also serve important strategic purposes. They provide continuity, maintain reform, assure accountability, assemble coalitions, educate the public, influence court decisions, and lobby legislatures and governors. Although community organizations entered the education policy arena relatively recently, they have clearly become key players in education reform in our country.

Chapter 11 Power and Perseverance: Organizing for Change in Texas

Albert Cortez

A recent *New York Times* article chronicling the history of school finance in the United States focused on the long-standing battles for school funding equalization in Texas. Today, the funding system is attempting to remain stable after a twenty-year state court battle, and no immediate end to the conflict is in sight. For three decades, a group of school funding reform advocates has led the battle for equalization in Texas, among them the author of this chapter.

The major obstacles to school funding reform encountered by community-based advocates have changed over time. They have included:

- the lack of general public awareness of the extent and effects of school funding inequalities;
- lack of access to data on school interest funding;
- myths and misconceptions relating to the causes of school funding inequality;
- limited expertise on the workings of the Texas funding system;
- perception of school finance as an issue that primarily affects minor-

ity (Mexican-American) communities rather than communities throughout Texas;

- resistance to change by entrenched proponents of the status quo;
- myths and misconceptions regarding possible solutions to the unequal status quo;
- ambivalence or reluctance toward supporting public school funding reform among many education interest groups;
- difficulties in accessing, compiling, and analyzing school funding data;
- competition for public policy priority with other educational issues and noneducation issues;
- gross misconceptions regarding perceived benefits derived from the unequal status quo;
- policy makers' insistence on phasing in reform over many years;
- holding funding reform hostage to demands for prompt improvement in school achievement;
- mixed messages contained in the Texas Supreme Court's rulings; and
- fatigue and disillusionment in the courts and among finance reform proponents.

This chapter chronicles and examines these obstacles, approaching the task in a decade-by-decade analysis that begins in the late 1960s and takes us to 1994. Although each era is treated as a discrete period, it is important to recognize that, as in all histories, there are no clear lines of demarcation; each era and its prevailing conditions melds into the subsequent period, and many obstacles have persisted over time.

The chapter closes with a presentation of the various strategies used by reform proponents in Texas and a discussion of the strengths and limitations associated with these approaches. Although the Texas experience is far from exemplary, the length of the struggle and the variety of issues that have surfaced in the bitterly contested battles that have raged around school funding reform may serve to inform other advocates engaged in similar efforts around the country.

THE GENESIS OF SCHOOL FUNDING REFORM
IN TEXAS: A PERVASIVE LACK OF AWARENESS

Texas has long been at the forefront of the national struggle to achieve greater funding equity in state public schools. The effort began with a lawsuit (*Edge-*

wood v. Kirby) filed by a sheet metal worker in San Antonio, Demetrio Rodríguez, a resident of the Edgewood Independent School District. Edgewood was then the poorest school district in Texas, measured in terms of the amount of taxable property available to support the education of local students. In that early effort, the plaintiffs originally sought to force the adjacent, "more affluent" San Antonio Independent School District (ISD) to share its wealth with the relatively poor Edgewood school system. The fact that the suit named the San Antonio ISD, itself a property-poor school district compared with other systems in the state, reflected the lack of awareness of the cause of school funding inequalities among the overwhelming majority of people in Texas. According to Jose A. Cárdenas, who was serving as superintendent of schools when the original *Rodríguez* suit was brought, attorneys for Rodríguez came to recognize that the answer to funding equalization did not lie in the forced sharing of resources among adjacent property-poor school districts but in shifting the focus to the state's role in creating and supporting the gross inequalities of the Texas funding system.

During the early days of school funding reform, one of the prevailing problems was the lack of information, especially detailed data on existing property wealth, revenues, and expenditures in Texas public school districts. So unavailable was data that the board of trustees of the Harlandale ISD—located in the same city and county as Edgewood—voted to contribute funding to the opponents of the *Edgewood* case out of concern that if Edgewood won, more affluent districts would be forced to share their resources with poor districts such as Edgewood. Ironically, in a wealth-order ranking of more than twelve hundred Texas school districts, Harlandale was later found to rank seventh from the bottom in terms of wealth per pupil and thus stood to benefit tremendously from the *Edgewood*-initiated challenge. This general lack of awareness concerning the Texas school finance system was partly due to lack of information and of access to information on funding at the state and the local level.

According to interviews conducted by the author with state legislators involved with public education in the 1950s and even as late as the early 1960s, state education funding policy was controlled by a handful of state legislators and special-interest groups who were relatively well-versed in state education funding formulas. During this period, information on state public school finance was not widely sought, and access to the data was tightly limited by staff of the central education agency and a handful of policy makers who controlled the funding formula process. Data and data access were so limited that the famous *Rodríguez* challenge was built on only a sampling of local school districts in the state, a factor that ultimately affected the strength and credibility of the case presented by the *Rodríguez* plaintiffs in federal court (Cárdenas, 1997).

School finance reform in Texas was initiated by a handful of educators and community activists in the early 1970s and eventually included active participation by a broad cross-section of players ranging from the governor and Ross Perot to grassroots community organizations throughout Texas. Although a number of groups eventually entered the fray, a handful of organizations formed the core of the Texas school finance reform movement throughout its twenty-year run. These equity advocates, listed in order of their entry into the battle, included

- Texas for Educational Excellence, which after three years reincorporated as the Intercultural Development Research Association (IDRA), a nonprofit research, training, and technical assistance group formed by Jose A. Cárdenas
- The Equity Center, an association spun off by IDRA and composed of representatives from the state's property-poor school districts.
- The Mexican American Legal Defense and Education Fund (MALDEF), a litigation group specializing in minority-focused cases.

Other notable groups and individuals participated over the course of the campaign. Organizations that took part in a more limited way, or for part of the process, included the Texas League of Women Voters and the Industrial Areas Foundation Network, a "Saul Alinsky–oriented" grassroots community advocacy network with chapters in major population centers in Texas.

LIMITED EXPERTISE CONCERNING THE WORKINGS OF THE TEXAS FUNDING SYSTEM

When equity proponents requested data from the state agencies involved in calculating state aid requirements, they joined a small pool of experts who possessed the capacity to tabulate and analyze what had been considered "privileged" information. Accessing key data proved to be a critical first step in future battles to reform the Texas system.

The filing of *Rodríguez* and the court battles and media coverage that followed raised public awareness about the extent of school funding inequity in the Texas system (Walker, 1977). But although this initial battle enlarged the circle of state school finance experts to include advocates of funding reform, the number of persons familiar with the working of the system continued to be limited to a handful of people. This in turn contributed to a general misunderstanding of the underlying causes of state funding inequalities.

In a school finance reform project jointly funded by the Ford and Carnegie Foundations from the mid-1970s through the early 1980s, the author had an opportunity to work with a wide cross-section of educational administrators, teachers, community organizations, and state legislators on the issue. Interactions with the various parties confirmed the author's suspicion that the lack of understanding of the finance system also affected educators—whom the system impacted directly—and state legislators who voted on the state funding formulas that drove the system. In session after session convened throughout the state, and in extensive interactions with the leadership of the education interest groups that followed the school funding debates, these groups showed little knowledge of the state funding system. Ignorance about the role of unequal property wealth, compounded by the absence of effective state finance mechanisms to offset tax-based disparities, constituted a great obstacle to the creation of a community-based movement to reform the system. With local educators and most community members uninformed or misinformed, the unequal status quo was not difficult to maintain. In an analysis of the Texas funding system following the 1973 *Rodríguez* decision, Morgan (1975) observed, "The Texas tradition regarding elementary and secondary education finance has been one of apathy bordering on non-cognizance. Before *Rodríguez*, only a handful of people in the entire State had understood the finance system. . . . But because of the publicity surrounding *Rodríguez*, the level of consciousness of the body politic has been raised appreciably; even in the legislative sessions of 1973, there was a general awareness, at long last, of the financing system's severe deficiencies." Despite increased understanding of the existence of funding inequities among some state political leaders and some members of the educational community and the general public, the overwhelming majority of Texans had no inkling of the causes of the great spending disparities found in Texas public schools. Even those aware of disparities were often guilty of gross misconceptions about the causes of the problem.

MISCONCEPTIONS REGARDING THE CAUSES OF FUNDING INEQUALITIES

One of the prevailing misconceptions during the early school finance reform battles was the notion that property-poor districts had lower revenues than more affluent communities because they made less of a tax effort. Since the lower tax effort of property-poor schools was assumed to be the cause of lower revenue levels, people thought they had only themselves to blame for their problems. Lacking contradictory evidence, the general public and state legislators could thus lay the blame for existing revenue inequalities on those communities, absolving themselves and the state of responsibility. A key component of presentations on the funding inequality issue was a discussion about what Cárdenas and others called the great "Texas tax paradox." Reformers provided examples in which property-poor districts were taxed at higher levels but, due to their limited tax bases, generated significantly lower revenues per pupil than their wealthier counterparts (who were taxed at below-average rates yet generated thousands more dollars for their local education programs). Public awareness sessions, coupled with more focused training of selected state legislators on the school funding system, set the stage for some of the ensuing legislative battles that addressed these inequalities.

New computer technology improved access to data on the Texas public school funding system throughout the late 1970s and 1980s. With better data and growing awareness among a broad cross-section of educators, community leaders, and legislators about the cause of the problem and prospective solutions, the stage was set for the next phase of the Texas campaign for funding equalization.

In conversations with Texas funding reform pioneers (Jose Cárdenas, former state senator Joe Bernal, and state representatives Matt Garcia and Carlos Truan, among others) it was commonly noted that in the early phases of the Texas funding reform campaign, reformers generally assumed that once people became aware of funding inequities and understood their causes a great groundswell of support for equalization would arise. These somewhat naive assumptions were quickly replaced with a growing recognition that there was a deep-seated resistance to change, particularly among state interests that benefited from the status quo. These included not only educators working in high-wealth districts but also large property owners and other members of the state's educational and political power structure.

Early victories at the federal district and appeals courts created momentum for reforming the state funding system as state and national attention was focused on the gross inequities created by the existing system. With the U.S. Supreme Court ruling that education funding equity was not within the purview of the federal court system, the momentum for reform slowed, not only in Texas but all over the country. Despite the Supreme Court ruling in the *Rodríguez* case, its observations that the Texas system was chaotic and unjust—

although not unconstitutional—helped to spur the first wave of state education reforms since the adoption of the Gilmer Aiken laws of 1949.

EARLY SCHOOL FUNDING REFORM INITIATIVES
IN TEXAS

The initial changes to the state funding system were integrated into House Bill 1126, which passed in the 1975 Texas legislative session. Spurred by the federal court litigation, the 1975 reforms included not only the creation of equalization aid funding but also a general increase in overall state funding of public schools, as well as the creation and funding of programs serving special student populations. This early legislation proved to be the forerunner of a pattern in which "equalization" funding came to compete with many other state education funding priorities for revenue earmarked for education-related programs. Perceived as a simple problem requiring increases in state funding rather than systemic change, equalization came to be considered by educators and legislators as competing with increases in funding for general education, teacher salaries, special programs funding, and similar educational needs identified in the state.

In the mid-1970s, Texas benefited from rising oil prices fed by unstable political conditions in the Middle East. This resulted in biennial budget surpluses totaling billions of dollars. Although state revenues had the potential to ease the pain of equalizing district revenues, a deep-seated resistance to significant structural changes meant that only small, insignificant changes were made to the funding system. This compounded the impression that the problem of equalizing revenues could be addressed simply by increasing state funding and that equalization was just one issue competing for the surplus revenue. Because educators were also concerned with many issues besides funding equalization, little progress was made toward equalizing the state funding system in the late 1970s.

During the state budget surplus era, Texans also displayed a growing disenchantment with the property tax system. Political pressure created by tax-reduction proponents (spawned in California, reflected in the infamous Proposition 13, and exported to states around the country) led to the eventual decrease in state-mandated local tax requirements, under the guise of "local property tax relief." In a report analyzing major issues confronting Texas lawmakers in the 1977 legislative session, the House Study Group (1976) noted, "This report discusses the major school finance issue of 1977—whether to proceed with the equalization movement or to make property tax relief the new priority." Although it benefited individual taxpayers, this movement provided the greatest tax relief to the state's wealthiest school districts, which the system had required to assume the greatest proportion of local education costs. Justified by recommendations that emerged from the Special House Committee on Alternatives to Public School Financing, the legislature proposed the inclusion of "property tax relief" in a school finance package. The fact that granting local property tax reductions in the form recommended by the committee would create more inequity did not deter the legislature from following what was perceived as a politically popular course, even as the Texas Research League warned that "any reduction in the local share reverses the equalization process, gives most additional State aid to rich school districts and threatens another serious legal challenge to the system." Despite this dire warning, the legislature adopted House Bill 750, which provided property tax relief in inverse proportion to district property wealth. This local share reduction (which led to increases in state funding for wealthy schools) neutralized the impact of increases in state equalization funding provided in the same legislation.

Another factor influencing Texas's reluctance to radically restructure the system was the contention by the state's wealthiest school districts that their high revenue levels enabled them to pioneer the development of innovative, cutting-edge educational strategies that could then be shared with their poorer counterparts. This educational "trickle-down" argument was often presented in legislative committee hearings to justify the continued disparities in the Texas system. This created a need to conduct research to confirm or invalidate such claims and served to divert public attention from the negative effects of funding inequality. Although the validity of the educational trickle-down argument was eventually challenged, it did succeed in providing justification for delaying action and postponing public commitment on significantly reforming the system.

Another obstacle to funding reform was the state's tendency to adopt funding reforms while at the same time providing for "hold-harmless" clauses that effectively neutralized the impact of legislated changes on wealthy school districts. Examples of hold-harmless clauses included guarantees that no district would receive less state funding than received in previous years or clauses that limited increases in local share requirements among the state's wealthier systems even as local share requirements were raised for most school districts. The integration of such clauses put Texas in the position of maintaining gross inequalities in educational funding despite significant increases in the overall level of state funding for education.

The potential for significant and relatively painless reform in Texas disappeared with the oil bust that followed the boom of the 1970s. Faced with severe revenue shortfalls, the state greatly slowed down funding increases for education. Funding reform efforts also slowed to a crawl in the face of resistance to equalization reform, which was often perceived as requiring revenue reallocation from high-wealth to low-wealth districts or significant increases in state taxes.

THE 1980S BARRIERS

Significant movement in Texas education reform did not reoccur until equity proponents, frustrated by six years of stagnation on the equalization issue, filed suit in state court challenging the constitutionality of the current funding plan and until Texas witnessed the emergence of a grassroots movement in support of statewide funding equalization. These developments, coupled with the governor's campaign promise to increase teacher salaries and to address the long-standing funding equalization issue, created pressure to address education funding in the 1983 session of the Texas legislature. Yet despite gubernatorial pressure to address the teacher salary issue, and grass-roots pressure for reform, Texas legislators resisted. Their reluctance was caused by three factors: (1) the recognition that increased salaries or equalization would have to be coupled with support for a tax increase to provide the additional state funding required; (2) growing skepticism that limited additional state funding for education in itself would resolve the long-standing equity issue; and (3) a growing belief that merely providing more money would not significantly improve the quality of public school programs. Faced with legislative resistance reinforced by the private sector's reluctance to support tax increases to finance education, the governor turned to Ross Perot, a business magnate and political ally, for assistance.

No committee since the historic Gilmer Aiken Committee of the 1940s has had a more significant impact on Texas education than the 1984 Perot Commission. Intended as a vehicle to garner private-sector and public support for increased education (particularly teacher salary) funding, the group, under the prodding of its chairperson, Ross Perot, undertook a review of the entire Texas education system. Literally taking over the committee, Perot challenged every sacred cow in Texas education, from eligibility for participation in football and other co-curricular activities to the number of days pupils could be exempted from class to participate in school-sanctioned livestock shows. As the Perot

Committee conducted its work, the IAF Coalition, led by the San Antonio–based advocacy group Citizens Organized for Public Services (COPS), mounted a statewide grassroots campaign urging the political leadership to drastically alter the state education finance system. Under his aggressive leadership, Perot's committee increased student testing requirements, initiated teacher testing, created a teacher career ladder based on merit and supervisor's ratings, reshaped the school accountability system to include more stringent sanctions for nonperformance by students, and—almost as an afterthought—recommended some major changes in the formulas used to finance the state's public schools. What started as a strategy to increase state support for teacher salary funding turned into a runaway reform wagon that eventually caused that governor's subsequent electoral defeat (Cortez, 1987)

Although the Perot committee's work eventually led to a trade-off involving greater "accountability" in return for increased education funding levels, observers noted that the committee did support some major changes in funding formulas. These reforms, passed in House Bill 72, the 1984 Texas Education Reform Package, included (1) the abandonment of an archaic funding mechanism based on personnel units that rewarded districts on the basis of the professional credentials and experience of staff; (2) the adoption of a pupil-based method of funding; (3) the integration of a "guaranteed yield" approach tied to local tax effort for enrichment equalization; (4) the use of "weighted pupil" funding formulas for special population (bilingual, compensatory, and gifted and talented) programs; and (5) other refinements to state financing mechanisms, including the creation of provisions for determining accountable costs of education (Cortez, 1987). Although it had the potential to reduce somewhat the inequalities that had plagued the Texas system for so long, the new system was significantly weakened by the legislature's subsequent refusal to appropriate the level of state funding needed to fully implement the plan.

Choosing to give the legislature the opportunity to respond to the filing of the legal challenge in state court, and subsequently disappointed by the legislature's waning commitment to equalizing funding, reform advocates decided to proceed with their initial legal challenge in the state court system, *Edgewood v. Kirby* (*Edgewood I*).

The *Edgewood I* decision to proceed with the state court challenge was supported by the removal of two important barriers to reform. The first was a change of justices in the state's elected supreme court and an assessment that the new court would support the equalizing of education funding; the second was expanded access to state and local education funding data, which made it much easier for reform proponents to analyze and present data on funding disparities. A third factor was a much greater public awareness of the extent and causes of funding inequity. This combination of expanded technological capacity, greater technical expertise and public awareness of the problem, a more favorable judicial climate, and growing public impatience for the development of a solution set the stage for the first legal challenge to the funding plan in the Texas court system.

The suit was brought by a coalition of thirteen low-wealth school districts, led by the Edgewood district in San Antonio. It included the original parent plaintiff in *Rodríguez v. San Antonio*. The plaintiffs charged that the state funding plan violated several state constitutional provisions. Following months of expert testimony, which included conflicting presentations of the status of funding equity by state witnesses—and experts supporting the plaintiff district—a state district court found for the plaintiffs and ruled that the Texas school funding system created significant and unconstitutional disparities in access to equitable educational revenues available for students in property-poor and property-rich school districts. Although reversed at the appellate level, the *Edgewood I* decision was ultimately upheld in December 1990 by the Texas Supreme Court, in a historic 9 to 0 decision. The court gave the Texas legislature until September 1, 1991, to develop a constitutional funding plan. This initial decision led to the formation of several reform plans that were adopted and subsequently overturned in a series of Texas Supreme Court rulings.

THE *EDGEWOOD II–IV* ERA: SECOND-GUESSING
THE STATE SUPREME COURT

Following the initial Texas Supreme Court ruling in *Edgewood I,* the Texas legislature adopted Senate Bill 1, which increased state equalization funding but offered little in the way of structural reform. In that plan, the politicians sought to appease the court with study committees that would eventually submit recommendations for funding levels and proposed formula changes. Unhappy with what were perceived as minimal changes to a fundamentally flawed system, equalization advocates challenged Senate Bill 1.

After several weeks of testimony highlighted by the presentation of data on inequities still permitted by the "reformed system," the district court declared that the new state funding plan violated the Texas Constitution. On appeal by the state, the state supreme court upheld the district court ruling on a 9–0 vote. In the more strongly worded *Edgewood II* opinion, the court noted that band-aids to the existing system would not suffice and that substantive structural reform was needed.

In 1993, the Texas legislature passed Senate Bill 351, a plan backed by major supporters of state funding equalization. A central feature of the plan was the creation of county education districts (CEDs), which would force tax-base sharing among the state's property-poor and property-rich school districts. Though it created substantial tax-base equity, the plan was challenged by the state's wealthy school systems, which took the offensive and launched their own legal challenge to the 1993 CED-based system.

Although equalization advocates supported the 1993 plan, Senate Bill 351 was eventually struck down by the Texas Supreme Court, not because of its impact on equity but on a technical point related to the governance of the new CEDs created by the plan and the lack of an election by local voters to approve the "sharing" of tax revenues across school district lines. Stung by what was perceived as a partial retreat from earlier court mandates, the Texas legislature once again struggled with the task of creating a school finance plan that would pass state constitutional muster.

The second successive rejection of a reform plan (a plan that even equalization proponents supported) led to increasing legislative resentment of court activism on the issue and consideration of options that would remove the courts from jurisdiction over school finance equalization. Tired of taking the initiative only to have its actions rejected by the courts, the legislature opted to address the constitutional flaws in the latest plan by authorizing a statewide election to seek voter approval of a constitutional amendment that would legitimize the CED-based system.

Actively opposed by wealthy school systems and some major taxpayers residing in wealthy school districts, who financed a major media campaign against the reform measures, the constitutional amendment ultimately failed. This once again left the reform issue squarely in the lap of the state legislature.

THE 1993 REFORM PROPOSAL

In an attempt to address the court's latest objections, the Texas legislature adopted Senate Bill 7, a plan that required wealthy districts to "voluntarily" share resources with less affluent districts or be subjected to involuntary state-mandated reallocation of taxable property or forced consolidation. This plan was opposed by both rich and poor school systems, with one side feeling that the plan went too far and the other that it did not go far enough. In December

1993, the district court upheld the plan in part but ruled that the legislature had still failed to provide sufficient mechanisms to equalize funding for school facilities. This ruling was reviewed by the Texas Supreme Court. Oral arguments were presented in May 1994, and the court issued a ruling upholding the 1993 funding plan in the winter of 1994.

Throughout the twenty-year battle to reform the Texas funding system, IDRA, the Equity Center (an association of property-poor school districts), the Mexican American Legal Defense and Education Fund (MALDEF), and key representatives from property- poor schools formed the core strategy group that led and coordinated funding equity activities in Texas. Advocates have used a variety of strategies to promote and sustain the equalization campaign in the state. Multifaceted and varying over time, these strategies have included public education efforts, support for school district and community organization advocacy, alignment and coordination of reform efforts, and the use of litigation as a means to spur reform.

One of the original strategies developed and maintained throughout the campaign was the use of public education to raise the level of awareness of funding disparities created by the state system. Target audiences included a cross-section of groups affected by the issue, specifically educators (particularly teachers and administrators working in these systems), community-based organizations whose children are affected, taxpayer groups affected by the tax and revenue disparities associated with inequitable funding systems, and public policy makers and their staffs, who ultimately must vote for the reforms. Over the years, strategies included the convening of conferences, symposia, meetings, discussion groups, and other informal gatherings in order to provide information and develop networks of proponents of school reform.

These training efforts were complemented by development of informational and educational materials designed to explain the problems in the state funding system and possible alternatives. Over time, organizations have developed "primers" on school funding (some now in their fourth edition), an array of informational research papers, and other documents designed to inform various audiences about relevant developments and the current status of the issue.

Although their success has varied, these public-education efforts collectively play a crucial role in raising general levels of public concern and in developing a statewide consensus that funding equalization is a continuing problem that needs to be addressed.

Because it was fruitless to depend on existing education power brokers to conduct research on equalization, equity advocates began to conduct and disseminate their own focused, independent research. Early experiences with state education researchers, who are often beholden to the political power structure for their own funding, also revealed the need for independent analyses of school funding data. The ability of advocates to conduct their own analyses of data and to issue reports, papers, and articles reflecting their point of view was central to the struggle to keep the issue before the public and the legislature. Independent research was particularly important because legislative debates often centered around data on the extent of the disparities permitted by the existing funding system. Conducting this research required the development of extensive expertise on the working of school funding systems and the array of available options, access to latest available school-district-finance-related data, and access to technology required for data tabulation and analysis.

A key feature of the Texas reform strategy has been the orchestration of advocacy in support of substantive school funding reform. The equity coalition in Texas has benefited from participation of a variety of sectors in school funding reform. These efforts have included integrating the community-based Texas Industrial Areas Foundation Network into the school funding reform effort, supporting the formation of the Equity Center—a school district-membership equity reform organization—and educating and selectively involving certain private-sector representatives.

Although members of the equity coalition agree on matters of general principle, it has been a continuous challenge to achieve consensus on major issues and maintain open channels of communication, particularly at key points in the policymaking or litigation process. Operating informally and using collaborative approaches, the equity coalition has remained a loose-knit group characterized by varying levels of participation by different members. The level of involvement has been affected by resources, extent of concern, leadership agendas, and the different contributions made, ranging from legal expertise to grassroots demonstrations of concern about the equalization issue.

School finance reform in Texas was the product of a well- orchestrated and sustained campaign conducted by a loose-knit coalition of organizations committed to changing the public school funding system. Different members of this coalition played different roles, each capitalizing on the relative strengths it brought to the struggle. Texans for Educational Excellence (later reorganized as IDRA) was involved in much of the research on the extent of the school funding problem, in organizing and disseminating information on the issues, and in educating the general public and state policy makers. The Equity Center eventually assumed some of the ongoing research and further organized and expanded internal pressure for reform from low-wealth school districts.

Together, MALDEF and IDRA initiated the legal challenges to the system and played the key role in the court hearings that eventually forced the legislature to implement significant changes in the state funding scheme. They also teamed up to monitor state legislative activities related to the finance reform issue, providing guidance and feedback to the legislative process and providing expert testimony on plans purporting to address the funding issues.

Other community-based organizations such as the League of Women Voters and the IAF network provided important links to voters and constituencies that were affected by the state's public school funding schemes. These public interest representatives raised the threat of public accountability for state policy makers and thus created pressure for the legislature to consider alternatives to the status quo.

Together, these disparate groups helped change Texas public education. The battles over Texas school funding reform are legendary, spanning more than twenty years and spawning an array of similar court challenges in states throughout the country. During its tumultuous history, Texas funding reform has encountered different obstacles. Reactions have varied from general receptiveness to outright hostility to challenging the status quo and from inadequate state responses to the problem to substantive systemic reform.

LESSONS LEARNED

Prolonged involvement with the school reform network and discussions with equity proponents indicate that continuity and long-term participation are crucial for maintaining momentum and a grounded understanding of the history of the issue. Given the extensive turnover among the various individuals and, to a lesser extent, organizations that have participated in the equalization battles in Texas, it is critical to maintain a core organization or group of individuals over the course of a reform effort. Any significant discontinuity in reform advocacy disrupts momentum and sustained public focus, both considered crucial to successful funding reform.

LITIGATION

A key element in the Texas equalization strategy was the monitoring and periodic assessment of litigation prospects in the state, along with the willingness to use litigation as one strategy for moving the equalization agenda forward. It is important to note that litigation, although a key for achieving or recovering momentum for funding reform, was only one part of a multifaceted strategy. The litigation effort itself included identifying prospective litigation-oriented groups to take the lead in legal matters, educating the legal experts on the workings of the Texas funding system, collaboratively analyzing the legal strategies employed in the challenge, and collecting the required data.

As the litigation strategy was implemented, it became crucial to align it with subsequent policy reform efforts to insure consensus on priorities and to agree on criteria for assessing the adequacy of state responses to the legal challenges posed. A related and critical need was the development of a financial resource base to help support the litigation effort in the interim, as well as in the event that court costs were not awarded to the plaintiffs' attorneys. In this area, the involvement of MALDEF, a public interest law group partially subsidized by legal fund contributions from plaintiff school districts, was important in the series of Edgewood challenges.

Taken collectively, long-term involvement, focused research, the organization and orchestration of equalization advocacy, and the use of litigation to spur legislative action have proved effective in moving a recalcitrant and conservative state down the road of funding reform. The fact that after a quarter-century Texas has still not arrived attests to the extent of resistance among those who would maintain the unequal status quo.

Experience in Texas over the years has taught the need for equalization advocates to remain vigilant against weakening resolve and subtle revisions that dilute previous gains or that restore advantages to one group over others. As in other struggles, such as those against forced segregation or to win the right to vote, activists must be constantly alert. Perseverance in pursuing the reform agenda and a dogged, unwavering commitment to the concept of equalization were critical elements in the Texas reform effort. Although coalition-building and collaboration with other key groups was an important part of the overall effort, participants were always careful to ensure that other priorities and agendas were kept separate from the equity issue. One potential distraction was the emergence of concerns over efficiency, adequacy, and accountability, which inevitably become a subset of the equalization discussion. Augenblick et al. (1990) have noted that, "in the next few years, schools' finance activity in the states is likely to grow as the litigation focuses both on inequities across school districts in particular states, and [on] the lack of sufficient funds to provide high quality education services. The tension between adequacy, equity and efficiency will continue to complicate the finance issue." In Texas, reformers have focused on equity, arguing that conversations about what is adequate or efficient can only be held by parties sharing a common reality with a similar commitment to solving problems. The ultimate lesson learned in Texas is that substantive reform of school finance is a long, hard struggle, yet one that is well worth it to those committed to making sure that concepts such as equity and equal opportunity are not words written in legal documents but realities that children in Edgewood can share with the children of Highland Park and similar children throughout our country. To accept less than equity for any one child is to accept inequality for all children.

REFERENCES

Augenblick, J., and K. Adams. 1979. *An Analysis of the Impact of Changes in the Funding of Elementary/Secondary Education in Texas: 1974/75 to 1977/78.* Denver: Education Finance Center.

Augenblick, J., and K. McGuire. 1990. *Education Finance in the 1990s.* Denver: Education Commission of the United States.

Cárdenas, J. A. 1973. The New Crisis in School Finance. *Texans for Educational Equity Newsletter* 1 (September):3–5.

———. 1974. Review of School Finance Litigation. *Texans for Educational Equity Newsletter* 2 (February):3, 6.

———. 1975a. Elements of Equitable School Financing. *IDRA Newsletter* (February):1–4.

———. 1975b. New School Finance Law Reviewed. *IDRA Newsletter* (June):1–5.

———. 1976. Texas School Finance: Past, Present, and Future. *IDRA Newsletter* (September):1, 4–6.

———. 1982. The State of the State. *IDRA Newsletter* (January):1.

———. 1984. Educational Reform and Dysfunctional Responses. *IDRA Newsletter* (April):1, 6, 8.

———. 1987. Remedies for Finance Equity. *IDRA Newsletter* (May):6–12.

———. 1988. Is School Consolidation the Solution to Achieving School Finance Equity? *IDRA Newsletter* (February):1–4.

———. 1990a. Tax Base Sharing: An Affordable Approach to Equalization. *IDRA Newsletter* (January).

———. 1990b. Unequalized, Unconstitutional. *IDRA Newsletter* (February):1–3.

Cortez, A. 1976. Inequities in School Facilities. *IDRA Newsletter* (December):1–3.

———. 1977a. CSHB 750 Maintains Status Quo Among Rich and Poor Districts. *IDRA Newsletter* (May):7.

———. 1977b. Equity Versus Tax Relief Causes Legislative Deadlock. *IDRA Newsletter* (June):2, 5–6.

————. 1977c. Senate Bill 1 Revises Distribution of State Aid. *IDRA Newsletter* (August):2–3, 5.

————. 1978a. Educational Spending: A Look at Texas and Other States. *IDRA Newsletter* (May):7–8.

————. 1978b. Major School Finance Issues to Be Debated in 1979 Session. *IDRA Newsletter* (February):1, 7.

————. 1979a. Education Studies Completed. *IDRA Newsletter* (February):1–3.

————. 1979b. Senate Bill 350 Continues School Finance Reform. *IDRA Newsletter* (June):5–6.

————. 1980. The Rise and Fall of Bilingual Education Funding in Texas. *IDRA Newsletter* (February):4–6.

————. 1981. School Finance Reform in Texas: Major Issues in the 1981 Legislative Session. *IDRA Newsletter* (January):1, 7.

————. 1982. Texas School Finance: Prospects for the 1983 Session. *IDRA Newsletter* (December):1–2.

————. 1983. Edgewood ISD Considers Litigation. *IDRA Newsletter* (June):6.

————. 1983a. School Finance Equity: The Challenge and the Chance Revived. *IDRA Newsletter* (January):1–2, 8.

————. 1983b. Texas Legislature Deadlocks on School Finance Legislation. *IDRA Newsletter* (June):3, 6.

————. 1984a. Constitutionality of Texas School Finance System Challenged. *IDRA Newsletter* (June):1, 9.

————. 1984a. School Finance Reform Advocates Present Testimony Before Governor's Select Committee. *IDRA Newsletter* (February):6, 8.

————. 1987. Texas System of Financing Schools Ruled Unconstitutional. *IDRA Newsletter* (May):1–2.

————. 1988. School Finance Alternatives Explored. *IDRA Newsletter* (October):1–3.

————. 1989. Seventy-first Texas Legislature Adopts School Funding Plan. *IDRA Newsletter* (June):9–10.

————. 1990a. District Court Rules Senate Bill 1 Unconstitutional. *IDRA Newsletter* (October):4–8.

————. 1990b. More Money, Little Change: Senate Bill 1: The 1990 Education Finance and Reform Bill. *IDRA Newsletter* (August):1–4.

————. 1991a. Texas Legislature Adopts School Funding Plan. *IDRA Newsletter* (May):1–5.

————. 1991b. Wealthy Districts File Challenge to Constitutionality of Senate Bill 351. *IDRA Newsletter* (June):5.

————. 1992. Supreme Court Overturns New Texas Plan. *IDRA Newsletter* (March):1–4.

————. 1997. *Texas School Finance Reform: An IDRA Perspective.* San Antonio, Tex.: Intercultural Development Research Association.

Cox, J. 1977. Review of School Finance Bills. *IDRA Newsletter* (March):1, 12–15.

Edgewood I.S.D. et al. v. Kirby et al., Case No. 362,516, 250th District Court, Austin, Travis County, Tex., Aug. 27, 1987.

House Study Group. 1977. *The School Finance Dilemma.* Special report. Austin: House Study Group.

Intercultural Development Research Association. 1980. IDRA Study to Address School Construction Needs. *IDRA Newsletter* (July):1–2.

———. 1975. Three Restrictions Make Equalization Aid a Disappointment. *IDRA Newsletter* (December):1–2.

———. 1976. Update on School Finance Reform Litigation. *IDRA Newsletter* (April):7–8.

———. 1982. Statewide School Finance Cases: 1982 Update. *IDRA Newsletter* (November):4–6.

Kelly, J. A. 1992. Making Things Happen. *IDRA Newsletter* (October):1–2, 6–7.

Martínez, J. H. 1975. Impact of House Bill 1126. *IDRA Newsletter* (October):7.

McGrew, J. W., et al. 1972. *Public School Finance Problems in Texas*. Austin, Tex.: Texas Research League.

Morgan, D. C. 1975. School Finance Reform in Texas: A Brief History and an Evaluation of Present Conditions. Working brief, University of Texas, Austin.

Policy Information Center. 1991. *The State of Inequality*. Princeton, N.J.: Educational Testing Service.

Rips, G. 1983. COPS Comes to Austin. *Texas Observer,* 14 January, at 1, 10–14.

Robledo, M. R. 1978. Analyzing Cost Elements of Bilingual Education. *IDRA Newsletter* (February):1, 7.

Texas Chamber of Commerce. 1990. Crisis in Texas School Funding: The Pieces of the Puzzle. Conference work materials, Austin, Tex.

Walker, B. D. 1977. A Comparison of Six Alternative Models for Equalization of Educational Expenditures in the Texas Public Schools. Ph.D. diss., Texas Tech University.

Weiberg, M. 1984. School Finance Reform and Educational Equity. *IDRA Newsletter* (March):1–2, 4, 8.

Chapter 12 The Prichard Committee and Kentucky School Reform

Robert F. Sexton

"Reform won't work unless it has legs" is organizer Anne Hallett's succinct metaphor for the value of citizens in school reform. Those legs, I explain here, must carry reform from public frustration to legislation, and then from legislation to the classroom. They must step across political transitions and election cycles, be prepared for a long march rather than a sprint, and scurry around keeping troops informed and focused.[1]

The organization I represent, the Prichard Committee for Academic Excellence, is one example of mobilized citizens being the legs for reform. In this chapter I talk about our strategies for encouraging reform and the challenges inherent in promoting comprehensive reform, and I conclude with a few observations about conditions that can make independent reform organizations more successful.

BACKGROUND

Our volunteer citizen and parent voice was born in earnest in 1983 when we became an independent, privately funded organization after two years as a state-appointed body. We had about sixty volunteer members and two staff persons from 1983 to 1990. We now have one hundred members, scores of active citizen volunteers, eighty-five local Community Committees for Education involving about one thousand people, and a much larger network of several thousand people. It's most useful to see the Prichard Committee more as a collection of volunteer advocates than as a traditional institution. Composed entirely of private citizens and funded by private donors, the Prichard Committee's mission is to promote improved education for all Kentuckians.

In 1984 the committee convened a statewide forum on education. On one November night about twenty thousand Kentuckians showed up in 176 school districts, linked together by Kentucky Educational Television. People talked about their hopes and concerns for their children and their communities: they said they wanted quality schools for their children; they wanted to break the historic cycles in their poorly educated state.

It is widely acknowledged that the forum and the political energy it created helped build the base for the sweeping 1989 Kentucky Supreme Court decision that found the entire school system to be unconstitutional and for the reform legislation that followed. The legislature responded with the comprehensive reform program Kentucky is attempting to implement at this moment. Those sweeping reforms require and measure high academic standards for all children, provide rewards and sanctions for school performance, push decision-making to the school level, control political hiring and nepotism, provide preschool for all four-year-olds, and much more. The tax increase that went with the reform has moved Kentucky toward the funding equity demanded in the initial court test. The gap in per-pupil expenditures between the poorest and the wealthiest districts has been cut by more than half.[2]

We have found that it's one thing to ring the alarm and rally the troops for reform in the abstract, as our organization did prior to 1990; it's another thing entirely to hold those troops together as specific actions in real schools play out where real kids, real teachers, and real parents experience daily the hard work of changing schools so that all children learn at high levels.

Why is this? Reforms such as Kentucky's challenge parental perceptions of what it means to learn and what schools should be. Parents of children who did well in the past do not readily buy the argument that *their* children need to learn more and work harder. Some parents may also believe that their children will get less if schools teach *all* students at high levels.

There was widespread agreement before 1990 that school improvement was needed. But the public did not reach consensus on every specific reform step.

Individual parents and teachers, despite the involvement of their statewide organizations, often felt that they were not consulted. People who study the change process remind us that this usually happens; policy makers have time to think things through before change occurs, but others need time to catch up.

So building grassroots support for reform in Kentucky has had two chapters. The first chapter meant inviting and channeling public, business, and parent frustration. The second chapter requires nurturing and mobilizing that public participation so that it sustains reform as it moves from statute to classroom. Strategies and lessons from those two chapters are the next topics.

BUILDING A MOVEMENT

A simple question I'm often asked—understandable but still surprising to me—needs an answer at the outset. Why, some wonder, did citizen volunteers need to organize themselves and do what they did in the 1980s? To our volunteer members the need to seriously challenge the status quo was apparent.

First, the problems were severe in Kentucky. There was a great deal of evidence that Kentucky's education system was much worse than the nation's. This came at a time when, said *A Nation at Risk,* American schools were in crisis.

Kentucky, meanwhile, was last in the nation in the percentage of adults with high school diplomas and first in adult illiteracy. It was second from last in the percentage of adults attending college and depressingly low on other indicators of educational performance, including spending.

One understandable result of this performance, plus the widespread perception—and reality—of political corruption, was lack of trust in public schools.

Next there was consensus that the school community was not equipped or inclined to solve these problems alone and that it needed encouragement. There was also consensus that community needed new ideas, a different view of the problem, and support when it moved in the right direction. The view was that schools, even if so inclined, couldn't reform themselves.

Third, politicians were reluctant and cautious. Talk about school reform and increased taxes was not popular. There was a stalemate among interest groups. Politicians were inclined toward quick and simple solutions that would not do much for entrenched problems such as Kentucky's.

Fourth, the public and parents were disengaged from public schools, feeling shut out, thinking that the problems were too complex for mere citizens to understand. They thought it was too hard to join in a technical conversation that sounded like gibberish. There was a feeling of hopelessness. "Things have always been this way and they always will," the public was saying.

Fifth and finally, we had a sense that we were engaged in something that went beyond improving schools. We were activist citizens, and, as such, we concluded together that many of the complex and intractable problems the state faced, like others across the nation, were not to be solved by changes in the structures of government or institutions alone. What was needed instead, we surmised, was a reinvestment in the community problem-solving institutions and social organizations that had become so weakened. We recognized that complex problems required communities and groups of individuals to think deeply about solutions and solve their own problems. We Kentucky volunteers were willing to consider new questions, to educate ourselves, to practice the skills of citizenship and encourage others to use those skills, to get people's attention, to take responsibility. We believed that many problems aren't "out there" caused by someone else but that they were our own responsibility.

We did not presume to have all the answers. But we did believe that it is the job of citizen leaders to mobilize other citizens to solve problems. And we volunteered ourselves to mobilize those resources and to force action on the problem of educational mediocrity and worse in Kentucky. When we got people's attention and, when, in 1990, Kentucky passed its comprehensive reform program, we changed our direction and mobilized citizens, parents, and business people to ensure that reform would move successfully from the statute to the classroom.

In the 1980s, we took advantage of the committee's independence to put pressure on the political and educational leadership and help set the policy agenda. We promoted public involvement by holding forums and organizing local grassroots groups. Using a time-consuming process, we formulated our own comprehensive school reform recommendations. The committee hosted forums for gubernatorial candidates and reached local people through hundreds of chicken dinners.

Another priority in the 1980s was to work closely with the media. The committee was a source of objective analysis, story ideas, and straight talk. Although our volunteer membership included much political talent (four former governors, for example), our strength rested in our regular citizen and parent members, many with local or regional credibility. The Prichard Committee staff and officers also kept up aggressive behind-the-scenes negotiations with state officials, urging them to take credit for bold action, on one hand, and providing political cover when they needed it, on the other.

Our independence from government and politics, our credibility, and our reputation for straight talk were our greatest strengths. The core strategy was to create characteristics required for high public impact: believability, sensible recommendations, focused selection of issues, alliances with other groups, and persistence. The public was the audience; the Prichard Committee was not a lobbying group. In effect, the committee became a symbol of citizen concern that energized other equally concerned citizens at the local level.

The result of this effort, from about 1983 through 1990, was to help build a political base for passing the Kentucky Education Reform Act. Although much of that reform was consistent with the Prichard Committee's recommendations, the committee did not write the reform legislation.

SHIFTING GEARS

The second chapter of citizen organizing in Kentucky began with the passage of reform in 1990. On balance, we got what we wanted in the Kentucky Education Reform Act. The immediate challenges for the Prichard Committee were to be persistent but to subtly change directions and to avoid being labeled cheerleaders, thereby losing the credibility we had earned in the 1980s.

Persistence is tough. Volunteers get tired. Funding is hard to find. And now that reform is in place, the toughest work, we've discovered, has just started. We see a situation something like the one in Eastern Europe, described as moving from the "politics of drama to the politics of endurance."

New challenges emerge for citizen reform groups as time passes. These include engaging a constantly changing public more deeply in conversation and helping it learn for itself what it means to be educated today, not yesterday.

A public view is unfolding in response to the new and difficult goal of setting and measuring academic standards. We see public confusion with the language of reform—terms such as *setting high standards, problem solving, continuous learning, authentic assessment.* Parents want more of what they believe they had themselves; what's important for many is memorization and rote learning. Many parents have trouble with talk about "high-order skills" and "critical thinking." Their main concern, says a recent report, is with order, discipline, and teaching the basics. To deal with this, parents need to be engaged in more fruitful conversation with teachers so that teachers can explain what they are doing in the classroom. Parents need direct, clear language and models of good teaching; they need to know what a good school really looks like.

We must also provide a bridge between elections, help policy stay on track, keep things from veering off in the wrong directions. We must counsel patience through work with the media and parents and encourage public comfort with long-term solutions rather than quick fixes. At the same time—and this is very difficult—we must learn from experience and make adjustments as we go along.

And, we have to engage more people, especially parents. This requires helping communities think about shared responsibility for raising children. Children won't reach the higher academic levels we expect without families and communities helping.

All of this is to be done in a highly volatile political atmosphere where terrifying rhetoric, fueled by a national political movement, bombards parents in the so-called culture wars.

An anecdote captures the challenge. In 1993, the state spelling bee, sponsored by the Kentucky Education Association and the Louisville *Courier Journal,* was canceled. In the news accounts, one sponsor incorrectly said that the spelling bee was inconsistent with the Kentucky Education Reform Act because it promoted competition. So the spelling bee, one of the most traditional education symbols, had been canceled, and school reform was "against competition," a core American value. For all who opposed reform the news was worth millions of advertising dollars. The news was understandably unsettling to parents. Combined with misstatements by some teachers who said they "can't teach spelling because of KERA," it confirmed the myth that academic standards had been lowered, when in fact they had been raised.

Politics is a world of symbols and perceptions. The spelling bee fiasco, said a friend, symbolized the gap between what schools used to be and what they need to become. It also symbolized the tendency toward extremes in education: "all past practice is bad" becomes the dogma instead of "use the best of the old and the best of the new."

Now the challenge is different, and our work has shifted to new strategies. First, we need to remind people of the problem reform is designed to solve. Second, as the specific pieces of reform are implemented, reform's constituencies shift. Advocacy for specific reform actions—many of them looking quite different than what parents experienced themselves—isn't the same as advocacy for reform as a general goal. As reforms reach the school level, we're reminded that opinion polls show dissatisfaction with public schools in general but also that "my school's OK." So, for example, the parents of gifted children, those who thought that their children were doing well and "getting into college," are alarmed about what their children might miss if teachers really teach all children.

One of the new challenges, then, is to explain that helping all children learn doesn't mean taking something away from some children, that education doesn't only come in strictly measured doses but is infinitely expandable. Parents are inclined, our research has shown, to believe the opposite: that if their child is doing fine then helping other children learn will diminish their fair share. This view is often confirmed by educators, so fear spreads.

And we have to build understanding that, if schools are to be accountable for high academic performance, then entire communities must take more responsibility for children than they do now. If school councils are to make decisions involving parents and to become more democratic institutions, then communities must learn how to help. Inherent in Kentucky's reform is a central question: Can schools become more democratic if their communities don't become more democratic as well?

But this runs against the grain of the times. Institutions for democratic decision-making are struggling. Confidence in government is low. Voter anger more than apathy runs high. And in this climate Kentucky government is being asked to implement change and solve problems, not just manage things as they exist.

LESSONS

There are several requirements, learned from experience, for creating a public voice that gives reform its legs. The first requirement is to get people's attention and to determine what that attention is for—what's the message? If people give you their attention, they're giving you considerable power. So what's to be said?

We committee members set out to collect our own thoughts as citizens and teachers and make our own statement about Kentucky's educational problems and our own recommendations for solving those problems. That statement took the form of a report published as part of a two-year process in which the committee tried to redefine a negative situation (an almost hopeless situation) as a problem that people could solve.

The committee got people's attention through giving hundreds of speeches on the chicken-dinner circuit, expressing the business community's concern, and encouraging supportive media across the state. It's been said that we— hundreds of volunteers—translated ideas to the public. This may be partly true, but even more we were asking the public to do the work itself.

The Prichard Committee engaged people directly and created a statewide classroom on education reform for the public. Anyone could enter that classroom, and people knew that. We did that with the town forums and gatherings.

The second requirement is to be credible. People must believe that you are sincere; they must give you their trust; they must take you seriously. (Note that to be credible you also have to be independent.)

Deeds, not image, are the source of genuine credibility. By engaging thousands of people through the town forums, we found that it is possible to gain immense good will, and also many good ideas, by asking people what they think and by taking them seriously. We've been listening for years, and we're trying very hard to keep on listening. We also trained local organizers, and our volunteer members became symbols to other local volunteers, long shut out by local political barons. One parent in a remote community said, "You're our hope down here. If you can do it across Kentucky, we can do it here."

Our volunteers also educated themselves. Citizen volunteers studied the issues, read tedious research, listened to experts, and met more than sixty times throughout 1983 and 1984.

In order to be credible, deeds must also show that you are above partisan politics, that there are no hidden political agendas. They must show, for instance, that you are not running for office. Another key is giving credit to others and not to yourself, the opposite of the behavior of a candidate for office and thus a demonstration that you are not a candidate. Given the current atmosphere of distrust, giving credit to others is essential.

And a major piece of the credibility puzzle is to work closely with the media. This means encouraging in-depth coverage of education and the investigation of problems. The press can do a great deal of work that a small organization cannot.

And finally, for credibility, you must be responsive. We try to respond through a toll-free telephone line, through visits in the communities, and through services to individuals who ask for them (seeing that those services are always of high quality).

And that leads to the third requirement, one that is easily skipped: to provide thoughtful, responsible, solid work and ideas that make sense. We have done this with numerous reports, with research on the progress of reform, with comments in the media, and with aggressive outreach to various constituencies. Too many organizations miss their opportunity to lead by only complaining and criticizing; they discredit themselves when they propose no solutions to the problems they identify.

Quality work must also engage the emotions. Our voice, joined by others', created a sense of possibility in a land of hopelessness. (That passion, however, is difficult to maintain over time.)

Fourth, it's critical to select issues and fights strategically. The rule is focus, focus, and stay focused.

For us, focusing means concentrating on how schools can change teaching so that all children can achieve at much higher levels. That's not just rhetoric. It's a radical idea that challenges directly the way schools have been organized and teachers prepared.

Focusing means also that we decline to fight about topics that others love to fight about. We do not, for example, fight about prayer in the schools, about abortion, about condom distribution, or even about how to teach subjects such as reading. We believe that there are many school matters people believe to be very important, and rightfully so. But these subjects don't all have equal power to improve what happens between teachers and students in the classroom; they won't help all children learn at higher levels.

Focus, though, doesn't mean rigidity. Flexibility is key as well. We must respond and adjust as new issues emerge.

Fifth, it is necessary to form creative alliances. We've done this with other education groups, with the business community through the Partnership for Kentucky Schools, and through association with groups such as the Kentucky Youth Advocates, the Kentucky League of Cities, the Kentucky Education Association, and the Kentucky Chamber of Commerce.

The sixth and final requirement is persistence. It is not trite to remember Woody Allen's homily that "95 percent of success is just showing up."

It's critical that reform advocates publicly commit to being there until the job is done. As reforms unfold in states across the nation, "showing up" allows independent advocates to provide coherence in policy and a bridge between one set of officials and another. The idea, writes Susan Fuhrman, is to keep policy from veering off in different directions.[3]

Those in positions of authority, we remind ourselves, will always be there, as the old quote from Tammany Hall's George Washington Pluckett indicates. His lesson to "reformers" (not, in his mind, a complimentary label) was that they "shouldn't be like morning glories, who look lovely in the morning and withered up in a short time, while the regular machines [keep] on flourishin' forever like fine old oaks."

CONCLUSION

School reform, like other democratic involvement, is not for spectators. The Prichard Committee is one among many models for involving citizens, although it may differ from others in its membership, organizing strategy, and choice of issues. It grew from the particular needs of Kentucky as a remedy for the hunger for educational excellence and equity that had been frustrated for so long. It may, by its existence and persistence, even have helped create hope in a people who, like others in their region, were beaten down by historic conditions and educational malnutrition.

NOTES

1. Portions of this chapter are adapted from Robert F. Sexton, *Communicating with the Public About Education Reform* (Washington, D.C.: National Governors' Association, 1994).
2. This chapter does not attempt to explain the Kentucky Education Reform Act or its history in detail. For more detail the reader should consult the following: Ronald Dove, "Acorns in a Mountain Pool," Prichard Committee, 1990; Edward Fiske, *Smart Schools, Smart Kids* (Washington, D.C.: Editorial Projects in Education, 1991); Editors of *Education Week, From Risk to Renewal: Charting a Course for Reform* (Washington, D.C.: Editorial Project in Education, 1993); *A Citizen's Handbook: The Kentucky Education Reform Act* (Frankfort, Ky.: Legislative Research Commission, 1994); *1994 Kentucky School Laws Annotated* (Frankfort: Kentucky Department of Education, 1994).
3. Susan Fuhrman, "Politics and Systemic Education Reform" (report for Consortium for Policy Research in Education, Rutgers, N.J. [1994], 3–4).

Chapter 13 Advocacy to Restructure the Chicago Public Schools Through State Legislation

Donald R. Moore

In December 1988, the Chicago school system was fundamentally restructured through state law by rewriting the section of the Illinois School Code that applies only to Chicago. Stanford political scientist Michael Kirst concluded that "this is the biggest change in American school control since the 1900s. . . . It is the most drastic change in any school system I can think of. It is absolutely precedent-breaking" (Wilkerson, 1989).

A coalition of parent, community, citywide advocacy, and business organizations has played a key leadership role not only in securing the passage of this law but also in pressing for its implementation. This chapter analyzes key events that illustrate *the interplay of political forces* that have had a significant impact on the law's passage and implementation, including *the role of this advocacy coalition*. This analysis covers three time periods: (1) 1983 to 1988, during which the campaign for the Chicago School Reform Act was carried out; (2) 1989 through 1994, during which the initial implementation of the reform act occurred; and (3) 1995, during which a new Republican majority in the Illinois General Assembly made substantial changes in the reform law.

THE CAMPAIGN FOR THE CHICAGO SCHOOL
REFORM ACT: 1983–88

Chicago has the third largest school system in the United States, after those of New York and Los Angeles. In 1993–94, the school system enrolled 409,000 students, of whom 56 percent were African American, 30 percent were Latino, 11 percent were Anglo, and 3 percent were Asian. Education is provided through 550 schools and supported by a $2.9 billion budget.

Prior to the passage of the Chicago School Reform Act in 1988, the system was administered centrally, from a school headquarters that is popularly called "Pershing Road." The system's eleven-member board of education was appointed by the mayor, and the board hired a general superintendent to administer the system. Although the school system was legally separate from city government, the Democratic political machine had always played a major role in the schools. For example, until the election of Mayor Harold Washington in 1983, applicants for the twenty thousand nonteaching jobs in the school system went first to city hall, where the real decisions about whether they would be hired took place (Washington Transition Committee, 1983).

Next to the mayor, the general superintendent and key leaders of the Pershing Road bureaucracy, including their administrative subdistricts, functioned as a second center of power and as a permanent government resistant to the initiatives of reform-minded board of education members and external reform groups.

There had been major civil rights protests in the 1960s about segregation and unequal resources for minority schools, but there was little community activism around the schools as of the early 1980s. During the 1980s, a reform process slowly grew that culminated in the passage of the Chicago School Reform Act in 1988. The history of educational reform during this period has been analyzed in two historical monographs, which tell essentially the same story (O'Connell, 1991; Kyle and Kantowicz, 1992).

Foundations of the Reform Movement

Perhaps the single most important event that laid in the groundwork for Chicago's school reform movement was the election of Harold Washington as mayor of Chicago in 1983 and his success in building a broad-based, multiracial coalition with a strong belief in democratic participation. In his first term, however, Mayor Washington confined himself largely to attempting to improve the school system through his appointments to the board of education.

Two independent advocacy groups that focused on Chicago's schools also helped lay the groundwork for basic reform by aggressively monitoring key aspects of school system performance and repeatedly advancing related reform recommendations in the early 1980s. The Chicago Panel on Public School Policy and Finance (the Chicago Panel) zeroed in on the system's budget, its dropout rates, and the quality of high-school education. Designs for Change (DFC), an educational research and advocacy organization, organized low-income and minority parents in South and West Side schools and analyzed and widely publicized findings on such issues as low reading achievement, high dropout rates, and the school system's substandard programs for children with disabilities.

Designs for Change developed its basic advocacy strategy through a research study of eight experienced advocacy groups that it carried out in the late 1970s for the Carnegie Corporation of New York (Moore et al., 1983a, 1983b). The study recommended that advocates focus attention on restructuring the main-streamed process that mediates between inputs and outcomes (including the family and community) rather than on aiding at-risk students after they had been shunted from the mainstream. Designs for Change's conclusions about effective advocacy strategies have had a major impact on the Chicago school reform campaign from the early 1980s to the present. In 1981, DFC committed itself to a long-term advocacy campaign to restructure the Chicago public schools, applying the advocacy methods identified in the study.

"The Bottom Line," A DFC advocacy report (Designs for Change, 1985), laid out a ten-point agenda for change that focused on shifting educational decision-making to the school level; this agenda reappeared later in many of the reform movement's proposals.

By summer 1986, DFC had concluded, consistent with the findings of its earlier advocacy studies (Moore et al., 1983a), that nothing short of a total restructuring of the legislative framework for the Chicago public schools would provide an adequate basis for needed improvements.

The resources for the often-controversial work of Designs for Change, the Chicago Panel, and other advocacy groups that became active in education reform in the early 1980s came from a number of Chicago foundations, such as the Amoco Foundation, the Joyce Foundation, the MacArthur Foundation, and the Wieboldt Foundation. A new generation of staff members at these foundations were sympathetic to these aggressive reform strategies.

In the summer of 1986, Michael Bakalis, the former Illinois superintendent of instruction, played an important role in moving the reform process forward when he convened school activists to discuss restructuring the system. Together, interested groups formed the CURE Coalition: Chicagoans United to Reform Education. Initially, Bakalis and other group members favored dividing the school system into twenty subdistricts with elected school boards, following the New York City model. Designs for Change, however, argued for a school-based governance plan, and the group swung around to this approach.

In fall 1986, CURE released the coalition's first position paper, "Needed: A New School System for Chicago" (Chicagoans United to Reform Education, 1986). Among the major reforms that the paper advocated were shifting power for key decisions about staff hiring and firing, school budgets, and school improvements to elected school councils with a majority of parent and community representatives; eliminating tenure for principals; and limiting the size and authority of the central administration. The coalition also took the position that the best strategy for change would be to convince the Illinois General Assembly to restructure the school system by law. All of the key elements of the CURE plan eventually became part of the Chicago School Reform Act.

Meanwhile, the business community was becoming increasingly concerned that the school system's failure would undermine Chicago's economy. In 1981, the business coalition called Chicago United had issued a set of 253 recommendations to improve the Chicago public schools (Chicago United Special Task Force on Education, 1981). When they reviewed progress in 1987, however, they found that their most important recommendation, focused on improvements in student learning, had not been carried out (Chicago United, 1987). Chicago United concluded that student performance could not be improved in a centralized system and called for a major shift to school-based decision-making. These bottom-up management concepts had recently been embraced within local companies when corporate restructuring shifted decision-making from centralized offices to plant floors and local stores. The ideas advocated by Chicago United were very similar to those of CURE, reflecting the communication that was beginning to take place between the business leaders and parent and community advocacy groups.

The turning point for school reform came in September 1987, when a teachers' strike nearly a month long, the ninth in eighteen years, catalyzed a level of parent and community activism that had not occurred since the 1960s. Parent and community groups sprang up across the city demanding an end to the school strike and improvements in the schools. The CURE Coalition sought to use the strike as an opportunity to build support for reform proposals it had made that focused on achieving fundamental changes in the school system. Unlike previous strikes, parent and community activism did not dissipate when school reopened.

The Push for the Reform Act

To lead and direct this substantial grassroots movement, Mayor Harold Washington expanded an education summit group that he had formed the previous year and charged the group with developing a plan for restructuring the Chicago public schools. The summit included members of the CURE Coalition and Chicago United along with representatives from the school board and the teachers' union. Mayor Washington died the following month, but the summit, under his weak successor, interim mayor Eugene Sawyer, became the key forum for debating school reform proposals.

There were large differences in the approaches advocated by the various interest groups in the summit. Slowly, a coalition composed of parent groups, advocacy groups, and business leaders developed within the summit and began to meet outside it to reach agreement on positions that were then advanced in summit meetings. This coalition ultimately emerged as the Alliance for Better Chicago Schools (ABC'S Coalition), which ultimately pressed successfully for the adoption of a sweeping school reform bill by the Illinois General Assembly.

The final report drafted by the education summit contained most of the proposals that had previously been developed by CURE and the business community, who had now joined with other organizations in the ABC'S Coalition. When Mayor Sawyer's staff failed to develop a legislative proposal that reflected the summit report, the ABC'S Coalition and other reform groups turned their attention to the Illinois General Assembly in Springfield. The CURE Coalition had developed a legislative strategy and had begun building support among legislators even before the mayor's summit concluded. After the summit broke down, business leaders committed themselves to devoting substantial resources to a legislative campaign in Springfield, including use of a public relations firm, financial support for a major rally in Chicago, and funds for bus trips to Springfield. The CURE Coalition, an active member of the ABC'S Coalition, had obtained financial support to hire a lobbying and public relations firm to aid them in Springfield. At the neighborhood level, support from parent and community groups continued to grow, as such organizations as the United Neighborhood Organization (UNO), which had strong grassroots support in several neighborhoods, joined the ABC'S Coalition.

During the months of May and June 1988, ABC'S carried out a legislative strategy that one Republican legislator called "the most effective grassroots lobbying campaign I have ever seen." Over a six-week period, the ABC'S Coalition organized a continual presence of ten to thirty key leaders in Springfield, backed by weekly bus caravans of 50 to 150 people, a petition campaign to sign up ten thousand supporters for the bill, and constant phone calling and face-to-face visits in the legislators' home districts. The coalition's strategy was to push Chicago legislators for support by organizing in every Chicago neighborhood and to convince legislators from outside Chicago that the bill would not affect their own schools while making Chicago's schools better.

The reformers were also aided by the fact that the Chicago Board of Education and the Chicago Teachers' Union were not being listened to, largely because their credibility had been damaged by the bitter school strike and by the fact that neither Chicago's interim mayor, Sawyer, nor the Chicago Principals' Association mounted effective lobbying efforts for their own proposals.

In 1988, both the state senate and the state house were under the control of the Democrats. In June 1988, the powerful Democratic speaker of the house, Michael Madigan, brought together all sides in the Chicago reform debate to hammer out a bill that could pass the legislature. The major interest groups active around school reform met daily with senate and house Democratic leaders to draft the bill. In the final days before the bill's passage, the Chicago Board of Education and the Chicago Principals' Association were the only Chicago groups in Springfield actively opposing the proposed reform bill; the Chicago Teachers' Union had agreed to support the bill when its passage appeared likely. On July 2, 1988, Senate Bill 1839 (the Chicago School Reform Act) narrowly passed in the senate and the house over Republican opposition.

While the reform coalition celebrated passage of the bill, Republican legislators urged Republican governor James Thompson to veto it, because they were angered by some of the tactics that the Democrats had used in pushing it through. Thompson did veto the bill, and for several months it looked as though Chicago school reform might die, because the Republicans insisted on some minor but controversial changes that were offensive to the Chicago Teachers' Union and the legislative black caucus. The reform coalition mounted a vigorous campaign once again and got the two sides to compromise, however. After minor changes, a new version of the bill was passed on December 1, 1988 (Illinois General Assembly, 1988).

Highlights of the New Law

The Reform Act, as passed, mandated a comprehensive restructuring of the Chicago school system. Key provisions of Senate Bill 1840 included the following:

- A Local School Council (LSC) consisting of six elected parents, two elected community residents, two elected teachers, and the school's principal is established at each school.
- The LSC appoints the school's principal to a four-year performance contract. Principal tenure is abolished. After four years, the LSC can decide whether to reappoint the school's principal or select a new one.
- The LSC helps develop and approves a school improvement plan, which must spell out how the school, under the principal's leadership, will boost student achievement and cut truancy and dropout rates.
- The LSC helps develop and approves their school's budget and may use funds as they wish within existing laws and collective bargaining agreements. The largest source of discretionary funds is a state-funded compensatory education program called State Chapter 1. The reform law requires the school district to use these funds to supplement, not supplant, a fair share of basic education funds for each school. As a result, the average school now receives more than $500,000 it did not receive before school reform, based on the number of low-income students it serves.
- With one modest exception, any vacancy in the position of teacher or other educational staff can be filled by the principal, without regard to seniority.
- The principal, with the assistance of a teacher advisory committee, has the authority to develop the specific methods and content of the school's curriculum, within systemwide curriculum objectives and standards.
- A School Board Nominating Commission, composed of twenty-three members elected from Local School Councils and five members appointed by the mayor, screens candidates for the permanent central board and recommends slates of three to the mayor for each board slot. The mayor must either appoint one of the slated candidates or ask for a new slate.
- The central board has specific powers in limited areas subject to other provisions of the law, including the powers of Local School Councils.
- The central board is required to develop a comprehensive plan for restructuring the central administration to support school-level initiative, with the plan

to be approved by the Chicago School Finance Authority (SFA), a financial watchdog group. The central board is required to implement this plan to the satisfaction of the SFA; otherwise the SFA can impose its own plan.

• The central board is required to meet an expenditure cap on central administration; this resulted in a substantial cut in central administration staff.

The overriding strategy behind this set of changes was to shift accountability for school improvement from the central board of education to elected councils at each school representing the "school community" and to give these LSCs, principals, and teachers concrete authority and resources to make major changes.

INITIAL IMPLEMENTATION OF THE REFORM
ACT: 1989–94

Whereas events leading to the legislation's passage took place primarily in a few public decisionmaking bodies (the mayor's summit, the General Assembly), the implementation of the law has occurred not only in central decisionmaking bodies but also at the 550 schools at which the reform process will ultimately succeed or fail. Below, the focus is on highlighting a few key issues in the initial implementation period that illustrate how key interest groups responded to the reform law and attempted to shape its implementation.

Local School Council Activism

When the first Local School Council elections took place in 1989, skeptics expressed doubts about whether a sufficient number of candidates would come forward and whether substantial numbers of parents and community residents would vote. In contrast, reform strategists were hopeful that the reform law would create and build its own permanent political constituency that could be mobilized in its defense (Moore, 1991).

Participation in the 1989 LSC election exceeded all expectations, with 17,000 candidates for 5,400 parent, community, and teacher positions on the LSCs and adult voter participation of 228,000. Further, the ethnic composition of the LSCs that were elected closely mirrored the ethnic composition of Chicago's student body (Designs for Change, 1989). Thus, there are two-thirds as many African Americans serving on Chicago's LSCs as on all the school boards in the United States and two-thirds as many Latinos on Chicago's LSCs as on all the school boards in the United States (Designs for Change, 1991a).

Candidate and voter participation has declined substantially since the first

LSC election, however. Candidate participation dropped from 17,000 in 1989 to 8,200 in 1991 and 7,600 in 1993. Further, the number of parent and community voters dropped from 228,000 in 1989 to 118,000 in 1991 to 86,000 in 1993. School reform groups credit some of the drop in participation to the fact that the 1991 election was held shortly after the Board of Education had made demoralizing budget cuts in the schools and that the 1993 election took place in the middle of a financial crisis in which it was uncertain whether the schools would even be open on election day. A bill backed by reform groups in the fall of 1994 moved the election to Spring Report Card Pick-Up Day in order to avoid the frequent fall financial crises and to target the elections to a day on which the majority of parents visit the schools to meet with their children's teachers.

The six thousand Local School Council members now constitute a significant political force in the city. A thousand or more LSC members have become actively involved during a number of crises while successfully supporting reform, such as a campaign to reinstitute the reform law after aspects of it were declared unconstitutional, efforts to oppose the diversion of the schools' discretionary funds to general revenue to balance the school system's budget, and efforts to fight central administration plans to reinflate the size of the central administration. The large-scale activism that has occurred in crises has not been sustained around less critical issues, however. A much smaller core of about two hundred LSC members has been consistently involved in systemwide policy issues, typically collaborating with reform advocacy groups (see below).

In addition to involvement at the central board level and in the General Assembly, LSC members are constantly seeking the aid of local elected officials on issues of concern to their particular school (such as improved physical facilities, police intervention to combat gangs and drug dealers, and relief of school overcrowding) by contacting city council members, state senators, state representatives, and the mayor. Although most elected officials seek to maintain positive relationships with LSC members and to help them resolve school problems, some work more quietly to marginalize their authority.

Sustaining the Reform Coalition

Reform strategists were keenly aware that most reform movements dissipate once a law is passed or a court victory is achieved and that the institutions that are supposed to be reshaped by a new law or court decision come to dominate the implementation process (Edelman, 1964). In contrast, effective advocacy groups studied by Designs for Change remained active over a period of years to monitor reform implementation, and reform groups active in the passage of the Chicago School Reform Act were determined to aggressively monitor its implementation—protecting, refining, and expanding it (Moore, 1991).

Parent, community, advocacy, and business groups active in securing the law's passage have remained consistently active in the Illinois legislative process, using the same combination of lobbying, data-based reports, parent organizing, complaints to government bodies, and the like that they used in passing the reform law. Such long-time school reform groups as Designs for Change and the Chicago Panel were joined by new groups such as the Citywide Coalition for School Reform, Chicago Association of Local School Councils, and Schools First. The business community formed its own advocacy organization to support reform—Leadership for Quality Education. Citywide advocacy organizations have thus far been able to convince funders that advocacy to protect and extend the reform process is essential, although support for this work has declined somewhat during the 1990s.

These reformers have annually built formal legislative coalitions that agree on legislative priorities, employ lobbyists, mobilize Local School Council members and other allies, and scrutinize almost all education-related legislation before the General Assembly. Through these efforts, they have been able to protect and in some cases extend the school-level autonomy established by the 1988 reform law, although they were not able to secure additional funding for Chicago's schools, which have faced a financial crisis at the beginning of virtually every school year (see below). In their efforts to give principals more control over staff selection and over the scheduling and supervision of custodial and food service workers, reform groups have worked with the Republican legislators, in opposition to Democrats tied to school employee unions.

Reform organizations similarly remained active in monitoring the central board and administration, analyzing its budget, advocating the restructuring of the central administration to support reform, opposing board of education rules that threaten LSC and principal autonomy, and the like. And they have secured substantial pro bono legal help that has enabled them to mount a major effort to defend the school reform law from a legal attack by the Chicago Principals' Association and to oppose in court board of education actions that violated the reform law.

One key controversy in the school system's 1991 funding crisis illustrates the nature of the reform groups' initiatives. In May 1991, Superintendent Kimbrough claimed that the school system faced a $310 million budget deficit for the fiscal year beginning on September 1, 1991, but he did not release details of projected revenues or expenses before launching a campaign to obtain more state funds for Chicago and (unofficially) to free up $80 million in state money earmarked for the education of low-income children that was under the control of the LSCs. The board of education wanted to use these school discretionary funds (called State Chapter 1 funds) to balance its budget. Schools reform groups questioned the accuracy of the superintendent's revenue and expenditure projections and the wisdom of asking for more state money without releasing a detailed school system budget that specified economies in such areas as central administration, and they expressed unanimous opposition to any diversion of State Chapter 1 funds. Nevertheless, the plan for diverting $80 million from the State Chapter 1 allocation for fiscal year 1991–92 was introduced in the Illinois House of Representatives on June 20 and quickly passed. Reform groups were told that this plan had the support of all four legislative leaders, the legislative black caucus, the mayor, and the governor.

Designs for Change and a spectrum of other reform groups played a central role in the successful campaign to defeat this plan over the next week, however. Within forty-eight hours of the plan's introduction, DFC had prepared and released to the media and LSCs a detailed school-by-school analysis indicating how much each Chicago school would lose under this plan, as well as the loss that would be experienced by individual legislative districts (Designs for Change, 1991b). Legislators received hundreds of calls from irate LSC members, principals, and teachers. As a result, this plan was repudiated by the Illinois house and senate.

Principals and Teachers Respond

Those skeptical about the school reform law predicted that principals and teachers would rebel when parents sought to carry out their new decisionmaking role. Immediately after the school reform law passed, the Chicago Principals' Association responded with vigorous opposition, while the teachers' union adopted a "this too shall pass" attitude.

The Chicago Principals' Association filed suit to have the reform law declared unconstitutional, and some principals pursued related legal actions (*Fumarolo et al. v. Chicago Board of Education et al.*). In the first round of principal selections in 1990, several principals who were not rehired charged racial bias and organized community protests among their supporters (Wilkerson, 1990). A study of the selection process showed that there was no pattern of racial bias in principal dismissals (Designs for Change, 1990).

By the spring of 1992, however, a careful study of the attitudes of principals concerning reform showed that they were generally positive, felt the reform process was improving their schools, and appreciated the new authority that they had received under reform. Of those who had been principals before the reform law was passed, 83 percent agreed with the statement "Since reform, this school is getting better"; 80 percent of principals agreed that "the LSC and I have a similar understanding of the principal's responsibilities and rights"; and only 29 percent agreed with the statement "Since reform, there is more conflict in this school" (Bennett et al., 1992).

A major factor affecting principals' responses to reform is that after the first round of selections, 30 percent of principalships had turned over, and by 1994, more than 80 percent of those who had been principals when the reform law was passed were no longer in their positions. Most of this turnover resulted from retirements, although a moderate percentage of principals were not re-hired by their LSCs (Designs for Change, 1990).

Thus, most school principals now in office have chosen to serve under the new ground rules for the principalship, and the Chicago Principals' Association has moderated its position on school reform.

During the initial years of implementation, the Chicago Teachers' Union pursued ways to reverse provisions of the law that limit teacher job protection. The union became supportive of many key provisions of the reform law, however, because it gives teachers more decisionmaking and leadership oppor-tunities in their schools and because teachers achieved a 29 percent increase in salary from its passage through the 1993–94 school year. According to a spring 1991 study of elementary schoolteacher attitudes, they tended to be positive about the impact of school reform. For example, 63 percent of elementary teachers agreed that "since reform, I am more optimistic this school will improve"; and 60 percent agreed that "this school is getting better." Such responses were not distributed equally across schools. The study concludes: "In about three-quarters of schools teachers are 'pro-reform.' Strongly pro-reform schools were found in every neighborhood" (Easton et al., 1992).

One major concrete initiative of the Chicago Teachers' Union in support of reform is their establishment of the Quest Center, an ambitious program to assist teams of teachers to restructure their teaching practices (Bradley, 1994).

Central Office Restructuring
and the New School Board

The cap on the size of the central administration imposed by the reform law resulted in a substantial reduction in the staff of Pershing Road and of the school system's eleven subdistrict offices. An independent analysis of the bureaucracy's size indicated a decrease from 2,528 in 1988–89 to 1,471 in 1994–95, a 42 percent reduction (Public Information Project, 1995).

This downsizing of the central office staff was not accompanied by a restructuring of the administration to enable it to carry out its new responsibilities, however. The first general superintendent under reform, Ted Kimbrough, served from 1990 to 1993. He did not carry out a comprehensive central office restructuring effort, typically making across-the-board cuts to meet the law's requirements and seeking support to reverse the limits on central administration size. The reform law's drafters anticipated the possibility of such resistance and required the board of education to get annual approval for a comprehensive central office restructuring plan from the Chicago School Finance Authority (SFA) for the first five years of reform and to implement this plan. The reform law also specified that if the board failed to submit a satisfactory plan, the SFA could impose a plan and direct the board to carry it out. The board never submitted a meaningful plan, however, and the authority, appointed jointly by the mayor and the governor, backed down from a confrontation with the board in which the SFA would have had to develop its own plan for central office restructuring.

Kimbrough's successor, Argie Johnson, who served from 1993 to 1995, did start a process for restructuring Pershing Road with the help of CSC Index, a consulting firm with a track record for successfully restructuring major corporations. This restructuring initiative remained in the planning stages, however, while stories of central office incompetence received wide publicity. Similarly, Johnson did not successfully come to grips with long-standing corruption within the Pershing Road bureaucracy, and a series of scandals involving the disappearance of school board equipment and alleged rigging of school board contracts dominated media coverage of Chicago education in the 1994–95 school year.

In part, these problems resulted from the failure of the selection process for the central board of education, which sought to balance authority between the mayor and the School Board Nominating Commission selected by Local School Councils. A number of individuals who won seats on the nominating commission were political enemies of the mayor and were able to put forth nominees who similarly opposed him. For his part, the mayor frequently delayed long past his legal deadline for acting on school board nominations and thus helped undermine the viability of the selection process. The net result was a board of education that did not press aggressively to eliminate corruption and restructure the central administration to serve the schools effectively.

The Politics of Gauging Progress

Given the controversial nature of Chicago reform, disputes about whether or not it is "working" have raged at every step since the law was passed. A new institution grew up specifically to study the progress of reform—the Consortium on Chicago School Research, headquartered at the University of Chicago (Consortium on Chicago School Research, 1991). The consortium has taken the position that in the early years of reform it is critical to understand whether changes are occurring in educational practice at the school level that are consistent with the reform strategy and that show promise of leading to improvements in student achievement. In the summer of 1993, the consortium carried out a comprehensive study of reform's impact titled *A View from the Elementary Schools: The State of Reform in Chicago* (Bryk et al., 1993). Among the study's key conclusions are the following:

- About 40 percent of Chicago's elementary schools are making what the study calls "systemic educational improvements" that are likely to boost student achievement. Such systemic improvements include new principal leadership with a priority on improving instruction, increased use of "best practices" for instruction by teachers, increased teacher involvement in staff development and in planning instructional change, and extensive parent and community involvement.
- Schools making such systemic educational improvements are spread throughout the city and cut across racial and ethnic lines. And they are as likely to be low-income as middle-income schools.
- An additional 20 percent of schools show some evidence of initiating systemic changes. The remaining 40 percent of schools are essentially unchanged by reform.
- Nearly one-third of Chicago's elementary schools have created "strong democracies" in which the principal, teachers, parents, and community leaders collaborate effectively on school improvement.
- These "strong democracy" schools are the schools most likely to be making systemic improvements in their educational programs. This connection between democratic participation and the likelihood of educational improvement lends support to one of the key ideas behind Chicago reform (i.e., that

changes in the process of educational governance will stimulate improvements in the quality of students' educational experiences).

The report concludes with a generally positive assessment of the progress of Chicago reform, given the time frame in which schools had had to change: "Is the restructuring of the Chicago Public Schools evolving in ways that can lead to major improvements in student learning? We answer 'yes'" (Bryk et al., 1993).

To many analysts and public officials, however, the consortium's data on changes in the process of education are irrelevant, and the only pertinent question is whether standardized test scores have risen. Schools in other cities that are now regarded as models for exceptional student achievement frequently have taken five to seven years to show significant test score gains after beginning to make basic changes in their educational practices (Levine and Lezotte, 1990; Comer, 1980). Test results for Chicago through the spring of 1994 showed achievement up slightly overall in the elementary schools and down in the high schools (Chicago Public Schools Department of Research, Evaluation, and Planning, 1994). A number of inner-city Chicago schools that made the kinds of changes identified by the consortium also moved above state and national averages on standardized achievement tests. Further, the high school dropout rate fell from a high of 51.5 percent in 1991 to 42.6 percent in 1994 (Pitruzzello et al., 1995), and serious violence in the schools declined by 46 percent (Williams, 1994).

Some key public officials concluded from this evidence that school reform was in fact working and needed more time and more consistent funding to succeed. Yet the failure of achievement test scores to rise substantially after five years of school-level implementation, coupled with continuing revelations of fraud and incompetence at Pershing Road, obscured the changes documented by the consortium in the mind of the general public and led critics of Chicago reform and some public officials to conclude that it had failed.

The Ongoing Financial Crisis

The initial implementation of reform was carried out against a backdrop of financial crisis in the public schools, both in Chicago and statewide, with more than one hundred Illinois school districts placed on a financial watchlist in 1995 (Illinois State Board of Education, 1995). The state's share of school support dropped dramatically from 1975, when the state contributed 49 percent of revenues, to 1994, when the state contributed 35 percent. As school districts became more dependent on property tax revenues, per-pupil revenue disparities among districts markedly increased (Coalition for Educational Rights, 1995).

Although not among the state's poorest school districts, Chicago received $400 per student less in basic unrestricted state aid and property tax revenues than the average Illinois school district in 1992–93. An independent financial analysis of Chicago school finances indicated a structural imbalance between revenues and expenses, even with economies in central office operation (Booz Allen & Hamilton, 1992). The beginning of the 1990, 1991, 1992, and 1993 school years were dominated by debate over impending financial shortfalls and the need to either increase revenues or cut expenses. In the worst of these crises, in the fall of 1993, Chicago cut four hundred high-school teaching positions, and the schools were kept open week by week by court order until the Illinois General Assembly and the governor agreed to allow Chicago to borrow $378 million to temporarily balance the budget over the 1993–94 and 1994–95 school years. The politics of this crisis were typical of the politics around Chicago school funding during the initial years of reform. The board of education and school reform groups pressed the Illinois General Assembly for more money, as did other cash-strapped districts statewide. The Chicago board was inept in making its case for more funds, as revelations of mismanagement and fraud continued to surface in the media. Republicans and Downstate Democrats, who were opposed to raising taxes in general, found it politically useful to oppose any "bailout" for Chicago schools, even as part of a plan that would bring more funds to school districts of their own with financial problems.

REPUBLICANS CHANGE THE REFORM LAW: 1995

In the fall of 1994, Republicans won control of both chambers of the Illinois General Assembly, and the incumbent Republican governor decisively won reelection by defeating a Democratic candidate who advocated more funding for Illinois schools. Chicago projected a $150 million deficit for the 1995–96 school year and an average deficit of $290 million for subsequent years (Chicago Public Schools, 1995). In the spring of 1995, nearly 150 bills were introduced that impacted Chicago school reform, including proposals, for example, to abolish the decisionmaking structure created in 1988, to divert the $260 million in school improvement discretionary funds to balance the school system's budget, to give Chicago's mayor control of the board of education, and to shift more control over school custodial staff to principals. During this period, the credibility of the Chicago Board of Education was virtually nonexistent with the General Assembly, as stories of central administration corruption continued to surface.

In this environment, school reform organizations, including advocacy groups, business groups, school principals, and Local School Councils, made an active effort to protect the basic structure of school reform. They prepared reports, sought media coverage, and met with legislators and with the governor's staff to document the reform progress indicated by research and by their direct experience, to document the key role of school discretionary funds in the improvements that had taken place, to urge that schools be given more control over their budgets and over custodians and other staff, and to urge more school funding statewide.

In the end, the General Assembly left the essentials of Chicago's school-based decisionmaking structure in place, including almost all of the school improvement discretionary funds. They also made some major changes in the Chicago reform law, including the following:

- The mayor was given direct authority to appoint a new board of education and a chief executive officer to carry out the board's responsibilities.
- Due to the elimination of restrictions on how state categorical funds and local tax levies could be used, the new board was given the ability to divert more than $100 million per year in revenues to help balance their budget, without cutting services to schools.
- Job and work rules protections for custodial workers and tradesmen were eliminated from state law, and all unions were prohibited from negotiating over scheduling and working conditions.
- The new board was given extensive powers to privatize services.
- Principals were given full control over the supervision and scheduling of custodial staff and food workers.
- The new board was given broad powers to intervene in failing schools.

The mayor appointed his former chief of staff as president of the new school board and his budget director as the school system's chief executive officer. Focusing initially on the budget and on union negotiations, the new leadership team moved quickly to propose a four-year balanced budget, negotiate a four-year contract with teachers that includes annual raises, eliminate 1,050 custodial and trade positions, and privatize school repairs. It also moved quickly on some flagrant examples of waste and incompetence in the central administration. And it espoused a back-to-basics educational strategy, with an emphasis on "direct instruction."

School reform groups, principals, and Local School Councils are highly encouraged by several of these initiatives, which are consistent with positions they pressed during the period of initial reform implementation. They were apprehensive, however, about the possibility that the new leadership will seek to recentralize the school system by mandating a specific curriculum built on their commitment to "the basics" and by misusing the central board's broad new powers to intervene in failing schools.

CONCLUSION

Although the jury is still out on the effectiveness of Chicago school reform in improving student achievement, the experience to date suggests several conclusions about the interplay of political forces around Chicago reform and their impact. First, it is clear that a state law that shifts important decisionmaking authority to the school level in a large urban school system can have a major impact on the day-to-day operations of a substantial number of schools, inducing them to carry out educational practices that show promise for improving student achievement. Second, it is clear that urban parents and community leaders will participate on a sustained basis if given the opportunity to make decisions about their children's education and that principals and teachers will accommodate to this new decisionmaking role, even if it dramatically changes their roles. Third, it is clear that, as documented in the study of advocacy groups published by Designs for Change in 1983, independent, skillful advocacy organizations focused on achieving educational reform can become major players in securing dramatic changes in public policy and in pressing for their implementation (Moore et al., 1983a).

REFERENCES

Bennett, A., Bryk, A., Easton, J., Kerbow, D., Luppescu, S., and Sebring, P. 1992. *Charting Reform: The Principals' Perspective.* Chicago: Consortium on Chicago School Research.

Booz Allen & Hamilton, Inc. 1992. *Financial Outlook for the Chicago Public Schools.* Chicago: Booz Allen & Hamilton.

Bradley, A. 1994. A Quest for Change. *Education Week,* June 22.

Bryk, A., Easton, J., Kerbow, D., Rollow, S., and Sebring, P. 1993. *A View from the Elementary Schools: The State of Reform in Chicago.* Chicago: Consortium on Chicago School Research.

Chicago Public Schools. 1995. *Closing the Gap: Financial Forecasts: FY96 to FY98.* Chicago: Chicago Public Schools.

Chicago Public Schools Department of Research, Evaluation, and Planning. 1994. *Report of the Chicago Public Schools Achievement Trends.* Chicago: Chicago Public Schools.

Chicago United. 1987. *Reassessment of the Report of the 1981 Special Task Force on Education: Chicago Public Schools.* Chicago: Chicago United.

Chicago United Special Task Force on Education. 1981. *The Chicago School System.* Chicago: Chicago United.

Chicagoans United to Reform Education. 1986. *Needed: A New School System for Chicago.* Chicago: Chicagoans United to Reform Education.

Coalition for Education Rights. 1995. *Adequacy and Equity in Illinois School Finance.* Chicago: Coalition for Education Rights.

Comer, J. 1980. *School Power: Implications of an Intervention Project.* New York: Free Press.

Consortium on Chicago School Research. 1991. *Achieving School Reform in Chicago: What We Need to Know.* Chicago: Consortium on Chicago School Research.

Designs for Change. 1985. *The Bottom Line: Chicago's Failing Schools and How to Save Them.* Chicago: Designs for Change.

———. 1989. *Shattering the Stereotypes: Candidate Participation in the Chicago Local School Council Elections.* Chicago: Designs for Change.

———. 1990. *Chicago Principals: Changing of the Guard.* Chicago: Designs for Change.

———. 1991a. *Closer Look: Chicago School Reform,* No. 1. Chicago: Designs for Change.

———. 1991b. *Devastating Inequality: The Impact of Senate Bill 158 on Low-Income Schools.* Chicago: Designs for Change.

Easton, J., Bryk, A., Driscoll, M. E., Kotsakis, J., Sebring, P., and van der Ploeg, A. 1992. *Charting Reform: The Teachers' Turn.* Chicago: Consortium on Chicago School Research.

Edelman, M. 1964. *The Symbolic Uses of Politics.* Urbana: University of Illinois Press.

Fumarolo et al. v. Chicago Board of Education et al., No. 89 CH 03105, April 17, 1989.

Illinois General Assembly. 1988. Public Act 85–1418.

Illinois State Board of Education. 1995. *Illinois State Board of Education News.*

Kyle, C. L., and Kantowicz, E. R. 1992. *Kids First—Primero los niños.* Springfield, Ill.: Sangamon State University Press.

Levine, D., and Lezotte, L. 1990. *Unusually Effective Schools: A Review and Analysis of Research and Practice.* Madison, Wis.: National Center for Effective Schools Research and Development.

Moore, D. R. 1991. *Chicago School Reform: The Nature and Origin of Basic Assumptions.* Chicago: Designs for Change.

Moore, D. R., Soltman, S., Steinberg, L., Manar, U., and Fogel, D. 1983a. *Child Advocacy and the Schools.* Chicago: Designs for Change.

———. 1983b. *Standing up for Children: Effective Child Advocacy in the Schools.* Chicago: Designs for Change.

O'Connell, M. 1991. *School Reform Chicago Style: How Citizens Organized to Change Public Policy.* Chicago: Center for Neighborhood Technology.

Pitruzzello, A., Turetsky, B., Gonzalez-Latin, C., and Rice, W. 1995. *School-Level Dropout Trends: 1989–1994.* Chicago: Chicago Public Schools.

Public Information Project. 1995. *School Reform's Heroes: Join Them.* Chicago: Public Information Project.

Washington Transition Committee. 1983. *Toward a Prosperous, Compassionate and Efficient Chicago: Policy Recommendations.* Chicago: Washington Transition Committee.

Wilkerson, I. 1989. New School Term in Chicago Puts Parents in Seat of Power. *New York Times,* 3 September.

———. 1990. Fate of Principals Splits Some Chicago Schools. *New York Times,* 2 March.

Williams, D. 1994. Violence in Schools Drops as Security Staff Grows. *Catalyst* 1, no. 3 (November):1.

Conclusion: Creating a School Reform Agenda for the Twenty-first Century

Marilyn Gittell

Demands for school reform have become a constant in American life and include three broad categories of concern: governance, teaching and learning, and finance. Seldom are these issues joined, although they are clearly interdependent, and only together do they offer the opportunity to change the way schools function. The failure to integrate reform demands reflects the dominance of the agenda by school professionals, who are the most active and influential stakeholders in the process. Almost half a century ago one of the most astute early analysts of school politics, Robert Conant, described the power of professional school elites as a result of the circulation of those elites in positions of power, from the local school districts to state and federal bureaucracies to the university schools of education. He attributed the insulation of school systems and education policy to the closed elite decision system (Conant, 1963). My own research on city school systems confirmed his findings (Gittell, 1967; Gittell and Hollander, 1968). In six urban school systems we found virtually closed political systems controlled by professional bureaucrats.

Other analysts of school policy have described the strong influence of private corporate interests in the determination of educational priorities and the structure of school funding. Bowles and Gintis (1976) describe the role of education as reproducer of the class structure and defender of capitalism. Tyack (1974) records the influence of corporate America on the structure and content of education. Katz's (1968) political economy interpretation of events attributes the early adoption of compulsory public education in Massachusetts in the middle of the nineteenth century to the powerful role of commercial and political elites. The adoption and support of vocational education has been explained as a product of corporate influence. Administrative and professional school reforms for the last century emulate corporate management styles, demonstrating the pervasive influence of business elites on education organization and practice. School historians appreciate that the professionalization of the school system, the development of centralized school bureaucracies, and the emergence of the school superintendent as a manager of the system are direct results of the influence of corporate practices. These new managers of the system, like their corporate CEO counterparts, were characterized as above or outside politics and recruited on the basis of their expertise. Centralized bureaucratic structures were promoted by the new corporate professionals as the answer to highly politicized, decentralized districts and independent local schools (Ravitch, 1987). The ideal of the apolitical school system ignored the fact that schools were competitors in the political arena because they competed for and spent public funds. Guided by the principles of Progressivism, the emphasis on insulating the school system had a lasting political impact: it discouraged the engagement of a broader group of stakeholders in participation in the system. Local elected school boards and parent and community activists performed limited roles, called on particularly when their support for taxes and funding was necessary.

The issue of school quality was greatly simplified by the school professionals who in the 1950s established the principle that the more dollars spent on schools, the better the school system. Comparisons of schools and districts were made in terms of per capita expenditures. School finance reform followed the Progressive model: remove school finance issues from the political agenda by creating fiscally independent school districts or school budgets that would be controlled by school managers. Support of schools would be assured by separate referenda in which the public would approve school budgets supported by local property tax revenues and supplemented by state funds. Coleman's extensive national study (Coleman, 1966) challenged the concept that school expenditures were the determining factor in the quality of schools. Responses to his research were highly critical of his conclusions, and he was largely ignored by the people who ran the schools.

States that were legally responsible for education as a function and providing 50 percent of the total cost of education were pressed in the post–World War II era to make adjustments in their school aid funding to equalize resource disparities that resulted from differential property values in local school districts. The struggle in state capitals to adopt new equalization formulae recognized the political underpinnings of the American education system. New actors and stakeholders were lured into the game of school politics. Only the most naive reformers thought it would be a simple task to construct an equitable state aid system to balance district resources. They soon faced the reality that wealthier districts were not committed to redistributive tax and spending policies. There was only limited success—and in very few states—in bringing poor school districts into line with the wealthier districts. The lack of progress demonstrated the limited ability of poor districts to win such a battle. The legislative leadership in most states responded to the interests of their major supporters in wealthy suburban districts even in the face of court action to the contrary.

Anticity politics, which was traditional in state politics, rationalized continued limits on funding for city school systems, although those schools faced the biggest problems and the greatest needs. Professionals in the urban communities used their increased powers in the state capitals to successfully press for more sensitive state urban school policies, recognition of their unions as bargaining agents, and increased salaries and expenditures in the 1950s and 1960s. As suburban growth exploded in the next several decades, teacher associations expanded their statewide constituencies and the suburban members soon exceeded their city constituencies, and there commitments to a city agenda faltered.

Teachers' unions emerged as a force to be reckoned with in state politics by the late 1960s; they were to become the largest spenders of lobbying and campaign dollars in many states. A state's education law, the content of which was increasingly determined by the ability of unions to influence state legislatures, set the parameters for collective bargaining contracts negotiated at the local school district level. The contracts set the ground rules for how schools were to be governed, how money would be spent, and how classes would be taught. Responsibility for the content of education and certification of professionals would reside in the state bureaucracy. It wasn't long before the teachers' unions and associations, organized statewide, would support legislative resistance to redistributive state school aid to achieve equity funding for poorer school districts. Professional school groups pursued increased state funding for all districts with fail-safe provisions to protect the funds of the suburban school systems.

In a small window of opportunity, from the late 1950s to the mid-1970s, the needs of city school systems received an unusual amount of attention, motivated by the *Brown* decision and the civil rights movement. More liberal state regimes in several heavily urban states responded to political pressures from cities. Several states revised their aid formulae, increasing their funding to city school systems. Federal compensatory education funding, at its maximum in 1978 at 9 to 10 percent of total school spending, was concentrated in cities. Questions of equity were broadened to include desegregation, equitable excellence and funding, more participation of new stakeholders, with emphasis on inclusion of parents and community in school governance and decision-making. The community control movement demanded a sharing of power with the professionals. A populist school reform movement arose out of the civil rights and school desegregation demands. For one of the few times in the history of school reform all three reform agendas were joined in demands for (1) a radical change in governance, including decentralization and parent and community participation in community-controlled schools; (2) changes in school aid formulae to increase funding for cities and poor districts, increasing equity with richer districts; and (3) changes in the curriculum and flexibility in teaching and learning to reflect diversity in the population and to individualize learning in open classrooms.

The school reform agenda mimicked the demands of the broader civil rights movement. Greater emphasis was placed on the political process and on school governance's relying on participatory democratic theory, which prescribes more direct citizen participation in decentralized institutions. This emphasis on the political process would result in greater responsiveness to the needs of students, a basis for establishing professional accountability, and a revitalization of citizen interest in the schools. Distinctions between education excellence and educational equity were avoided by joining the two issues. Excellence was recognized as not meaningful if it did not include everyone in the system.

The new reform movement was not greeted enthusiastically by professionals and their leaders. In fact, their resistance turned to opposition and criticism directed at the comprehensive demands for governance changes, which they viewed as a challenge to professional power. The system responded to defend the status quo. The investment of energy and resources in comprehensive school reform during this era, however, accomplished some significant results. Federal programs, which proved most capable of achieving equity goals through compensatory funding, also gave impetus to curriculum changes and increased parent participation, the model being the Head Start program. The opening of school systems to public view and the demands for data and accountability created a new ecology of school politics and the potential for active new stakeholders to become engaged. Actual reform of school systems to achieve a redistribution of power, however, was minimal. Attempts to shift decision-making and control of budgets and curriculum from central bureaucracies to the city and to individual schools failed. In several cases the defeat took place in the state capital. The 1969 New York State legislation for decentralization of the New York City school system fell far short of the recommendations of the Bundy Panel (created in 1968 by the governor and the mayor to come up with a decentralization plan for the New York City school system), which proposed governance structures in each school, controlled by a majority of parents. Bundy recommended a devolution of power from the central bureaucracy to the school or to a smaller local school district. The legislation that was passed created thirty-three local districts (Bundy had recommended sixty-five) with elected school boards and districts with a single devolved power: to choose a community superintendent. The school professional associations, particularly the United Federation of Teachers and the Council of Supervisors Associations, had little difficulty defeating fragmented community organizations from New York City, who had waning support from the reform mayor and the governor and no consistent support from their own legislative delegation, the media, foundations, or the business community (Gittell, 1994). The tradition of Progressive politics in New York City that protects professional prerogatives and centralized bureaucracies was able to stay the course and deny any shift to an open, participatory school system and comprehensive school reform.

Attempts to create community-controlled school districts in Watts and Harlem came to the same fate within the next several years. It was not until 1988 that a successful comprehensive school reform took place in a major American city. Chicago decentralized its school system with a radical governance change centered on the individual school. Boards of majority parents and teachers were elected in each school with the power to select their principal, assign teachers, and reallocate part of their budgets and reorder the curriculum. The coalition organized around Chicago school reform was a broad one, and it presented itself with strength and consistency in Springfield. The reform mayor, Harold

Washington, was committed to the battle and helped rally the troops. And the strong tradition of activist community-based organizations willing to create and join in a coalition with corporate leaders provided a broad base of articulate defenders of more comprehensive reform. School professional associations, although they did not support the reform, did not muster their energies to oppose it; the teachers' union had used much of its credit in securing a new contract after several debilitating strikes, and the supervisors lacked sufficient energy on their own. Finance reform was the missing piece of the Chicago reform plan, and by 1995 a newly elected conservative governor and a similarly unsympathetic legislature passed legislation capping the city school funds and giving the mayor control over the whole system.

The 1980s rhetoric of school reform shifted with the rightward thrust of American politics. Equity became the enemy, and school excellence became the byword. Basic skills and a traditional curriculum replaced the multicultural curriculum and the inquiry method of learning. An open and participatory political system was no longer a goal, and community-run schools were replaced by the new reformers with professionally organized charter, alternative, and collaborative schools. Professional reformers abandoned their efforts to achieve systemwide change, seeking instead to reform individual schools. Smaller alternative schools created and run by teachers were to be the panacea. Ted Sizer and Debby Meier, the new professional gurus of educational reform, won strong foundation as well as professional support for resetting the school reform agenda. Small schools run by teacher collaboratives could not be achieved systemwide. Governance and finance equity were abandoned, as was systemwide reform of teaching and learning. The goals of the new professional reform movement, including smaller, teacher-led schools not subject to selected system constraints, formed a more palatable reform agenda. It posed less of a threat to teacher unions; in fact in New York City the union responded by including a provision in its 1994 contract for schools, by vote of their staff, to avoid teacher seniority standards. The new alternate schools approach also fit nicely with the declining state interest in systemwide reform, which would have required significant shifts in funding away from suburban districts. Equity goals as determined in the courts in some states were beginning to pose an even larger threat to the suburbs, requiring larger metropolitan school systems to achieve equity with desegregation. Minnesota and Connecticut court cases moved in that direction.

Support for charter school legislation increased, although the teacher associations and unions opposed freewheeling state legislation, which they viewed as a threat to their contract provisions. Four hundred twenty-eight charter schools were operational as of January 1997. The professional associations equated charter schools with the voucher system that was often supported by business groups, who generally support any alternative school plan. Both efforts seemed to encourage bypassing the public school structure, and the professionals struggled to limit the number of schools that could be created under each category. State charter school legislation differs with regard to the number and character of the charter schools permitted and whether they are subject to any or all of the constraints of the local system. Legislation was passed in almost half the states establishing procedures for creating these new schools and generally calling for teacher governance. The foundations also weighed in heavily in support of alternate schools; the new strategy eliminated the political issues attendant on systemic and governance reform. It encouraged discrete foundation funding for individual or small groups of schools. It also gave the foundations or their education program officers a more direct role. In Philadelphia, the Pew Charitable Trust allocated $8,000,000 in 1993 for charter schools. The Diamond Foundation in New York City created a competition for the creation of what they called New Vision Schools and allocated $750,000 for those schools. And then, dramatically, in 1995 the Annenberg Foundation contributed $500,000,000 to support teacher-run alternative schools, fashioned after the Sizer-Meier model, in large cities. Annenberg support came with restrictions, dictated by the foundation, stating which schools would be funded and stating the need to maintain a separate entity to receive the funds. The Annenberg schools would be separated from the rest of the system to avoid the kinds of controls exercised by the system. In addition, funds were to be matched on a 2:1 basis with funds contributed by local foundations. Evaluation of the schools' progress is to be tightly controlled by self-selected evaluators.

Activist groups in several cities continue to struggle with changing their school systems' governance, personnel policies, and even curricula. Other groups continue the difficult task of seeking equity, particularly in state funding formulae. They even win court decisions as a result of remarkable briefs and excellent legal strategies. Joining school adequacy definitions to equity goals was a stroke of creative genius by a couple of young civil liberties lawyers. The results were court findings of inadequacy in schools and court-ordered action establishing outcomes that included proof of school adequacy, which demands more comprehensive strategies for reform, including new financial, governance, and teaching and learning arrangements. Only one statewide comprehensive reform resulting from a court decision on equity financing has actually been implemented, however. That is in Kentucky, a remarkable example of successful implementation of court action that resulted at least in part from sustained coalition-building with organized parent and community activism and vital corporate support. Some analysts belittle the Kentucky success and its identification as a model for other states, noting the benign role of the teachers' union in that state and the low funding levels, teacher salaries, and standards they started with. It is also notable that city suburban conflict is not as much of an issue in Kentucky as it is elsewhere.

Imaginative court decisions in Alabama and Connecticut remain decisions, unenforced by the states. Decades spent in litigation to pressure states to enforce court decisions to correct unconstitutional funding formulae frustrate activists and litigators in Texas and New Jersey, as well as several other states. These frustrations suggest even more pointedly the need to recognize the interdependence of reform agendas. Comprehensive school reform, combining finance and governance reform with teaching and learning improvements, requires the support of a broader group of stakeholders and construction of coalition politics at the state level that can pursue and achieve an equitable reform agenda. Separation of these interests or conflict among them minimizes the pressure on state legislators and bureaucrats to address change. Agreement on priorities for systemic change in Kentucky and strong coalition-building around those priorities proved to be the basis of the successful effort there to achieve reform.

Social change movements often struggle with whether their efforts should stay constant in pursuit of systemic change or seek to establish alternative models, within the system or outside it. The school reform movement in the United States has throughout its history reflected differences in perspective about a viable approach to reform. Activists who become disillusioned with the difficulty of achieving systemwide change are encouraged to accept piecemeal efforts, rationalizing that these experiments can then be used as a model for systemwide change. Excuses for abandoning systemwide reform also result from differences in priorities and timing. In the 1990s a major campaign was mounted by school professionals and their associations to address what they described as the abandonment of public education, justified, they said, by the threat of the voucher system and privatization of schools. Voucher plan recommendations have several faces: they can include only options within the system, as is true in Minnesota, and they can include parochial schools or not. Teachers' groups made the battle against vouchers their top priority, and they were successful in defeating an open statewide plan in many states, including California and Pennsylvania, and in reducing the size of voucher efforts in Ohio (to Cleveland), Milwaukee, and Minnesota. The courts overturned a voucher plan for Cleveland. In Washington, D.C., efforts have yet to be settled. Privatization of schools was recently abandoned in Baltimore and Hartford. The campaign to deter privatization, however, marginalized urban school reform as an issue.

The new reformers and the professional groups have been diverted from the issues surrounding the radical regime changes in the states. This has dramatically reduced support for city school systems, creating even greater inequities in some states. Conservative political regimes in the states have renewed and intensified anticity school policies. These new regimes disclaim the special needs of urban schools. Drastically reduced state aid, along with elimination or block granting of federal compensatory programs, has created major problems for city school systems. Not only are the new state regimes not interested in school finance equity, they have taken to city-school-bashing. Suburban interests and power are pervasive in almost all state legislatures and in the state education bureaucracies. Anti-immigrant and nativist policies undermine school programs in large cities even in formerly sympathetic states such as Minnesota and California. The division between city and suburban stakeholders is intensified, and competition for dollars overrides any common concerns for social goals.

The collaborative and charter school movement currently represents the best-funded (though externally funded) efforts nationally to change schools. Two criteria seem constant: the schools are teacher-governed, and they are established independent of the local school system. They are also small in size, not more than three hundred students. These schools receive district funding and, in five large cities, additional Annenberg Foundation and matched local foundation support. Staff development is the single most-often-mentioned priority for use of new funding. Also of concern is creation of a system of teacher certification, self-evaluation, and assessment. The emphasis in all of these efforts is on professional criteria. Interesting as some of these schools appear to be, it is difficult to think of the reformers or their reforms as different from the professional reforms of their predecessors the Progressives. There is no doubt that energy, dollars, and leadership for comprehensive state- and city-wide school reform have been siphoned off by these efforts.

It is difficult to argue against reforms or changes that improve the education environment and opportunities for even a limited number of students. And so alternative models of change can contribute to resistance to systemic change without even being aware of their role. Most important is the need to rethink how compromises in experimental or collaborative school reform can contribute to broader and more comprehensive reform efforts that rely on creating common goals and coalitions of stakeholders in the cities and the states. To the extent that the alternative model reduces opportunities for broader support, repeating the dangerous and historic practices of professionally closed schools, it will contribute to the undermining of the efforts at comprehensive reform. When the current leaders and funders of those schools disappear they will once again become marginal institutions looking for greater system funding and protections.

A school reform agenda for the twenty-first century requires recognition that school reform, like schools, cannot be separated from other community reform efforts. We are witnessing an ever-increasing awakening to the fact that we have segmented our communities by separating service areas, professional empires, and targeted populations, ignoring the essential element of engaging citizens in the political process to achieve common goals. The result is declining community capacity to address major problems that are necessarily interdependent. To the extent that we separate policy areas, exclude citizens from the political process, and narrow the class of stakeholders, we will ultimately destroy cities. Twenty-first-century reform requires a new paradigm, based on integration within the community through a revitalization of institutions and an enhancement of citizen roles. Narrowing the context of school reform contradicts that effort. Broadening our perspective of the context in which schools function, as well as our definition of education, will encourage new stakeholders to form coalitions to create new institutions at the community level.

Reformers in many cities recognize that segmentation of interests and services has not served their community's needs. More important, it has minimized opportunities for the development of strong constituencies around community issues. Segmentation of services diffuses the energies and the strength of citizen action. Building parent and community school constituencies at the grassroots level has been labeled a top priority by a group of foundations working together in New York City called the Donors Education Collaborative. Selected foundations and reformers recognize that strong local constituencies are essential to institutional change. Putnam's (1993) study of provincial governments in Italy confirms de Tocqueville's early recognition of the vital role of local voluntary organizations in American democracy (de Tocqueville, 1966). The past fifty or more years of professional reforms in schools and in other urban policy areas, in addition to overemphasis on the welfare state, have undermined the vitality of local community organizations and their ability to influence the organization and substance of government. The development or redevelopment of community capacity in American cities and neighborhoods requires reconstruction of community constituencies at the neighborhood level with enough political interest and concern to act to change what doesn't work for them, to initiate coalitions of neighborhoods and cities that can join a variety of stakeholders to seek comprehensive reform.

REFERENCES

Bowles, Samuel, and Herbert Gintis. 1976. *Schools in Capitalist America.* New York: Basic Books.

Coleman, James. 1966. *Equality of Opportunity.* Washington, D.C.: U.S. Government Printing Office, Office of Education.

Conant, James. 1963. *The Education of American Teachers.* New York: McGraw-Hill.

de Tocqueville, Alexis. [1835] 1966. *Democracy in America.* New York: Harper & Row.

Gittell, Marilyn. 1967. *Participants and Participation: A Study of School Policy in New York City.* New York: Praeger.

————. 1994. School Reform in New York and Chicago: Revisiting the Ecology of Local Games. *Urban Affairs Quarterly* 30, no. 1 (September):136–51.

Gittell, Marilyn, Mario Fantini, and Richard Magat. 1970. *Community Control and the Urban School.* New York: Praeger.

Gittell, Marilyn, and T. E. Hollander. 1968. *Six Urban School Districts: A Comparative Study of Institutional Response.* New York: Praeger.

Katz, Michael. 1968. *The Irony of Early School Reform.* Beacon.

————. 1987. *Reconstructing American Education.* Cambridge, Mass.: Harvard University Press.

Putnam, R. D. 1993. *Making Democracy Work: Civic Traditions in Modern Italy.* Princeton, N.J.: Princeton University Press.

Ravitch, Diane. 1987. *The Great School Wars: A History of the New York City Public Schools.* New York: Basic.

Tyack, David. 1974. *The One Best System: A History of Urban Education.* Cambridge, Mass.: Harvard University Press.

Contributors

John Augenblick serves as president of Augenblick & Myers, a Denver-based consulting firm founded in 1983 that works primarily with state-level policy makers on education issues, particularly those concerning finance. Since 1976, Dr. Augenblick has provided assistance to numerous states and other entities on issues related to education finance. In the past few years he has served as a consultant to legislative study groups in Indiana, Kansas, Mississippi, Nebraska, New Mexico, and Pennsylvania; the Office of Education Accountability in Kentucky; departments of education in Alabama, Alaska, Maine, Minnesota, and Ohio; and the Louisiana Board of Elementary and Secondary Education. He has also served as a consultant to the Alliance for Adequate School Funding (Ohio), Greater Phoenix Leadership (Arizona), the Kansas City School District, and the World Bank.

Thomas Corcoran is co-director of the Consortium for Policy Research in Education (CPRE) at the University of Pennsylvania. Prior to joining CPRE, he served as the Policy Advisor for Education for New Jersey governor Jim Florio. His major research interests focus on the relationships among state and local officials, teachers, parents, and citizens in decentralized governance systems, the impact of changes in work environments on the productivity of teachers and students, alternative approaches to teacher development, and the role of the states in promoting education improvement.

Albert Cortez is director of the Intercultural Development Research Association (IDRA) Institute for Policy and Leadership. In his role as director, Dr. Cortez coordinates its activities to support reform efforts impacting the education of minority, low-income, limited-English-proficient, and recent immigrant populations. Institute activities include providing information on policy issues, training in the effective integration of research information and advocacy, and technical assistance in identifying policy issues and developing impact strategies. In legislative sessions from 1977 to 1995, Dr. Cortez served as a technical advisor and resource person to the Texas Mexican-American Legislative Caucus and the Senate Hispanic Caucus on education-related issues.

Martha Darling staffed former Boeing CEO Frank Schrontz on the Governor's Council on Education Reform and Funding from 1991 to 1993. Currently with the Boeing Commercial Airplane Group, she has more than ten years' involvement in education policy issues through the Washington Roundtable and Seattle's Alliance for Education, as well as service on national and local boards concerned with education reform. A graduate of Reed College and Princeton's Woodrow Wilson School, she is a former White House Fellow and was a senior legislative aide to Senator Bill Bradley.

Marilyn Gittell is professor of political science at the Graduate School and University Center of the City University of New York and director of the Howard Samuels State Management and Policy Center. She has written extensively on the politics of education. She is currently conducting research on state political regimes and urban school reform. In addition, Dr. Gittell has written on state and urban politics, welfare, and economic development. She has published articles on urban problems, race and gender in community development corporations, welfare and higher education, and community capacity. Her books include *State Politics and the New Federalism: Commentaries and Readings; Choosing Equality: The Case for Democratic Schooling; Limits of Citizen Participation: The Decline of Community Organizations; Six Urban School Districts: A Comparative Study of Institutional Response; School Boards and School Policy; Local Control in Education; Participants and Participation: A Study of School Policy in New York City; Community Control and the Urban School.*

Margaret E. Goertz is a professor in the Graduate School of Education at the University of Pennsylvania and a co-director of the Consortium for Policy Research in Education. Her research focuses on the allocation of federal, state, and school-level education resources, the design and implementation of state education reform policies, and state and federal programs for special-needs students. A past president of the American Education Finance Association, Dr. Goertz has studied school funding systems in nearly a dozen states and was vice-chair of New Jersey's Education Funding Review Commission. She is co-author of *Politicians, Judges, and City Schools* and *From Cashbox to Classroom: The Struggle for Fiscal Reform and Educational Change in New Jersey.*

Helen Hershkoff is an assistant professor of law at New York University School of Law. Before coming to NYU, she served as an associate legal director of the American Civil Liberties Union. A leading civil rights lawyer, Professor Hershkoff participated in a number of groundbreaking educational equity lawsuits in Alabama, Louisiana,

Connecticut, and other states. She graduated from Harvard Law School and Radcliffe College and studied modern history as a Marshall Scholar at St. Anne's College, Oxford University.

Laura McKenna is a Ph.D. candidate in American politics and theory at the Graduate School at the University Center of the City University of New York and a research associate at the Howard Samuels State Management and Policy Center. She is currently working on a dissertation on political culture and education reform and is project director of a ten-state study on political regimes and education for the Samuels Center.

Donald R. Moore is executive director of Designs for Change, a Chicago-based children's research and advocacy group. He holds a doctorate in education from the Harvard University Graduate School of Education and has conducted five major national research studies analyzing strategies for improving urban education. His major focus has been on finding ways to provide quality education to low-income and minority children and children with disabilities and on empowering and involving parents in decision-making at their schools.

Peter D. Roos is co-director of Multicultural Education, Training and Advocacy (META), Inc., a public interest law firm with offices in San Francisco and Boston. He was previously director of education litigation at MALDEF and a senior attorney at the Harvard Center for Law and Education. He has been active in litigation concerning the rights of immigrant children to school, bilingual education, desegregation, and equitable school funding and was a lead attorney in the Los Angeles case discussed here.

Nathan Scovronick teaches education policy and directs the program in New Jersey affairs at the Woodrow Wilson School of Public and International Affairs of Princeton University. He has had wide experience in the New Jersey state government, where he most recently served as executive director of the Treasury Department in the administration of Governor Jim Florio. He has also been the policy director of the General Assembly and the principal staff person for the legislative committees on education.

Robert F. Sexton, a Louisville native, has been executive director of the Prichard Committee for Academic Excellence, a nonpartisan advocacy group dedicated to improving Kentucky public schools, since its creation in 1983. He graduated from Yale University and received his doctorate in history from the University of Washington. He is a founder of Kentucky's Governor's Scholars Program, the Commonwealth Institute for Teachers, and the Kentucky Center for Public Issues. In 1994 he received the Charles A. Dana Award for Pioneering Achievement in Education.

Clarence N. Stone is professor of government and politics at the University of Maryland. His most recent book is *Regime Politics: Governing Atlanta, 1946–1988,* winner of the American Political Science Association's Ralph Bunche Award in 1990. His current research interests center on the politics of school reform, and he is directing an eleven-city study, "Civic Capacity and Urban Education," funded by the National Science Foundation.

Kirk Vandersall is coordinator of assessment, evaluation, research, and planning for the Paramount Unified School District in Paramount, California, and a Ph.D. candidate in American politics and public policy at the Graduate School and University Center of the City University of New York. His current research includes work on the state politics of urban school reform in California and dissertation research on the changing politics of suburban communities in Los Angeles.

Thomas Vitullo-Martin is a New York City-based consultant specializing in policies affecting the organization, finance, governance, and performance of public, charter, and private schools, with a special emphasis on access and services for lower-income and inner-city students. Since 1992, he has provided planning and research to Michigan organizations promoting education choice policies, assisted in developing Michigan's charter school legislation, and monitored changes under the new law. He received his Ph.D. in political science from the University of Chicago.

Index